Rama X

Rama X

The Thai Monarchy under King Vajiralongkorn

PAVIN CHACHAVALPONGPUN
Editor

with a Foreword by
TYRELL HABERKORN

Monograph 69/Yale Southeast Asia Studies

Library of Congress Control Number: 2023949264
International Standard Book Number: *paper* 978-1-7326102-2-4
                                                                    cloth 978-1-7326102-3-1

Distributor:
Yale University Southeast Asia Studies
P.O. Box 208206
New Haven, Connecticut 06520-8206
USA

Printed in USA

Contents

Figures

Foreword

ON 3 AUGUST 2020, lawyer-poet Arnon Nampha took to the stage at a Hogwarts-themed protest at Democracy Monument in Bangkok and gave a speech that permanently transformed both politics and history in Thailand. A few weeks earlier, following the enforced disappearance of Wanchalearm Satsaksit, an exiled republic critic, people took to the streets to call for democracy. They demanded that the prime minister, Prayuth Chan-ocha, who had occupied office since the 22 May 2014 coup, resign and a new election be held; a new constitution be drafted through a participatory process; and the state stop threatening dissidents. Dressed as Harry Potter and wielding his unwavering voice and direct words like a magic wand, Arnon added a fourth demand to the mix and called for an end to persistent public silence around the monarchy. The People's Party–led transformation from absolute to constitutional monarchy on 24 June 1932 theoretically placed the country in the hands of the people and the monarch under the constitution. But in practice, this transformation has remained both incomplete and ambiguous, leaving the people without the sovereignty they were promised and rendering the monarchy beyond question, let alone oversight.

Rather than the whispers and gossip that surround both the institution and the figure at its head, Rama X, Arnon urged the people to speak frankly: "Out of honor and respect for myself, and to honor and respect the brothers and sisters who have come to listen, and with the greatest honor and respect for the monarchy, it is of the utmost necessity that we speak about how the monarchy is involved in Thai politics today. We have shoved this problem under the carpet for many years, brothers and sisters. There is no mention of the actual problem, which means that the solutions miss the mark."[1] The immediate response of royalists was to accuse Arnon of calling for the overthrow of the monarchy, but they misheard. His call was at once simpler and perhaps more challenging: to clarify the position and role of the monarchy in the Thai polity.

On 10 August 2020, a new protest group, the United Front of Thammasat and Demonstration (UFTD), concretized and expanded Arnon's call into ten demands for specific reforms of the monarchy.[2] The UFTD's suggested reforms included, for example, the removal of military units from Rama X's control, the explicit distinction between the private funds of royals and publicly provided funds, and the revocation of Article 112 of the Criminal Code. Article 112 prescribes a punishment of three-to-fifteen years of imprisonment for anything deemed to defame, insult, or threaten the king, queen, heir apparent, or regent, and it has been used increasingly to silence any public questioning of the monarchy since the 19 September 2006 coup. On 19 September 2020, the sixteenth anniversary of the coup, Panusaya Sitthijirawattanakul, one of the founders of the UFTD, wrote an open letter to Rama X conveying the demands to him and inviting him to join the people as partners in creating a Thailand in which everyone is an equal member of the polity. Rama X did not respond, but the people did. Over the next two months, sustained protests around the country—with expansive participation from high school and university students to veteran Red Shirts, LGBTQIA+ activists, and more—echoed and expanded Arnon's and the UFTD's demands.

For a moment in 2020, the completion of the transformation started by the People's Party in 1932 seemed imminent. But then began a sustained state crackdown on the protests, including the most extensive use of Article 112 to date. Between 24 November 2020 and 28 October 2022, at least 217 people were charged in 236 cases.[3] To be clear: these are grave criminal cases being brought against citizens for peacefully expressing their political views. As is typical in Article 112 cases, many of those accused have been denied bail, at least initially; those who are granted bail usually must agree to no longer join protests as a condition of release. The first round of leaders face numerous cases, including Arnon, with fourteen cases, and Panusaya, with ten cases. The crackdown has not ended protests, but it has made the potential cost for dissenting much higher. The possibility of reform of the monarchy and the completion of the People's Party's work is no longer imminent, and instead those who continue to dissent know that they are part of a struggle that may take their entire lifetime. They know that they may face years in prison for daring to question the monarchy, and yet they continue.

Arnon's call to speak frankly about the monarchy and the harsh prosecution under Article 112 of anyone who dares to do so are at once grave political problems and also urgent analytic ones. What are the effects on the polity when a key social, political, economic, and cultural figure—the king—cannot be spoken of? How can scholarship about Thai society, politics, economy, or culture be completed without carefully examining the role of both Rama X himself and the institution of the monarchy? What does it mean—for individual lives and the entire society—when those who peacefully and carefully raise questions about the monarchy may go to prison for daring to imagine themselves as equal to the king? Does scholarship about Thailand have any meaning or worth if scholars maintain silence about the monarchy when activists who break this silence face decades behind bars for doing so?

This is the context in which Pavin Chachavalpongpun, who has been directly and continuously targeted by both the Thai state and royalists for his dissidence since the 22 May 2014 coup, edited this important volume. Across nine essays, the contributors take up Arnon's call to speak directly and examine Rama X in relation to law, military, property, intimacy, and memory. Each author does precisely what scholars and journalists do best: bring empirical evidence and rigorous thought to bear on thorny questions. Just as solutions to political problems in Thailand miss the mark when they fail to account for the monarchy, so too does scholarship. I read this book as an academic response to the request with which Arnon closed his speech on 3 August 2020:

> Do not leave it to those on the margins to have to talk about the monarchy and then face threats and harassment all alone. Do not leave it to the political exiles to talk about the monarchy and then be brutally murdered and disappeared. From now on, this is not going to happen anymore. From now on, no one who comes out to talk about the monarchy will be accused of being crazy or insane and scooped up and put in the hospital even though they spoke the truth. Brothers and sisters, this is not going to happen anymore.[4]

Let this book be the beginning of a wave of critical scholarship about both the monarchy and the repression experienced by those who have broken silence about it under Rama X and the kings who preceded him. Our work as scholars does not exist in a privileged space beyond society and politics, but unavoidably within it.

Tyrell Haberkorn
Professor of Southeast Asian Studies
Department of Asian Languages and
    Cultures
University of Wisconsin-Madison

Notes

1 Arnon Nampha, *The Monarchy and Thai Society* (London: PEN International, 2021), 12.

2 "The Demonstration at Thammasat Proposes Monarchy Reform," *Prachatai English*, 11 August 2020, https://prachatai.com/english/node/8709.

3 Thai Lawyers for Human Rights, "Statistics of Those Prosecuted Under Article 112," 28 October 2022, https://tlhr2014.com/archives/23983.

4 Arnon, *The Monarchy and Thai Society*, 22.

the current government's disdain of academic freedom. Thailand has become a fearsome place for academics, democracy activists, and human rights advocates.

The "patriarchal bias" that has emerged in critical studies of the Thai monarchy needs to be addressed seriously and systematically, not necessarily for the sake of this specific project, but rather for the overall state of Thai monarchy studies. Over the last decade, female academics have not been shielded from Article 112, and have faced serious political consequences and threats to their safety. For example, Suda Rangkupan from Chulalongkorn University was forced to flee Thailand on lèse-majesté charges in the aftermath of the 2014 coup. Meanwhile, others were imprisoned or detained because of their opposing political standing. Sudsa-nguan Suthisorn of Thammasat University was imprisoned for a month for her alleged insult of the court. I interviewed two female political activists who were detained for lèse-majesté; they told of the horrendous abuses against them in prison. Some of the abuses were sexual in nature. Following the current wave of protests, the Thai state has begun to target women on the ground of violating the lèse-majesté law. The increasing number of females charged under Article 112 has been alarming, particularly among younger female political activists and journalists, including Panusaya "Rung" Sithijirawattanakul, Benja Apan, Patsaravalee "Mind" Tanakitvibulpon, Chonticha "Lookkate" Jangrew, Ravisara "Dear" Eksgool, Tantawan Tuatulanonda, Supitchata "Menu" Chailom, Baipo Natthanit, and Benjamaporn "Ploy" Nivas.[38] According to Thai Lawyers for Human Rights, of the 195 cases currently charged under the lèse-majesté law, there are 53 females.[39] Although none of them is working directly in academia, the surge of the lèse-majesté cases and harassment against female individuals has left a chilling effect among scholars of Thai studies. Two of the female scholars who dropped out of this project cited the systematic punishment against females charged with lèse-majesté as a reason for their withdrawal.

Other female scholars declined my invitation to participate in the project because of the gender-related currents of this topic and scholarship. They told me of their intention to boycott the topic in protest of Vajiralongkorn's maltreatment of the women around him, which is often portrayed by the palace itself and the international media as devoid of agency. This includes the uncritical use of certain terms in references to women in the royal court, such as "harem," "mistress," and "concubine." Such portrayal reflects not only

Vajiralongkorn's degrading stance toward women, but also the tabloid-esque language and the framing of events and practices in the palace that perpetuates a patriarchal lens for understanding the gender dynamics. The concerns echoed among female scholars resonate with a recent study by Rosalind Dixon on gender and monarchy. Dixon raised pertinent points in her work, such as the connection between the operation of the monarchy and norms of gender equality and the attitudes of male monarchs toward female leadership and gender justice. One of her key messages is that many feminists are committed to republicanism over monarchy as an inherently more democratic, less patriarchal institution.[40]

How can this be remedied in the future? I humbly suggest a few options, some of which were adopted in this volume to compensate for the lack of contributions from female scholars. First and foremost, it has long been my personal agenda to help, in whichever ways I could, "scholars at risk," the status of which I myself have assumed since the 2014 coup. The voice of the academic community is utterly important as it can serve as a shield for both male and female scholars working on sensitive and prohibited topics, such as the monarchy. Second, I urged all contributors to this volume to consider citation politics and engagement of diverse scholarship, particularly from women academics, given that women and non-binary gendered people have been active and prominent in the political protests of recent years. Third, I called on individual chapters to consider feminist approaches to social movements and historiography of Thailand (and Southeast Asia as a whole), of which much has been written. This allows us to think more profoundly about the institution rather than the projection of Vajiralongkorn himself, and in turn to avoid employing conceptual frameworks that would further entrench the patriarchal bias.

Outline of the Book

This book is the product of a workshop held at the University of California, Berkeley, on 14 and 15 November 2019. I would like to thank the university for hosting the workshop, as well as Sarah H. Maxim for her kind assistance during the event. My deep gratitude goes to the Free Future Foundation for its generosity in providing financial support for this project. The participants include me, David Streckfuss, Paul Handley, Claudio Sopranzetti, Gregory

Raymond, and Michael Ruffles, as well as others who unfortunately have since withdrawn. I would also like to thank other individuals who made this project a reality: Federico Ferrara and Chatri Prakitnonthakan for their eventual participation in the project, Erik Harms for having trust in our endeavor, Kristine Mooseker for her assistance with the manuscript, Nakrob Moonmanas for a brilliant cover design, and Virakri Jinangkul for his artworks in this introduction.

The original idea behind this book project stems from the fact that Thailand had recently entered the new reign under Vajiralongkorn. It was clear that even during its formative years, the Vajiralongkorn reign dramatically transformed the political landscape, including through the rise of royal absolutism. Although the workshop was organized prior to the protests in Thailand, all authors took into account the dynamism of the protests and how it has affected the monarchy. Following is a brief description of each chapter.

A biography

Paul M. Handley, the author of *The King Never Smiles*, condenses the life of the seventy-one-year-old Vajiralongkorn into a short biography. Handley has been firm on his view of Bhumibol as a very important political actor in Thailand. Bhumibol was identified with democracy, the most recent embodiment of a long "tradition" of democratic kings. His acts in support of a democratic culture were transposed back to previous kings, to the beginning of the Chakri monarchy in the eighteenth century, and—leapfrogging the Ayutthaya era—to King Ramkhamhaeng. This conscious construction began in the nineteenth century. But it was accelerated and cemented into place with Bhumibol by the canny high princes of the ninth reign's early decades. By the twenty-first century, after six decades under one king, the monarchy and government were inseparable from the monarch himself. In fact, Bhumibol survived only because successive governments were willing to uphold him as symbolic head of state in exchange for his endorsement of their power. But the end of the Bhumibol era was looming. This created a state of anxiety among stakeholders of the monarchy, resulting in the coup of 2014. Two years later, Bhumibol passed away, marking the interregnum in which the new king began to explore his reign employing a different approach. Handley asks: Could this be a fresh start for Thailand? In answering this question, Handley discusses a long list of controversies, past and present, of Vajiralongkorn. The past is haunting, but it is the present that will determine the future of the Vajiralongkorn reign. The present controversies include his open intervention in politics, his lacklustre attitude toward democracy, his family affairs, and his lack of vision in the future succession.

Extra-constitutional monarchy

Federico Ferrara examined in his chapter the concept of "extra-constitutional monarchy," well founded during the Bhumibol reign, to lay a foundation for an in-depth discussion of the current Vajiralongkorn era. The possible democratisation in the 1990s might have set Thailand apart from other developing nations struggling with authoritarianism. But the 2006 coup unravelled the remaining fragility of Thai democracy. While the liberal constitution of 1997 was exploited by political elites, and while the middle class decidedly turned its back on democracy, the crisis in Thailand could also be attributed to the Thai monarchy—designated as Thailand's "peculiar institution." Federico explained the peculiarity of the monarchy, viewing it as inimitable in its own operation and functionality. The demise of absolute monarchy in 1932 posed a challenge for subsequent kings regarding the survival of the institution. The abdication of King Prajadhipok and the mysterious death of King Ananda Mahidol exacerbated such a challenge. When Bhumibol took the throne in 1946, the future of the Thai monarchy was therefore uncertain. Astonishingly, Bhumibol, within the period of over a decade, transformed a near-death institution into one with hegemonic power. The success stemmed from his ability to rebrand the monarchy into a functional extra-constitutional institution. This chapter investigates the origin of an extra-constitutional monarchy, a system in the cleavage between absolutism and constitutionalism. In this seemingly strategic positioning, Thai monarchy à la Bhumibol functioned above the constitution, yet legitimately. Federico asserts that the reason why Thailand's monarchy is best described as an extra-constitutional monarchy is that while the king exercises a varying set of formal, constitutional prerogatives, its most significant powers are still extra-constitutional in nature. This was best demonstrated in his role as a *de facto* arbiter in political conflicts. But the legacy of Bhumibol is now being defied under new political circumstances. All the king makers are to be blamed for the decay of extra-constitutional monarchy for they corrupted the royal power to empower themselves. Vajiralongkorn, too, must be held responsible for the demise of the extra-constitutional monarchy concept due to his unbounded political ambitions. When the protesters called for royal reforms with ten demands in 2020, not only was their wish ignored, but they were also cracked down and thrown in jail on lèse-majesté charges. The Thai monarchy has come full circle, from its fall and rise under Bhumibol to a new fall under Vajiralongkorn. To survive, the palace must rethink the concept of extra-constitutional monarchy. Reforms are a key to begin the rethinking process. This process needs to place the monarchy strictly under the constitution without "extra" that has made the institution an adversary to constitutionalism in the first place.

The legal status of Vajiralongkorn

In this introduction, I have alluded to several questions pertaining to the legal rights of Vajiralongkorn in his macro- and micro-managements. David Streckfuss enlightens us by tackling the issue of the legal status of King Vajiralongkorn. Like Ferrara, Streckfuss finds that the problems involving the legal status of the monarchy predate the Vajiralongkorn reign. Bhumibol, as a monarch and a monarchy, was made inviolable and stringently protected by the lèse-majesté law. Vajiralongkorn, like his father, has been protected under the same condition and by the same instrument. Streckfuss takes us back to the origin of sacredness of the monarchies in Western Europe to establish the case of the inviolability of the royal institution. The notion that "the king can do no wrong" has its root in the inviolability of the monarchy. In the Thai case, although the People's Party abolished the absolute monarchy, what has never been dismantled has been the legal status of the monarchy. Streckfuss restates Bhumibol's record to understand the legal legacy passed on to Vajiralongkorn. Rama X gave himself new powers, and the legal status of the "royal decree" has become normalized as shown in the cases of Ubolratana (nominated as prime minister by the Thai Raksa Chart Party), the dismissal of Sineenat, and the transfer of troops, for example. In 2021, Thai protesters put forward their ten demands, which are unswervingly related to King Vajiralongkorn's dubious legal demands.[41] The protesters wanted the king to return what had been taken, thus repealing his unconstitutional legal power.

The military-monarchy connection

For decades, the monarchy has formed a "working relationship" with the military. Gregory Raymond argues that King Vajiralongkorn is establishing a fundamentally different relationship with the military to what has existed. First, he is aggressively personalizing control of the military in a way that Bhumibol never did. In this endeavor, he is advantaged by his professional background as a soldier, including his own network of trusted aides and his significant knowledge of the inner workings of military organizations. It is noteworthy that he graduated from a military school in Australia—Duntroon. Second, confident in his own military training, he is influencing very directly the structure, training, and image of the Thai military. Third, Vajiralongkorn is fostering a public image as a "military king," whose vision is to make the military, and in fact the nation, more disciplined. Raymond asserts:

> The establishment of the Royal Security Command is Vajiralongkorn's most significant reform in the sphere of defense and security, but not the only one. It is paralleled by Vajiralongkorn's creation of a new volunteer force, the Jit Arsa (Volunteer Spirit), in 2017. Although unarmed, the Jit Arsa is managed through the Kings Guard 904 and provides Vajiralongkorn with a massive workforce under his direct control. There are now a reported four million members, across the country and social strata.

This military-monarchy partnership, through new initiatives of Vajiralongkorn, has continued to flourish in the face of the protests in 2020 and 2021. Fundamentally, the ongoing protests have reinforced the partnership, as the two institutions are facing an imminent threat to their position of power. But this partnership is not without tension. The king's attempt to overpower the military could cause frictions in the future.

The Crown Property Bureau

Michael Ruffles, in his chapter, "What's Yours Is Mine: Transformation at the Crown Property Bureau," shows how King Vajiralongkorn has taken a strikingly different approach to royal finances than his predecessors in the Chakri dynasty. He argues that Vajiralongkorn, with the help of a pliant military-led government and powerful palace mandarins, has ushered in the most radical change to the way the crown's property and money have been managed since the 1932 revolution. In the process, Vajiralongkorn has also enriched himself. Ruffles outlines how this began before the death of Bhumibol, with the sale of a significant stake in a major international hotel chain. To explain how significant the changes have been since Vajiralongkorn's ascension, it was important to go back to the start. For more than a century, the crown's wealth has been underpinned by banking, cement, and land ownership. The Crown Property Bureau (CPB) had rather mundane bureaucratic origins in the Finance Ministry during the time of absolute monarchy and went through an upheaval in the 1932 revolution and its aftermath when the royal family was pushed to the periphery of Thai politics.[42] Under Bhumibol, both the CPB and the monarchy went from strength to strength. In 1946 when Bhumibol was named king, the bureau was bereft. Yet, by the end of his reign, it had evolved into a conglomerate with more corporate and business savvy. A significant turning point was the 1997 financial crisis, when palace finances were battered. In the aftermath, the CPB was much more focused on the core businesses that generated income, and Bhumibol was catapulted to the top of royal rich lists. Where his father enabled if not cultivated an air of ambiguity over ownership of crown property, with possession held in some nebulous zone between the person and the state that few dared to question, Vajiralongkorn has made it explicitly his own. He has taken direct control of the CPB, made its holdings part of his personal wealth rather than that of the state, and transferred significant shareholdings into his name. The changes in personnel at the organization are also telling, with loyal military men and hard-line royalists ousting technocrats in key board positions. More visibly from the outside, he has altered Bangkok by reclaiming and expanding royal land, with institutions including Parliament, the 80-year-old Dusit Zoo, and a 102-year-old turf club forced to relocate. Control of Sanam Luang, a public square adjacent to the Grand Palace and the Temple of the Emerald Buddha, has returned to the crown rather than the Bangkok Metropolitan Administration.

Vajiralongkorn has more control over a larger share of the country's wealth than any king since the revolution. But the wealth is also under unprecedented scrutiny, making it arguably more precarious than ever. For now, he controls the board, but others are making moves to counter his monopoly.

Fear as the new royal governance

Claudio Sopranzetti examines the shift from love to fear as tools of royal governance in contemporary Thailand. Over the course of the last decades, there has been a tendency in Thai studies to explore political shifts and emerging conflicts looking at material explanations, in particular shifting alliances among the elite, political-economic transformations, or regional inequalities. Sopranzetti argues that cultural elements have played a central role in contemporary Thai politics and that failing to acknowledge them means missing an important part of the picture. In this chapter, he focuses on the role of love and fear in shaping the relation between Thai citizens and the ruling monarch across the recent royal succession. He refers to the important work of Marshall Sahlins and David Graeber on kingship—"The ordinary balance of power between king and people is often maintained through intense emotional engagement"—showing that Thailand has not been an exception. Consequently, Sopranzetti discusses changes in the form of emotional engagement between the reigns of King Bhumibol and King Vajiralongkorn and explores what he calls the "affective governance" deployed by the two monarchs. Contrary to what it may seem, Sopranzetti does not see this shift as a degeneration from a positive form of governance to a negative one, nor from a less to a more desirable form of control. "Love" should not be considered, as intuitively we may do, as a positive emotion, while "fear" a negative one. Both emotions have been and continue to be equally productive forces that generate different systems of affective governance and management of the relation between king and his subjects, defined by specific forms of emotive participation and repressive mechanisms. This chapter's objective is not to express moral or pragmatic judgments but rather to analyze the features of each form of affective governance and the systems of participation and repression that they generate.

Erasing political memories

The chapter by Chatri Prakitnonthakan investigates the destruction and removal of buildings, monuments, and symbolic political artefacts related to the memory of the People's Party. The destruction and removal began to gain importance after the 2006 coup d'état. The basic questions posed by Chatri are: What is the reason for the destruction and removal, and why did it suddenly occur after the 2006 coup? His study shows that these acts occurred for clearly political reasons as an attempt to erase the historical memory of the People's Party, which has been revived as a symbol of the struggle for democracy after the 2006 coup. This chapter resonates with the argument of Kasian on the conflict between a disguised republic and a virtual absolutism—a struggle of the monarchy, pursuing the latter, against the revolutionists, pursuing the former. But this time, the struggle is portrayed through the destruction and removal of historical buildings and monuments. What is intriguing, as underscored by Chatri, is the fact that the intensity of destruction is undeniably related to the declining image of the monarchy in Thai society, particularly under the current reign of King Vajiralongkorn. In other words, as the king suffers his image problem, there appears to be an intensified elimination of memory through the destruction and removal of representations of the People's Party.

On Vajiralongkorn's life overseas

The world's view of Vajiralongkorn has remained unstudied and unknown. I tackle this issue by tracing his interactions with the world, from his childhood until the present day. As a young king, Bhumibol sought international allies to support his throne. The Cold War allowed Bhumibol to complete his mission. This international alliance was imperative for the survival of the monarchy. Allying with the Free World, Thailand forged ties with the United States in squashing the threat of communism. Domestically, the monarchy worked closely with the military in thwarting their enemies by branding them communists. It can be said that King Bhumibol played a significant role in redefining Thai diplomacy throughout the Cold War. But Vajiralongkorn is a different king and there is no threatening international environment to be exploited. The post–Cold War world with its global retreat from democracy has for the time being, as I argue, set King Vajiralongkorn free from conditions and expectations of the world vis-à-vis the Thai monarchy. Vajiralongkorn can behave with few international constraints. As a result, the prestige and dignity of the monarchy, once an asset of the Thai diplomacy, clearly does not rank high in the consciousness of Vajiralongkorn, as seen in the incident in Tokyo in the 1980s, or the controversies that surround Vajiralongkorn over his long-term stay in Germany. But Vajiralongkorn is not without a position in international politics. He has tilted toward China at this critical juncture in Sino-US relations, a stance supported by the royalists.[43] A tilt toward authoritarian China reflects the less pluralistic governance under Vajiralongkorn.

Conclusion

Under Bhumibol, political stability was key to authority. Politics was predictable. Benefits were shared among major stakeholders. Underpinning Bhumibol's strength was his unsurpassed ability to accumulate moral authority through the invigoration of the royal nationalist ideology, his powerful network, and loyalty from the populace. The Bhumibol consensus was the rule of the day. With this lacking under Vajiralongkorn, the new reign is using fear, among other tactics, as a mechanism reinforcing his position. Vajiralongkorn has also proven to be a political strategist. He redefines his relationship with the army, taking control of the royal wealth, eliminating political parties critical of the monarchy, and cooperating with senior bureaucrats to maintain the elites-based power politics. More than Bhumibol, Vajiralongkorn seems to be on the road to re-establishing royal absolutism.

The accumulated effect of the royalist narrative, which built a huge edifice of legitimacy to uphold the Bhumibol legacy and spurred use of the lèse-majesté law in defense of it, may have run out of steam. Power elites must fawningly change their loyalties and are now forced to support the much lesser vehicle of Rama X, masking, perhaps, the precipitous decline of the institution—a process that began in the early 2000s. It is true that Vajiralongkorn has consolidated his ties with other key institutions and relied upon repression and the lèse-majesté law to crush enemies. In this zero-sum game, the monarchy has become strengthened against any democratic aspirations many Thais may have harbored. Its use of naked power unconstrained by law or legitimacy marks a period of growing absolutism in an age of creeping authoritarianism.

Notes

1 Pavin, Introduction to *Coup, King, Crisis*, 4–5.

2 Ibid.

3 McCargo, "Network Monarchy and Legitimacy Crises in Thailand."

4 Thongchai, "Thailand's Royal Democracy in Crisis," 282–307.

5 Kasian, "The Irony of Democratization and the Decline of Royal Hegemony in Thailand."

6 Thongchai, *Thailand's Hyper-royalism.*

7 Katewadee Kulabkaew recently argued that Vajiralongkorn's recent enthusiasm in religious matters could be seen as a move to manage his lost moral authority. See Katewadee, "Managing Moral Authority."

8 Vajiralongkorn was elevated to become the crown prince (heir apparent) in December 1972.

9 See "Thailand: Ambassador Engages Privy Council Chair Prem," *WikiLeaks.*

10 Kobkua, *Kings, Country, and Constitutions*, 208.

11 Head, "Thailand's Constitution."

12 "Germany Says Thai King Cannot Rule from There," *Reuters.*

13 "Thailand's King Takes Personal Control of Two Key Army Units," *Reuters.*

14 "Thai King Takes Control of Some $30bn Crown Assets," *BBC News.*

15 Safwan, "From Thai King's Third Wife to a Nun while under House Arrest."

16 "Pongpat Sent to Prison for 6 Years in First Case," *Bangkok Post.*

17 Wassayos and Aekarach, "Royal Household Dismisses, Charges Shamed Ex-Chamberlain Distorn."

18 "Thai Palace Removes 'Extremely Evil' Official, Police General Jumpol Manmai," *Bangkok Post.*

19 "Ex-Deputy National Police Chief Jumpol Dies Age 72," *Bangkok Post.*

20 See https://news.thaipbs.or.th/content/295976.

21 Ruffles, "Thai King Reinstates 'Flawless' Consort."

22 Pavin, "Dhaveevatthana Prison."

23 Pavin, "The Case of Thailand's Disappearing Dissidents."

24 "Demonstration at Thammasat Calling for Reform on Politics and Monarchy," *Prachatai.*

25 Head, "The Mystery of the Missing Brass Plaque."

26 Hewison, "Managing Vajiralongkorn's Long Succession."

27 "Satharanarath Chamlang Kab Samuen Sumburanayasitthiraj," *Prachatai.*

28 "Thongchai Winichakul," *Prachatai.*

29 Fukuyama, *The End of History and the Last Man*, 15.

30 Fukuyama, *The Origins of Political Order,* 406.

31 See Arendt, *The Origins of Totalitarianism,* 306.

32 Gunia, "A Thai Opposition Party that Pushed for Democratic Reform Has Just Been Disbanded."

33 "[Full Statement] The Demonstration at Thammasat Proposes Monarchy Reform," *Prachatai.*

34 Punchada, "Hope over Fear."

35 McCargo, "Disruptions' Dilemma?," 175.

36 Baker, Review of *Coup, King, Crisis,* 804.

37 Ockey, Review of *Coup, King, Crisis,* 2.

38 I had an opportunity to respond, in April 2021, to the call of the United Nations to supply information and analysis on the safety of (female) journalists working in Thailand. See the UN call at https://www.ohchr.org/en/safety-of-journalists. Also see my report on this subject at https://112watch.org/wp-content/uploads/2021/10/1-Threats-to-Journalists.pdf.

39 Email interview with Sirikan Charoensiri, Thai human rights attorney with Thai Lawyers for Human Rights, 26 May 2022.

40 Nixon, "Gender and Constitutional Monarchy in Comparative Perspective," 2.

41 See Hathairat and Streckfuss, "The Ten Demands that Shook Thailand."

42 See Chollada, "Investment of the Privy Purse, 1890–1932."

43 Thai royalists even praised Russian President Vladimir Putin for invading Ukraine. See Janjira, "In Denial against Democracy."

References

Arendt, Hannah. *The Origins of Totalitarianism*. San Diego: Harcourt Brace Jovanovich Publishers, 1951.

Baker, Chris. Review of *Coup, King, Crisis: A Critical Interregnum in Thailand*, ed. Pavin Chachavalpongpun. *The Journal of Asian Studies* 80.3 (2021):802–4.

Chollada Wattanasiri. "Investment of the Privy Purse, 1890–1932." MA thesis, Silpakorn University, 1986.

"Demonstration at Thammasat Calling for Reform on Politics and Monarchy." *Prachatai*, 13 August 2020. https://prachatai.com/english/node/8717, accessed 4 June 2022.

"Ex-Deputy National Police Chief Jumpol Dies Age 72." *Bangkok Post*, 2 November 2022. https://www.bangkokpost.com/thailand/general/2427620/ex-deputy-national-police-chief-jumpol-dies-age-72, accessed 5 November 2022.

"[Full Statement] The Demonstration at Thammasat Proposes Monarchy Reform." *Prachatai*, 11 August 2020. https://prachataienglish.com/node/8709, accessed 4 June 2022.

Fukuyama, Francis. *The End of History and the Last Man*. New York: Free Press, 1992.

———. *The Origins of Political Order: From Prehuman Times to the French Revolution*. New York: Farrar, Straus and Giroux, 2011.

"Germany Says Thai King Cannot Rule from There." *Reuters*, 8 October 2020. https://www.reuters.com/article/uk-thailand-protests/germany-says-thai-king-cannot-rule-from-there-idUKKBN26T1P0, accessed 4 June 2022.

Gunia, Amy. "A Thai Opposition Party that Pushed for Democratic Reform Has Just Been Disbanded." *Time*, 21 February 2020. https://time.com/5788470/thailand-future-forward-party-disbanded/, accessed 3 June 2022.

Hathairat Phaholtap and David Streckfuss. "The Ten Demands that Shook Thailand." *New Mandala*, 2 September 2020. https://www.newmandala.org/the-ten-demands-that-shook-thailand/, accessed 3 June 2022.

Head, Jonathan. "The Mystery of the Missing Brass Plaque." *BBC News*, 20 April 2017. https://www.bbc.com/news/world-asia-39650310, accessed 4 June 2022.

———. "Thailand's Constitution: New Era, New Uncertainties." *BBC News*, 7 April 2017. https://www.bbc.com/news/world-asia-39499485, accessed 3 June 2022.

Hewison, Kevin. "Managing Vajiralongkorn's Long Succession." In Pavin, *Coup, King, Crisis*, 117–44.

Janjira Sombatpoonsri. "In Denial against Democracy: Thailand's Royalists See Putin as 'Decolonizer.'" *Fulcrum: Analysis on Southeast Asia*, 11 May 2022. https://fulcrum.sg/in-denial-against-democracy-thailands-royalists-see-putin-as-a-decoloniser/, accessed 3 June 2022.

Kasian Tejapera. "The Irony of Democratization and the Decline of Royal Hegemony in Thailand." *Southeast Asian Studies* 5.2 (2016):219–37.

Kastner, Jens. "Germany Doubts Thailand's King will Return to Bavaria." *Nikkei Asia*, 11 December 2020. https://asia.nikkei.com/Politics/Turbulent-Thailand/Germany-doubts-Thailand-s-king-will-return-to-Bavaria, accessed 3 June 2022.

Katewadee Kulabkaew. "Managing Moral Authority: Thai King's Revived Devotion to Buddhism." *Fulcrum: Analysis on Southeast Asia*, 23 July 2021. https://fulcrum.sg/managing-moral-authority-thai-kings-revived-devotion-to-buddhism/, accessed 3 June 2022.

Kobkua Suwannathat-Pian. *Kings, Country, and Constitutions: Thailand: Political Development, 1932–2000*. London: Taylor and Francis, 2013.

McCargo, Duncan. "Disruptions' Dilemma? Thailand's 2020 Gen Z Protests." *Critical Asian Studies* 53.2 (2021):175–91.

———. "Network Monarchy and Legitimacy Crises in Thailand." *Pacific Review* 18 (2005):499–519.

Mérieau, Eugénie. "Thailand's Deep State, Royal Power, and the Constitutional Court (1997–2015)." *Journal of Contemporary Asia* 46.3 (2016):445–66.

Nixon, Rosalind. "Gender and Constitutional Monarchy in Comparative Perspective." *Royal Studies Journal* 7.2 (2020):1–9.

Ockey, James. Review of *Coup, King, Crisis: A Critical Interregnum in Thailand*, ed. Pavin Chachavalpongpun. *Journal of Tropical Geography* 42.3 (31 August 2021):1–2.

Pavin Chachavalpongpun. "The Case of Thailand's Disappearing Dissidents." *New York Times*, 14 October 2019. https://www.nytimes.com/2019/10/14/opinion/thailand-dissidents-disappearance-murder.html, accessed 3 June 2022.

———. "Dhaveevatthana Prison: Hell on Earth in Thailand." *Japan Times*, 2 June 2017. https://www.japantimes.co.jp/opinion/2017/06/02/commentary/world-commentary/dhaveevatthana-prison-hell-earth-thailand/, accessed 4 June 2022.

———, ed. *Coup, King, Crisis: A Critical Interregnum in Thailand*. Yale Southeast Asia Studies Monograph 68. New Haven, CT: Yale Southeast Asia Studies, 2020.

"Pongpat Sent to Prison for 6 Years in First Case." *Bangkok Post*, 30 January 2015. https://www.bangkokpost.com/thailand/general/462642/pongpat-gets-reduced-6-years-in-first-case, accessed 3 June 2022.

Punchada Sirivunnabood. "Hope over Fear: The 2020 Student-led Protests in Thailand." *Fulcrum*, 29 October 2020. https://fulcrum.sg/hope-over-fear-the-2020-student-led-protests-in-thailand/, accessed 3 June 2022.

Ruffles, Michael. "Thai King Reinstates 'Flawless' Consort." *The Sydney Morning Herald*, 3 September 2020. https://www.smh.com.au/world/asia/thai-king-reinstates-flawless-consort-20200902-p55rub.html, accessed 3 June 2022.

Safwan. "From Thai King's Third Wife to a Nun while under House Arrest." *Hype*, 9 November 2020. https://hype.my/2020/202653/from-thai-kings-third-wife-becomes-a-nun-while-under-house-arrest/, accessed 4 June 2022.

"Satharanarath Chamlang Kab Samuen Sumburanayasitthiraj: Song Naewnom Fungfang Ti Kadyang Kannai Rabob Rachathippathai Tai Ratthathammanoon Thai" [Disguised republic and virtual absolutism: Two trends that collided under the Thai constitutional royalism]. *Prachatai*, 24 June 2021. https://prachatai.com/journal/2021/06/93654, accessed 7 June 2022.

"Thai King Takes Control of Some $30bn Crown Assets." *BBC News*, 16 June 2018. https://www.bbc.com/news/world-asia-44507590, accessed 3 June 2022.

"Thai Palace Removes 'Extremely Evil' Official, Police General Jumpol Manmai." *Bangkok Post*, 28 February 2017. https://www.smh.com.au/world/thai-palace-removes-extremely-evil-official-police-general-jumpol-manmai-20170228-guna5p.html, accessed 4 June 2022.

"Thailand: Ambassador Engages Privy Council Chair Prem, Other 'Establishment' Figures on Year Ahead." *WikiLeaks*, 25 January 2010. https://wikileaks.org/plusd/cables/10BANGKOK192_a.html, accessed 1 June 2022.

"Thailand's King Takes Personal Control of Two Key Army Units." *Reuters*, 2 October 2019. https://www.reuters.com/article/us-thailand-king-idUSKBN1WG4ED, accessed 4 June 2022.

Thongchai Winichakul. *Thailand's Hyper-Royalism: Its Past Success and Present Predicament*. Trends in Southeast Asia 7. Singapore: ISEAS–Yusof Ishak Institute, 2016.

———. "Thailand's Royal Democracy in Crisis." In *After the Coup: The National Council for Peace and Order Era and the Future of Thailand*, ed. Michael J. Montesano, Terence Chong, and Mark Heng, 282–307. Singapore: ISEAS–Yusof Ishak Institute, 2019.

"Thongchai Winichakul: Prachachon Nai Rath Sakdinamai Khong Chao Nuea Hua" [Thongchai Winichakul: The people in the new feudal state under the

king]. *Prachatai*, 13 September 2021. https://prachatai.com/journal/2021/09/
94971, accessed 4 June 2022.

Wassayos Ngamkham and Aekarach Sattaburuth. "Royal Household Dismisses,
Charges Shamed Ex-Chamberlain Distorn." *Bangkok Post*, 9 November 2017.
https://www.bangkokpost.com/thailand/general/1356979/royal-household-
dismisses-charges-shamed-ex-chamberlain-distorn, accessed 1 June 2022.

1

A Short Biography of King Vajiralongkorn

PAUL M. HANDLEY

> The case is worse when he comes to [the throne] old or middle-aged. He is then unfit to work. He will then have spent the whole of youth and the first part of manhood in idleness, and it is unnatural to expect him to labor. The only fit material for a constitutional king is a prince who begins early to reign—who in his youth is superior to pleasure—who in his youth is willing to labor—who has by nature a genius for discretion. Such kings are among God's greatest gifts, but they are also among His rarest.
> — Walter Bagehot, *The English Constitution*

ON 4 MAY 2019, Thailand crowned a new sovereign, Maha Vajiralongkorn, or Rama X, three years after the death of his father, King Bhumibol Adulyadej.

Bhumibol, the ninth king of the Chakri dynasty, passed away at eighty-eight years old, and had ruled Thailand for seventy years; he was the only king almost any Thai had ever known. He was the constant, when prime ministers and political parties came and went. He, and his predecessor kings, embodied the state, the culture, continuity, and stability. He was likewise identified with democracy, which was described officially as the "tradition" of the kings of Siam, or, under Bhumibol after 1948, Thailand. By the twenty-first century, after decades under one king, the institution of the monarchy, and the monarch himself, seemed inseparable from government.

According to Vernon Bogdanor, the British historian and expert on constitutional monarchy: "The crucial function of the monarchy in a democracy is to sustain the legitimacy of the state."[1] Bhumibol went well beyond this, establishing a symbiotic relationship with politicians, bureaucrats, and especially the generals of the Thai armed forces, who allowed him tangible powers in exchange for his endorsement, which they used and abused to sustain very often corruptly privileged positions. Bhumibol was threatened several times during his reign, when headstrong generals and politicians sought to wield power without his endorsement. But the longer he was there, the more the weight swung the other way. The politicians and generals needed his imprimatur for legitimacy, which he could leverage to his advantage.

After Bhumibol's storied intervention in 1992 against an unpopular military junta, it became accepted that he favored a democratically elected government for Thailand. That appeared to settle the country's political trajectory, once and for all. But in 2006, the year that the kingdom celebrated the auspicious twelfth cycle of Bhumibol's reign and the triumph of his restoration of a consequential and respected monarchy, the institution, and the democratic system of government, lost their footing. Faced with a choice between the democratic processes he had become so identified with, and conservative forces that viewed elected Prime Minister Thaksin Shinawatra as a threat to the monarchy and their own privilege, Bhumibol appeared uncertain and indecisive. When he finally lent his support to the military overthrow of Thaksin, the country was once again reminded of the real bargain that has underpinned Thailand's constitutional monarchy. The throne depended on the army's support to survive, and the generals held more power than any institution.

In a sort of interregnum, for the next thirteen years, the monarchy was essentially vacant. Its moderating role failed and gave way to two military coups, repeated bouts of deadly violence on the streets of Bangkok, atrophy of the political system, deterioration of the judicial system, and splintering of the civil society that had become stronger over the preceding two decades. His political weakness matched by physical frailty, Bhumibol was less and less visible, and frequently hospitalized, until he could not even wave his own hand to adoring subjects. His queen, Sirikit, immobilized by a stroke that had left her partially paralyzed, could not substitute for him to project the Ninth Reign's presence.

On the streets, royalist Yellow Shirt campaigners, backed by the military and the old elite, readily hijacked and abused the monarchy's name to justify the military's power grab. Their opponents, the pro-Thaksin Red Shirts and others, a younger generation more habituated to post-1992 democratic party politics than relying on a king's course-setting, only grew more doubtful of the monarchy's value.

As they fought, both sides were equally concerned about the future of the royal institution after Bhumibol passed. Crown Prince Vajiralongkorn, Bhumibol's only son, designated the official heir in 1972, was barely present. He passed most of his time with his multiple consorts and young son, Prince Dipangkorn Rasmijoti, in Germany, where he eventually bought two baronial homes near Munich. Vajiralongkorn's record as king-in-waiting was long a source of concern for royal-watchers. Mostly known to the people by tales spread by word-of-mouth, he was understood already in the 1980s to be abusive of his power, a serial womanizer, deeply vengeful, and violent, possibly homicidally so.

As the years passed, the constant stories of his familial troubles, and his disinterest in performing the royal duties that his father and sisters carried out with discipline, sustained this picture. The Thai people made their views of him known with open expressions of support for his younger sister Princess Sirindhorn, the designated alternate for succession. But, she was never a real choice. In 2006 she was fifty-one, unmarried, and childless, and so unable to sustain the hereditary monarchy on her own. She also never displayed any ability to temper her brother. Liked or feared, Vajiralongkorn was Bhumibol's successor, the future of the Chakri dynasty.

The interregnum was a period when the palace and military elite sought to extinguish the threat of Thaksin and protect their own power. They felt the need to ensure that the transfer of the crown, when Bhumibol did pass, went off without challenge or dispute. Meanwhile, their opponents sought to restore democratically chosen government, which they hoped could insulate the people from a likely capricious and impervious monarch after Bhumibol, and from his military allies.

The coup of 19 September 2006 failed to resolve this conflict. While Thaksin went into exile, his movement remained strong, taking advantage of the coup leaders' pledge to restore elected government to stage a comeback under his sister Yingluck Shinawatra, who became prime minister in 2011. While she and her brother took pains to demonstrate that they did not oppose Vajiralongkorn or harbor republican sentiments, they were distrusted by core factions in the military who allied themselves with the palace. Indeed, among the Shinawatras' supporters were many who had become deeply anti-military and anti-monarchy after years of fighting for a stronger democracy.

The second military coup, on 22 May 2014, sought to eliminate any path to power for the Shinawatras, the Red Shirts, and their allies. It ensured that generals supportive of Vajiralongkorn were in full control of government when Bhumibol died. They were committed to the concept of the traditional monarchy, to the king as head of state, and to protecting Vajiralongkorn. But they were equally committed to the deal by which the throne guaranteed their own special powers and benefits. They needed the succession to take place smoothly to ensure those benefits remained in place.

༄

Constitutional monarchy has been Thailand's choice, as it is Japan's and England's, where that system of government functions well as a modern democracy with an elected head of government. There is no real need, nor much justification, for a hereditary monarchy in a democracy, as the examples of France and the United States have proved, after bloody revolutions to dispense with it. But the cultural bedrock of monarchy can contribute to a nation's unity, and so can arguably be worth the cost of upkeep for pampered princesses and gilded palaces, and the occasional embarrassments wrought by reckless members of the royal family.

The coronation of the late Bhumibol's only son on 4 May 2019 ended the interregnum by resolving one key issue. It placed a new, active, and healthy king, with the new title Maha Vajiralongkorn, on the throne, with his attractive new queen. And he had children who, theoretically, could sustain the dynasty further. On the surface of it all, the Thai people were assured their monarchy and kingdom would endure. Theoretically, it was an opportunity for a fresh start, for the people, for politics, and for Vajiralongkorn, who had waited in the wings for many decades.

Several constants that arced through his life offered potential insights into how Vajiralongkorn would approach kingship. First was his formal preparation, learning the rituals and the ceremonies of a king, and the power and message they can project, with nothing explicitly spoken. Second was his military training, which is most important to his self-identity, giving him confidence, discipline, and command. Third was his unremitting indulgence in women and carnal pleasures that endowed him with an extremely turbulent marital history and, ironically, left the dynasty without a clear course after him.

Vajiralongkorn was born at 17:45 on 28 July 1952, a Monday, at Dusit Palace. It was a dynastic landmark, the first birth of a celestial prince since the reign of King Chulalongkorn, who died in 1910. Military bands struck up the royal anthem outside the palace, cannons thundered salutes, and thousands who waited throughout the day cheered. Over the next weeks newspapers and magazines ran photographs of the Chakri heir, shot by doting King Bhumibol himself.

Given the family's wealth and the constant presence of coddling and protective courtiers, a normal upbringing was impossible. But his parents were fairly attentive and sought to raise Vajiralongkorn and his three sisters based somewhat on the semi-Westernized middle-class values of the day. He went to school and played games with other children, learned sports, and had pets. He had all manner of toys, collected miniature cars, and flew kites with the king. He "liked drawing"—as did his father—and was "good in English" in primary school, according to official accounts. When he was older his father took him sailing, and sought to interest him in jazz music; the king played clarinet and saxophone in his own regular pickup combo. At least once they went to a university soccer match together.

From early on Vajiralongkorn also regularly took part in rituals, both those of a normal Thai child and those of a king-to-be. Buddhist and Brahman ritual practice was a duty of the royals, and also a signal of superior virtue. In a famous photograph, five-year-old Prince Vajiralongkorn crouches in front of his father to make an offering. His early education took place in a very small school created in the palace for Bhumibol's and Sirikit's four children, and a sprinkling of the children of the palace elite. (In 1958, it became the Chitralada School.) Bhumibol wanted an international education, like his own, for his only son. On 20 December 1965, at the age of thirteen, Vajiralongkorn addressed the Thai nation in a broadcast. Two weeks later, he underwent a Buddhist ceremony and departed for school in England.

The next nine months were spent at King's Mead Preparatory School in Sussex, which may have proven too much a challenge for his level of English and abilities in other subjects. In September 1966 he transferred to Millfield School in Somerset, often the choice for wealthy parents from Europe, the Middle East, and Asia whose children were not academically strong. His three-and-a-half years in England were not, by his own and others' accounts, completely happy years. He said he learned to be on his own, making his own bed, cleaning his clothes, even tying his own shoes. But he does not appear to have made friends, and reports of discipline problems seeped back to Bangkok.

One traditional path for Siam's high-born princes was military school in the West. His grandfather Prince Mahidol, Bhumibol's father, studied at Harrow and then attended two imperial military academies in Germany. Mahidol's half-brother King Vajiravudh, Rama VI, attended Britain's Royal Military College at Sandhurst for a year, and another half-brother, King Prajadhipok, Rama VII, attended Eton before studying at the Woolwich Royal Military Academy.

With Thailand surrounded by countries battling communist insurgencies and Bhumibol's alliance with, and dependence on, the Thai military deeper than ever, a military career path was unsurprising for Vajiralongkorn. On visits back from England, he joined his father on regular trips to army camps, where, dressed in army fatigues, they watched martial demonstrations and practiced shooting. In 1968 news reports, the sixteen-year-old prince is seen assembling combat rifles and firing a grenade launcher. In January 1971, he is seen with his father, both in fatigues with pistols on their belts, shooting M16s at Phuping, Chiang Mai. In May 1971, he underwent basic parachute training at Naresuan Camp in Hua Hin, receiving honorary wings for a parachutist first class. These were not just outings for fun; they were part of Vajiralongkorn's royal training, carried out in ritual form, to effect his socialization with the soldiers who would eventually serve him and protect him.

Both Sandhurst and the West Point military academy in the United States were options for the next stage of Vajiralongkorn's education. The United States was actively currying favor with the royal family at the height of the fight against communists in Southeast Asia. But both schools were likely far too academically rigorous for the young prince, and a third path, still challenging but possibly less so, was Australia's premier military school Duntroon. Canberra, too, saw advantage in building relations with Thailand through the monarchy.

In 1971 Vajiralongkorn entered King's School in Sydney for a year to prepare. In early 1972 he began the grueling four years of field and classroom training at Duntroon, a program in which the weakest, physically and academically, often dropped out after the first or second year. By multiple accounts of classmates, he should have been a dropout, but was given a "diplomatic pass."[2] That said, he learned the discipline and rigors of military training, and gained experience in leading combat squads. He completed the course in January 1976 in a ceremony attended by Queen Sirikit, and was made a lieutenant in the Royal Thai Army, with equal ranks in the navy and air force.

While his trainers and classmates at Duntroon did not think much of his royal blood, his stature grew back home in Thailand. In December 1972 Bhumibol had Vajiralongkorn return to Bangkok for his coming-of-age ceremony. Nine days of Brahman ritual inside the palace formally designated him as a future sacred ruler. On 28 December, he was formally invested as the crown prince, and presented to the public as the heir to the Chakri throne.

Just after completing Duntroon, he traveled to Thailand and made his presence known, partaking in several royal events with and on behalf of his parents. It was just at the beginning of the turbulent year 1976. But within days he returned to Australia for nine more months, studying special forces tactics at the Special Air Service Regiment in Perth. He then returned to Bangkok in October 1976 as the city was exploding with protests aimed at the military and increasingly the monarchy itself. He plunged into the situation as his father's liaison among the palace, military, and police, and with the Village Scouts, when the massacre of students at Thammasat University occurred on 6 October.

At the time there were already diverging views of the prince's suitability as heir to the throne. Many Thais accepted the official presentation of Vajiralongkorn as a budding warrior king, but among others, including students, his reputation was of a not-too-bright, asocial, imperious, and possibly violent prince, based on stories that had circulated back to Thailand since his school days in England.

A key incident that precipitated the Thammasat massacre reflected these diverging views. A newspaper, *Dao Siam*, published a picture of a mock hanging staged by student activists the day before, in which the effigy hanged resembled Vajiralongkorn, enough so to allege that students were attacking the monarchy.

After the Thammasat bloodshed, with the recent memory of the fall of the monarchy in Laos in December 1975, and Thai students fleeing the cities to join up with the Communist Party of Thailand (CPT), Bhumibol's palace went into crisis mode. It was suddenly essential to ensure the monarchy's future, by extinguishing the CPT threat, and by making sure there was a next generation of royals. As generals again seized political power in a coup, the royal family strengthened its key alliances in appearances and rituals, with Vajiralongkorn taking part. Four days after the massacre, he presided over a ceremony for the Village Scouts, who had contributed to the violence. He also made formal visits to military and police institutions, to provincial seats, and to key temples. Late that October he joined his parents to open a new session of the newly constituted, military-dominated legislative assembly. And weeks later, he accompanied his parents in a formal review of the armed forces, the annual trooping of the colors, where in a speech King Bhumibol highlighted the dangerous threats to the kingdom.

At the same time, attention returned to a priority set earlier that year: to get Vajiralongkorn married so he could produce royal heirs of his own.

While in Australia he had become enamored with the daughter of a diplomat and minor royal, Laksasubha Kridakara. But his mother the queen had someone else in mind: her own niece, his cousin, Soamsawali Kitiyakara. Their engagement was announced on 17 December 1976, and the wedding took place on 3 January 1977. Nearly two years later she gave birth to the first royal of the next generation of the Mahidol family, Princess Bhajarakitiyabha.

Yet, from the beginning the prince had little time for his wife. He joined some army field activities against the CPT, and stopped living together with Soamsawali by late 1977 when he entered the Army Staff College. Meanwhile he began enjoying the company of other women, mostly from outside the ranks of high society, supplied by powerful men and his military mates. Nine months after Bhajarakitiyabha's birth, he had a son by his favorite, Yuvadhida Polpraserth, later better known as Sujarinee Vivacharawongse.

Stories of his behavior spread while his younger sister Sirindhorn grew in popularity. Though unmarried, she was seen as a rival after she was designated in 1977 as alternate successor, via a constitutional change undertaken in 1974 to allow for a regnant queen, as a practical safeguard for the dynasty should something happen to Vajiralongkorn.

The palace remained focused on Vajiralongkorn's development as the crown prince. In November 1978 he was ordained at the royal temple, Wat Bovornives, under a top monk; present for the ceremony was Deng Xiaoping, just on the cusp of taking power in China. Hoping to get Vajiralongkorn on a disciplined track, in 1980 ex-army chief and prime minister Prem Tinsu-lanonda, one of Bhumibol's closest allies, arranged for the prince to go to the United States for training in special forces operations and flying heli-copters, at bases in Georgia and North Carolina. That, according to one person who was there, boosted his confidence and standing.[3] He earned a promotion to commander of the 1st Infantry Regiment, the King's Own Bodyguard, when he returned to Thailand, and began training on fixed-wing aircraft, quickly moving from a propeller-driven plane to the Cessna-37 trainer jet. In October 1982 he returned to the United States to train at US Air Force bases in Texas and Arizona on the F5E fighter jet. One year later, he flew a Royal Thai Air Force jet in a "live fire" air show in Lopburi. Such accomplishments elevated him well past age-group peers in the armed forces, aside from his special status as a royal. He was quickly promoted to special colonel and then, in 1987 and 1988, was made a major general and command-ing officer in the King's Own Bodyguard.

But what also was clear, those who have known him said, was that the military training, and especially flying, became a very important part of his life and identity. He appreciated the discipline, the command aspects, and, with flying, the freedom and the thrill. He was asked about it in a 1986 interview in *Dichan*, the leading magazine for women and high society.[4] "Do you like to fly?," *Dichan* asked. Vajiralongkorn replied: "I like it. Because it is something that requires skill, using your knowledge and ability at the same time. It requires, one, learning; two, decision-making ability; three, courage; four, your physical strength."

༺༻

While Vajiralongkorn's proto-military career advanced, his family life and reputation with the public went in another direction in the 1980s. In gently negative comments in a US magazine interview, his mother dubbed him a playboy. He was almost never seen with Soamsawali, and after their first daughter they never had another child. Meanwhile he had four more children by Sujarinee, for a total of four boys and one girl, the last born in 1987. He gave Sujarinee and their children royal names, indicating he considered their relationship official.

With his father experiencing serious health problems, and abdication under consideration in the mid-1980s, the crown prince made an effort to

rehabilitate his image and persuade his parents to accept his family with
Sujarinee. This involved undertaking more royal duties, which ranged from
visiting slum areas to offer assistance, to sitting as a judge in several court
cases, to a series of visits to foreign countries. (After 1967 his father never
again traveled abroad, except for one one-day trip to Laos.) In 1986 Vajiralongkorn made official trips to Indonesia and Canada, and in early 1987 to
China.

Even so, scandal followed him. He and others in the royal family were
tied to business scandals and rivalries in military cliques that sparked two
failed coup attempts. An official visit to Japan in late 1987 was a diplomatic
disaster. He cut it short, angry that his hosts, stressing formal royal protocol,
did not invite Sujarinee to travel with him because she was only an unofficial
consort. Nine years later he remained angry and took revenge, holding up
the visit of Japan's prime minister to Bangkok.[5] And in early 1988 he mostly
snubbed the visit of Britain's Prince Charles and Princess Diana, leaving
them in the hands of his sister Princess Sirindhorn.

Even so, he continued his efforts to show himself a worthy heir of his
father and have Sujarinee accepted. From 1988 to 1990 he made official visits
to a number of countries. He made several trips to rural areas to distribute
Buddha Navarajabophit statues, a symbol meant to demonstrate his father's
power and protection over the nation.

Important to this effort at rehabilitation were his 1986 and 1987 inter-
views with *Dichan*. In both, he cleverly showed that he had learned well the
lessons of a *dhammaraja*, a Buddhist king, sounding somewhat like his
father. And, as part of his campaign, he felt confident enough to openly
disparage Soamsawali.[6] He did not name her but very clearly indicated his
view that she did not respect him or the royal institution, and did not
perform her duties as a high princess.

In the 1986 *Dichan* interview, Vajiralongkorn, when asked about his life
and the pressures on him as a crown prince, replied, with a weary Buddhist
acceptance, that it is his fate. Further, the things people say about him, that
is his karma. "What is it like to be the crown prince?," the magazine asked.
"I don't know what it is like, because I have been born—the first second of
my life—I am a prince. It is difficult to say what it is like to be a fish, when
you are a fish, or what it is like to be a bird, when you are a bird."

People do things in his name, and he cannot control it, he says. Nor can
he control gossip about him.

> We have the duty to serve the king to the best of our abilities .... We are taken by the king to be used. And we present our abilities for use .... Maybe in the previous life we did not make merit enough. Or maybe at some time we did deeds that attracted reproach .... Things that are not true, or not correct, I feel, whatever, nothing. Just leave them. This is detachment. We do our duty ... in the name of the king, as his representatives. If no one comes, we still have to do it. Our feelings about this are something aside.

In the 1987 *Dichan* interview, he was asked whether he was a "black sheep" in the royal family, as some had said. He replied equally stoically. "It is funny. Sometimes a black sheep has its purpose. I want to reiterate, a black sheep has a purpose. Sometimes it's like making merit for someone else, being a black sheep for someone else. Or someone else designates you as the black sheep—other sheep might not be so white, but this makes them look whiter."

The theme of no-fault fatalism echoed through a third interview that he gave the magazine five years later, in 1992. Gossip had put him at the center of shady businesses and financial scams that accompanied the economic boom. A group of Thai reporters was called in and coached to ask specifically about his reputation as a *chao pho* (godfather).[7]

"For some time some people have said too much that the crown prince has businesses like pubs, bars, discotheques, whatever—this is the prince's, that is the prince's, and that is the prince's. ... The prince is a *chao pho*, in trust companies and finance companies, and chit funds ... a great tycoon with billions," he said.

"I don't have any experience in these things. If I really did it, the business would lose millions and millions, probably lose it all," he continued.

"No one's life goes smoothly all the time. But it is important to remember that it is never too late to work for good things. It is never too late to start working or searching for responsibility. There is a Buddhist saying that no karma is more important than present action."

At the end of 1989 he resumed his military education to burnish his preparation for the throne, enrolling in Britain's highly respected Royal College of Defence Studies. The course was designed to broaden the world vision of those destined for leadership. The British made special efforts to keep him apace with brighter students, but after a time he began to slip, not doing all the work. While there were troubled relations with his classmates, and some bad reports in the British press, when he completed it he was finally rewarded for all his efforts. On Queen Sirikit's birthday in August

1991, Soamsawali's official title was downgraded, from "royal consort" to "mother of the king's grandchild."

With his eye on getting a divorce and marrying Sujarinee, he continued in his royal duties, joining his parents in rituals for Vishaka Puja and taking official trips to Vietnam, North Korea, and Belgium. In December 1992, he presided over the much-heralded, multimillion-dollar project to cast an auspicious, solid gold Buddha footprint for the Queen's sixtieth birthday. And in mid-1993 he cast images of the Buddha and Chinese goddess Guan Yin to be installed in Wat Bovornives.

There were numerous other official functions and rituals that he led or joined, and in 1994 Sujarinee and their five children also took part, publicly. By that time his parents could not help but accept them: the four boys were the only heirs of the royal mantle in the next generation. Finally, with apparent blessing from the king and queen, he petitioned for divorce from Soamsawali in January 1993. The allegations detailed in the court filing were brutal, accusing her of numerous personal offenses against him, and failures as a wife and princess dating to the outset of their marriage.[8]

> Starting from living together as husband and wife, plaintiff and defendant had disputes and continually failed to get along, owing to the defendant not showing interest in caring for the plaintiff as her husband, and otherwise behaving aggressively to defame the plaintiff in front of other people, both in behavior and speech, and did not respect or obey the plaintiff, when the plaintiff advised or warned her in good faith.

In a rebuttal, Soamsawali denied all of the accusations while charging that he was involved with other women from the very beginning of the marriage. But her defense was in vain, and the divorce was finalized in July 1993. Seven months later the prince married Sujarinee in a quiet palace ceremony presided by Bhumibol, and she was given the right to append "Mahidol" to her name, formalizing her position, and that of her children, in the royal family. Thais expected that she would one day become the queen.

Yet, his relationship with Sujarinee was already fraught. Even in the 1980s she was only one among multiple women in a sort of "harem" Vajiralongkorn kept, in a pleasure house he retired to almost every afternoon in the back of his Nonthaburi Palace compound.[9] By the time they were married, he already had new favorites, including another young woman of modest commoner background, Srirasmi Suwadee.

Within two years the marriage with Sujarinee crumbled, a victim of his capricious temper and paranoia and constant desire for younger women. Suddenly in May 1996, while she and their children were abroad, he very publicly declared her persona non grata. He forcibly brought their daughter back to Thailand, and left Sujarinee and their sons to fend for themselves as political refugees in the United States, warned never to return. In charges equally merciless to those against Soamsawali, he accused her of defrauding the royal institution, sleeping with his also-defenestrated military aide. He spread a story that she and her family were involved in smuggling heroin, and he released a collection of nude pictures of her.[10]

For just a moment after that, it appeared that, at forty-four, Vajiralongkorn had finally grown into his position as crown prince. He reappeared in public several times with Princess Soamsawali and their daughter, suggesting that they were permanently reunited. He stood in for his father in royal duties and rituals. On the very day he ejected Sujarinee, he presided over the creation of more auspicious Buddha images at the royal Wat Phra Kaew. Months later he undertook a 15-day tour of South America. But this kind of activity lasted only a few months. By the end of 1996, he was no longer seen with Soamsawali and sharply curtailed official activities. He began traveling to Germany for what was widely believed to be a seriously threatening medical condition, which many thought was HIV infection. In public and photographs he appeared haggard and weakened, though there was never any confirmation that he was unhealthy.

As he spent more and more time in Germany—meaning he was less available for official duties—he took a new wife, his third: Srirasmi. They married in 2001, the prince telling reporters the following year, "I am now 50 years old and think I should have a complete family."

Over time the prince's health appeared to slowly improve. Four years after they married, Srirasmi gave birth to a boy, Dipangkorn Rasmijoti. With Vajiralongkorn's other sons banished to the United States and stripped of their titles, the future of the Mahidol line on the throne was pinned on him. None of his cousins, all women, nor his half-sister, Soamsawali's daughter Bhajarakitiyabha, had married or had children as of the end of 2020. Yet there remained a significant question mark over the dynasty, because, it was understood, Dipangkorn has significant learning disabilities that would make it impractical for him to assume the throne. He was raised and attended school in Germany, and for much of the first two decades of the twenty-first century, he and parents were rarely in Thailand.

Even as he spent much time abroad, in the 2000s Vajiralongkorn understood the political challenges facing the kingdom he would one day inherit. He sought at various times to moderate and resolve the break between the military and Thaksin, though without result. Thaksin remained in exile after 2006, and his influence waned as the opposition to the military junta evolved without him. Vajiralongkorn also appeared conscious of the need to avoid taking sides in the Red Shirt–Yellow Shirt fights, given that the monarch was supposed to be a unifying figure.

But, by the time his father died in 2016, the central themes of his life remained in place. He stayed mostly in Germany, seemingly oblivious to the massive costs that the palace and country shouldered, for the multiple aircraft that flew him around, for the luxury hotels he commandeered, and for the lakeside mansions he bought in Bavaria. He surrounded himself with military officials and ran his own palace and retinue as if it were an army unit. After becoming king he had uniforms for the police and military redesigned and issued them spartan new haircut rules, including for women. He also ordered a new method of saluting. He ran his staff and the "harem" he kept with military discipline, severely punishing those who crossed him. Several people in his orbit died suddenly after reportedly angering him.

His marital life was still tumultuous, and he continued to resolve conflicts with his wives with brutal treatment. In 2014, he summarily ejected Srirasmi from the palace, exiling her internally to a ramshackle farmhouse and having members of her family jailed.[11]

Replacing her as the new favorite was Suthida Tidjai, a former Thai Airways flight attendant in his retinue since the early 2000s. Suthida was named his queen after he was crowned in 2019. Shortly after that, in July 2019, he designated another regular companion, Niramon Ounprom, his official consort and gave her a royal name based on his own, Sineenat Wongvajirapakdi. Three months later, after Sineenat reportedly acted in a way to offend Queen Suthida, Vajiralongkorn stripped her of her title and positions, and then she disappeared for 10 months, thought to be confined or even jailed. In August 2020 she was suddenly rehabilitated, and thereafter made regular appearances with the prince. Suthida was still officially queen, but Sineenat was apparently his preferred companion, at least for a short while. She disappeared from public view again in late 2021.

ॐ

Beginning in late 2020 King Maha Vajiralongkorn began spending nearly all of his time in Thailand, due in part to the restrictions of the COVID-19 pandemic, and possibly also due to heightened public criticism in Germany of his residence there.

But in Thailand he faced visible criticism of the monarchy and its military allies almost daily that challenged him to weigh more seriously his position. There was a resurgence of anti-royalism, and palpable republicanism, partly rooted in domestic electoral politics, but also in the sense that, if the king was absent, what was his value? In response, Vajiralongkorn undertook more royal rituals, using them to demonstrate his power, to show who was in or out of favor, and to underscore that he was determined to reign, and in his own way.

The government met the rise in public and online protests with expanded application of internal security and lèse-majesté laws. Yet the experience of filing scores of lèse-majesté cases against government critics a decade earlier was that it only added to anti-monarchy sentiment. The primary issue was the military's continued control of the government, and repression of any popular movement or political party that would challenge that. It placed Vajiralongkorn in the same place his father was several times during his reign, torn between his military guarantors and principles of democratic government.

While the king's hand was not always clear, there were indications that his answer was to go backward toward the era of absolute monarchy. Unlike his father, he raised no questions about the military's abuse of political power or its deep corruption. Instead, there were multiple efforts to erase the memory of the 1932 revolution that established the constitutional monarchy.

His model, many thought, was the monarchy of King Vajiravudh, from 1910 to 1925. Rama VI likewise was enamored with military discipline and ceremony, and was less given to the Buddhist *dhammaraja* underpinnings of the monarchy. He also appeared to indulge himself carnally, though with men, not women. And he failed to provide an heir to the throne, though his own father's profligacy ensured that he had several brothers in line for succession.

Yet, pushing back against popular democratic forces with a turn toward the pre-revolution monarchy and a militarist style of government invites overt challenges to Vajiralongkorn's throne. Those could elevate the risks of facing the institution. Vajiralongkorn's personal behavior also creates risks. His profligacy, and his seizure of full, direct ownership of the assets of the massive Crown Property Bureau, which Bhumibol had shaped as a kind of national investment fund, also stir questions and criticism. Will Vajiralongkorn, as his father and mother had done, muster royal wealth for the good of the people, or deploy it mainly for his and his throne's benefits?

In addition, Vajiralongkorn's turbulent personal life has left the monarchy and Chakri dynasty without a clear future—another potential source of instability. He has no clear heir who could sustain the monarchy. His heir apparent, Prince Dipangkorn, is not likely suitable given his apparent developmental disabilities. His royal daughters and nieces are all unmarried and show no sign of producing their own heirs. And his four other sons by his second wife, Sujarinee, remain exiled in the United States, with no sign that he will accept them back.

Vajiralongkorn has given no indication of how he plans to ensure succession, leaving the possibility of a serious crisis if he dies suddenly with no replacement. The question would not only be whether there is a legitimate and viable successor, but whether the monarchy should be continued altogether.

Notes

1 Bogdanor, *The Monarchy and the Constitution*, 302.

2 Confidential interview with a Duntroon schoolmate of Vajiralongkorn's, Bangkok, March 1996.

3 Confidential interview with US diplomat, August 1994.

4 *Dichan*, 15 August 1986.

5 Handley, *The King Never Smiles*, 321–22 and 402.

6 *Dichan*, 15 August 1986 and 15 October 1987.

7 "CP Denies 'Chao Pho' Gossip and Lashes Out," 30 December 1992.

8 Divorce Court Case #79/2536, at Juvenile and Family Court, 27 January 2536.

9 Confidential interview, Washington, DC, 2019.

10 Handley, *The King Never Smiles*, 403–4.

11 Pavin, "Dhaveevatthana Prison."

References

Bagehot, Walter. *The English Constitution*. Cambridge: Cambridge University Press, 2001.

Bogdanor, Vernon. *The Monarchy and the Constitution*. Oxford: Clarendon, 1995.

Handley, Paul M. *The King Never Smiles: A Biography of Thailand's Bhumibol Adulyadej*. New Haven, CT: Yale University Press, 2006.

Pavin Chachavalpongpun. "Dhaveevatthana Prison: Hell on Earth in Thailand." *Japan Times*, 2 June 2017. https://www.japantimes.co.jp/opinion/2017/06/02/commentary/world-commentary/dhaveevatthana-prison-hell-earth-thailand/, accessed 7 July 2022.

2

The Making of Thailand's Extra-Constitutional Monarchy

FEDERICO FERRARA

Introduction

FEW COUNTRIES EPITOMIZE the adversities non-Western nations have met with in their quest to build stable liberal democracies as compellingly as the kingdom of Thailand. During the so-called Third Wave of democratization alone, Thailand underwent no less than three democratic transitions, the first of which was occasioned by the massive demonstrations that toppled a venal military regime in 1973.[1] And though the country's democratization suffered two major reversals as a consequence of military coups staged in 1976 and 1991, the "People Power" protests that last restored Thailand to the ranks of the world's "electoral democracies" in 1992 had once appeared to have discredited the armed forces so thoroughly as to make another coup virtually unimaginable. Following the promulgation of the so-called People's Constitution in 1997, Freedom House rewarded Thailand with the "Free" rating it reserves for real, liberal democracies—a designation the country had attained only twice before, in the "Freedom in the World" issues covering the years 1975 and 1989/90.[2] At long last, by the turn of the century, democracy in Thailand had seemed on the verge of becoming "the only game in town," especially after it endured the devastation wrought by the Asian Financial Crisis without succumbing to authoritarianism.[3]

The crisis, however, had also set in motion a sequence of events that caused Thailand to lose its "Free" rating in 2005 and its formal democracy in 2006, turning the country from a success story to a cautionary tale in the

space of a single electoral cycle. The run-up to the military coup staged on
19 September 2006—and the years of conflict that ensued—exemplify several
of the tribulations experienced by non-Western, developing nations during
the period of democratic recession, retreat, or retrenchment that followed
the end of the "Third Wave."[4] On the one hand, Thailand's sharp illiberal
turn under the leadership of wildly popular elected prime minister Thaksin
Shinawatra (2001/06) fit the narrative popularized at the time by commen-
tators such as Fareed Zakaria regarding "the rise of illiberal democracy" in
countries where democratic institutions were being hollowed out of their
"liberal" substance by elected leaders with little patience for the constitutional
rights of individuals and minorities.[5] On the other hand, the conflict that
unfolded in the years since has demonstrated that a large and influential
portion of the country's electorate and civil society—above all, Bangkok's
middle and upper-middle class, its organizational expressions in the nation's
political and associational life, and its intellectual vanguard of statesmen,
civil servants, activists, labor leaders, pundits, and academics—have yet to
accept the legitimacy of competitive processes governed by principles of
universal suffrage and majority rule. These actors and constituencies played
a crucial role in laying the groundwork for the royalist military coups staged
in 2006 and, with far more egregious consequences, in 2014. Indeed,
Bangkok's middle and upper-middle class has by and large remained
supportive of General Prayuth Chan-ocha's regime despite the efforts made
by Thailand's entire royalist establishment to rig the 2019 general elections,
which have allowed General Prayuth to stay in office beyond the formal
restoration of civilian rule. On this count, too, Thailand is hardly a unique
case, as underscored by the literature on the "revolt of the middle class"
responsible for instances of democratic breakdown or backsliding across the
developing world.[6]

Despite having many similarities with the rest of the developing world,
Thailand's reiterated failure to build a consolidated democracy cannot be
understood without reference to something decidedly more peculiar to the
nation's political development—namely, the role that the monarchy and the
reigning dynasty have played in its repeated oscillations between alternative
regime types, whose most visible manifestation is the succession of twenty
constitutions promulgated since 1932. Only a few decades removed from
having presided over the kingdom of Siam's transformation into a bounded,
centralized nation-state around the turn of the last century, Thailand's

monarchy was seemingly consigned to irrelevance upon succumbing to the unintended consequences of its own state-building reforms. Having been stripped of most of its powers and property in the years following the inauguration of the country's first constitutional regime in 1932, the monarchy went on to stage a most improbable comeback during the seventy-year reign of King Bhumibol Adulyadej (1946–2016). Over the course of his reign the palace and its allies exploited the "bureaucratic polity's" deficit of legitimacy,[7] as well as the Central Intelligence Agency's search of a local bulwark against the onslaught of communism in the region to restore the king to a position outside—indeed, decidedly *above*[8]—the country's ever-changing constitutional order, presiding over a hierarchy of karmic merit and purity,[9] which the state-sanctioned ideology of "royal nationalism" (*rachachatniyom*) had substituted for more egalitarian conceptions of the Thai nation.[10]

By the late 1970s, Bhumibol had become the country's most popular—and in many ways most powerful—political figure. Widely regarded as the ultimate arbiter of Thailand's political conflicts, his assent would henceforth be decisive to the survival of any government, the longevity of any regime, and the success of any coup d'état. Meanwhile, a network of royalist officials came to dominate the civilian and the military bureaucracies, carving out for themselves "reserve domains" that fixed the limits of the authority of duly constituted civilian governments well short of those set by the constitution.[11] Indeed, military coups were not only consistent with the idea of "democracy with the king as head of state," as underscored by the fact that the king was understood to retain his authority even in the absence of a constitution enumerating his powers; what is more, coups formed an integral part of the royalist establishment's arsenal of extra-constitutional powers, especially as elected politicians increasingly mistook their success at the ballot box as a mandate for exercising the prerogatives formally vested in them by the constitution. Holding the system together was the hegemonic status of "royal nationalism" and the cult of personality built around King Bhumibol through decades of taxpayer-funded propaganda as well as the enforcement of one of the world's harshest lèse-majesté laws. In the twilight of the king's life, an article in the *London Review of Books* ventured the assessment that "there is no deeper or more enduring cult of leadership outside North Korea."[12]

As it turns out, King Bhumibol's popularity and mild mannered, well-intentioned image—though periodically belied by the atrocities committed in his name and by the stridency of his actual speeches—kept the contradictions inherent to this state of affairs from spiraling out of control. On the day of his passing, 13 October 2016, Bhumibol had been the world's richest and longest-serving monarch for some time, and by some distance. And yet, it had long become clear that Bhumibol's succession with a less capable, less disciplined heir apparent—the erstwhile Crown Prince Maha Vajiralongkorn—would, in time, come to present an existential threat for the institution. Most obviously, Vajiralongkorn's accession instantiated anxieties that had troubled Bhumibol's uncle and predecessor, King Prajadhipok (1925–35), to the point of committing them to print. Years before he was forced to relinquish his absolute powers at the barrel of a gun, Prajadhipok had worried about the dangers that the Chakri dynasty would come up against should a "bad king" ascend the throne in a legal context that provided for no remedy other than, as he put it, "to chop off his head."[13] If anything, the actions Vajiralongkorn saw fit to take upon becoming king exacerbated this context, such as dismantling most of the legal constraints on the king's management of palace affairs and security, or his disposal of tens of billions of dollars' worth of crown property. In this sense, Thailand appears to be approaching full circle, for if the monarchy has never been more wealthy and powerful since 1932, its survival has never been more in doubt.

In fairness, the blame does not rest entirely—or even primarily—with the throne's current occupant. The monarchy's extra-constitutional status is not of Vajiralongkorn's own making. Nor can the increasingly widespread realization that the monarchy is—and has been for some time—an obstacle to the country's democratization be ascribed to the new king's admittedly bizarre behavior. On the contrary, the responsibility lies with those who repeatedly allowed the monarchy to be used as an all-purpose excuse to abridge the civil and political rights of individuals, and to strip the people as a whole of their right to self-determination, despite knowing full well that the tenuous legitimacy of these actions hinged on the popularity of an aging monarch. That Vajiralongkorn would not be up to the task of preserving the monarchy against the contradictions of the extra-constitutional role asserted by his father and predecessor was common knowledge in and around the palace throughout his long tenure as crown prince—at any rate, long before his Caligula-esque proclivities became tabloid fodder in Europe and elsewhere.[14] Just how hard King Bhumibol's aides really tried to prevent

Vajiralongkorn from inheriting the crown is the subject of dispute. What appears certain is that, as the Ninth Reign was coming to a close, none of the officials entrusted with the monarchy's protection—the apotheosized King Bhumibol foremost among them—showed any willingness to forego immediate expediency in order to safeguard the institution's future: *Après nous, le déluge.*

This chapter traces the historical construction of the Thai monarchy's extra-constitutional role over the past century and a half, focusing on the events and processes that have contributed to the formation, the development, and ultimately the decay of Thailand's own "peculiar institution," to borrow an expression from a different time and place. After contrasting Thailand's "extra-constitutional monarchy" with absolute and constitutional varieties of monarchical regimes, the chapter dedicates separate sections to its historical and intellectual origins, its apogee and decline, and its future prospects, which are shown to hinge on the capacity of the palace and its allies to undertake the reforms required to inaugurate a genuine constitutional monarchy. Many of these issues also form the subject of the wide-ranging comparative analysis carried out by David Streckfuss in this volume's next chapter.

Of Monarchies Absolute, Constitutional, and Otherwise

King Vajiralongkorn Bodhindradhebayavarangkul, the Chakri dynasty's tenth, ascended the throne in 2016 in circumstances that did not prefigure an especially successful reign. Though the Thai state's propaganda machine had kicked into gear in the last decade of King Bhumibol's life to promote the image of the then crown prince, it was clear that Vajiralongkorn would not inherit his father's domestic popularity and international respectability. Between the dubious associations, the messy separations from each of his three ex-wives, the reputation for cruelty and violence, the well-documented pattern of bizarre public behavior, and the rumors alleging poor intelligence, drug abuse, serial philandering, inveterate gambling, terminal illness, and even murder,[15] it has long been certain that no amount of propaganda could remake Vajiralongkorn—now seventy-one—into a plausible *dhammaraja.*[16] What is worse, his inheritance included historic challenges to the monarchy's power and legitimacy few had ever thought him to be properly equipped to handle. Indeed, the coup staged on 22 May 2014 has often been interpreted as motivated by the desire of conservative royalist officials to manage the succession, thereby ensuring that the new king could not be lured or bribed into an arrangement with former prime minister Thaksin and his allies, or otherwise preside over the destruction of the royalist political order built in the Ninth Reign. And while there were some who went so far as to delude themselves—despite the mountain of evidence to the contrary—that Vajiralongkorn harbored secret sympathies for the "red," pro-democracy side of Thailand's political divide, his clear preference for living in Europe and apparent disinterest in public affairs did give rise to more generalized expectations that his reign would be passive and listless, if not altogether helpless.

Such expectations, however, were disappointed as Vajiralongkorn acted swiftly, not just to protect the monarchy's "extra-constitutional" status, but also to enshrine into law the king's direct control of the royal household, palace security, and crown property. The opportunity to take actions of this sort was created by a favorable conjuncture that provided the new king with considerable leverage over General Prayuth Chan-ocha and his henchmen. At the time of Bhumibol's death, the junta was in the process of enacting a new "permanent" constitution whose provisions were of crucial importance for the generals. First and foremost, the new constitution would grant the coup-makers complete immunity from prosecution for seizing power unlawfully as well as blanket impunity for any and all actions taken before and after the 2014 coup. Almost equally important, particularly given the failure of the previous coup, royalists hoped that the new charter would institutionalize the military's continuing influence over the country's government long past the elections that would soon sanction Thailand's formal return to civilian rule, while denying elected politicians the chance to govern the country. As Prayuth himself had boasted,[17] in stark contrast with the efforts made by the junta's spin doctors to make the planned "reforms" palatable to domestic and international audiences, the goal was to restore Thailand to how it had existed five or six decades prior, rolling back the clock to a time before economic development and foreign ideas had fooled its people into chasing fantasies of empowerment.[18] Panitan Wattanayagorn publicly expressed his hope that the new charter should reflect "Thainess, the submission culture, the belief in seniority and military hierarchy."[19] Coupled with the measures taken to suppress all oppositions, which have amounted to the most expansive rollback in the Thai people's civil and political rights since the 1970s, the new constitution was supposed to ensure that no electoral, civilian force would ever again be in a position to challenge the country's "monarchy-centered hierarchical political order."[20]

Vajiralongkorn exploited the process's vital importance for the generals to extract substantial concessions, holding up the promulgation of the new constitution until significant changes were made to the charter itself—it mattered little that the main text had been approved in a public referendum months earlier—and new legislation was passed for the personal benefit of the king. The changes to the constitution, which were made public only after the charter had been promulgated and published in the *Royal Gazette*, relieved the king of the obligation to appoint a regent in his absence from the country, while increasing the king's control over the process by which a regent is appointed in other circumstances.[21] Almost concurrent with the constitution's promulgation, the junta's handpicked National Legislative Assembly approved measures that granted the king personal control over the Royal Household Bureau, the Office of His Majesty's Private Secretary, and palace security agencies previously under military or government control.[22] Later, two crucial infantry regiments stationed in and around Bangkok (the 1st and the 11th, collectively known as the King's Guard) were detached from the army's chain of command and assigned to the king's personal control via emergency decree.[23] Within three months of the constitution's promulgation, moreover, the junta's legislature amended the Crown Property Act, which now granted the king complete control over the Crown Property Bureau, unencumbered by any form of government oversight, and clarified the previously ambiguous status of crown property by declaring it the king's personal property.[24]

Commenting on this series of measures, an article in *The Economist* concluded that Vajiralongkorn is in the process of restoring the absolute monarchy in all but name.[25] Indeed, there can be no doubt that the reforms introduced at the king's behest have made the monarchy more powerful in a formal sense than it has been at any point since 1932. Substantively, however, the truth is somewhat more complicated. As a matter of fact, King Bhumibol had long arrogated in practice some of the prerogatives that were formally transferred to the king early in the Tenth Reign, such as the exclusive control of crown property. And while Bhumibol had attempted a similar power play in advance of the promulgation of a "permanent" constitution

in 1952, with decidedly mixed results, by the second half of his reign he had
evidently seen little need to oversee palace affairs and security personally.[26]
Similarly, while Vajiralongkorn's takeover of the King's Guard makes it
virtually impossible for any military coup to succeed without the king's
assent, in practice that had long been the case during the Ninth Reign.
Vajiralongkorn, then, is not so much engaged in an effort to restore the
absolute monarchy, or make the king more powerful in substantive terms,
as much as he is trying to ward off challenges to the monarchy's power and
status—some of them inherited, and some stemming from his own unpop-
ularity—by enshrining into legislation prerogatives Bhumibol had already
exercised in practice, or had never bothered personally to exercise.

Even at the height of Bhumibol's powers—in the period when the king
came close to running the country by proxy, in the person of the trusty
general and former prime minister Prem Tinsulanonda (1980–88)—it is
arguably more appropriate to describe the Thai monarchy as an "extra-
constitutional monarchy," which sets it apart from both "absolute" and
"constitutional" varieties of monarchical regimes. In a "constitutional monarchy," sovereignty is typically understood to rest with the people and its
representatives, and the monarchy's authority is limited to what is provided
in the constitution. In an "extra-constitutional monarchy" as in an "absolute
monarchy," conversely, the monarchy's status and power do not hinge on the
presence of a constitution that formally spells out its prerogatives. In the
specific case, the Thai monarchy's authority exists independently of what the
constitution *du jour* happens to provide. The fact that the king conserves his
authority even after the constitution is abrogated—as is typically the case in
the aftermath of military coups—indicates that His Majesty reigns by something more akin to natural right than positive law. A noted royalist stated as
much in a best-selling book published in 2005,[27] in which he argued that
"the constitution is not above the king in any way. ... [T]he status of the king
does not come under the constitution."[28] Whereas the stated intent of the
revolution that overthrew the absolute monarchy on 24 June 1932 had been
to place the king "under the law of the land" (*yu tai kotmai thammanoon kan
pokkhrong phaendin*), Bhumibol's seventy-year reign gave rise to a system of
government that effectively elevates the king *above* the constitution.[29]

Then again, while all absolute monarchies are also extra-constitutional
in nature—indeed, as Streckfuss's chapter in this volume suggests, many
"constitutional monarchies" also have extra-constitutional elements or

prerogatives—not all extra-constitutional monarchies qualify as "absolute." An "absolute monarchy" is by definition a system of government where the king, as sovereign, can dispose of all land and all life within the kingdom's confines, whether as "divine right" or based on the Hobbesian assumption that the people, if they knew their true interests, would themselves irrevocably delegate their sovereignty to a single Leviathan wielding absolute powers. This, however, is clearly not the case of Thailand's "extra-constitutional monarchy," where the king's authority may not derive from, nor is meaningfully hindered by, the constitution, but whose powers are still well short of "absolute"—both in theory, as all constitutions since 1932 have referred to the concept of popular sovereignty, and in practice, where the king is not the sole locus of legitimate authority.[30] Indeed, the political instability Thailand experienced throughout the Ninth Reign reflects at once the depth or expanse as well as the limits of royal authority. On the one hand, the network of power and influence presided over by the king has proven sufficiently entrenched to maintain its effective control of much of the state apparatus, despite the vicissitudes of the country's formal constitutional structure, while the hold of its official ideology has permitted it frequently to undo governments and constitutions that threatened its interests. On the other hand, the alliance formed under the aegis of King Bhumibol among the monarchy, the military, and business elites has never achieved, internally, the levels of cohesiveness required to build a strong state and a durable authoritarian regime,[31] and it has never asserted, externally, the levels of dominance required to prevent challenges to its power from routinely cropping up.[32] Nor has its "royal nationalism," successful though it was in shaping the worldview of millions, ever managed to extinguish popular demands for greater democracy.

Above all, however, the reason why Thailand's monarchy is best described as an "extra-constitutional monarchy" is that while the king exercises a varying set of formal, constitutional prerogatives, its most significant powers are still extra-constitutional in nature. Among the Ninth Reign's signature accomplishments was to assert the king's role as the ultimate arbiter of disputes that cannot—or for different reasons would not—be resolved in accordance with the law of the land, as in the wake of military coups. Recent constitutions have acknowledged as much in provisions such as Article 7 of the 1997 and 2007 charters, which famously states:[33] "Whenever no provision under this Constitution is applicable to any case, it shall be decided in accordance with the constitutional practice in the democratic regime of government with the King as Head of the State."

As Connors explained, the provision served to (1) sanction the king's right to render lawful any unlawful seizure of power comporting the suspension or abrogation of the constitution and (2) supplement the king's "right to warn and advise with extra powers."[34] Likely in an attempt to prevent the monarchy from publicly being dragged into potentially damaging controversies, as it was when royalist street movements such as the People's Alliance for Democracy (2005–6) and the so-called People's Democratic Reform Committee (2013–14) called upon the king to invoke the provision in order to remove popular if embattled elected governments, the draft constitution General Prayuth put before the voters in the referendum held in August 2016 replaced the vague Article 7 with a new "crisis management clause" (Article 5). The new clause assigned the resolution of cases for which the charter ostensibly featured no applicable provision to a meeting to be held among the heads of the Constitutional Court, the Senate, the Supreme Court, the Supreme Administrative Court, "independent" organizations, the house speaker, the prime minister, and the leaders of opposition parties. It is no coincidence that this was one of the provisions changed at the behest of King Vajiralongkorn in advance of the constitution's promulgation in April 2017. By changing Article 5 back to the text featured in Article 7 of the 1997 and 2007 constitutions, Vajiralongkorn ensured that Thailand's new "permanent" constitution would continue to recognize the monarchy's extra-constitutional authority.[35]

The Origins of Thailand's Extra-Constitutional Monarchy

The expression "democracy with the king as head of state" (*prachathippatai mi phramahakasat pen pramuk*) was first employed as the official moniker for a regime in which the king operated *above* the constitution in the short-lived royalist charter promulgated in 1949 (Article 2). The 1949 constitution officially sanctioned the failure of the 1932 revolution and the success of the royalist counter-revolution, which had culminated in a military coup staged with the cooperation of the palace and prominent royalists in 1947. In the aftermath of the 1947 coup, politicians affiliated with civilian revolutionist Pridi Banomyong were definitively removed from the country's political scene, whether through exile, imprisonment, or murder. The change marked by the language of the 1949 constitution was far more than a matter of semantics, for the document restored many of the prerogatives that had been stripped away from the monarchy since 1932. Indeed, the constitution's royalist content proved too much for the men who dominated the country's security forces—it was only a decade later that the monarchy and the military entered into a durable alliance, upon which Thailand's royalist order has rested ever since. Having failed to prevent the text of the 1949 constitution from being approved in parliament,[36] the leaders of the "Coup Group" abrogated the charter in the silent "Radio Coup" staged in November 1951. The 1949 constitution's abrogation, however, did not completely roll back the inroads royalists had made through their successful counter-revolution, their most lasting achievement having been the replacement of a regime in which the king was described as being "under" the constitution with one where the king was recognized to sit squarely "above" it. Notably, the amended version of the 1932 constitution introduced in the months following the Radio Coup now listed (in Article 37) the preservation of "democracy with the king as head of state" among the duties of every citizen.

The development of Thailand's extra-constitutional monarchy has its roots in the state- and nation-building reforms undertaken by King Chulalongkorn (1868–1910) and King Vajiravudh (1910–25) around the turn of the last century, which formed the kingdom of Siam into a modern, bounded nation-state governed by an absolute monarchy. For our purposes, the period in question is significant in two major ways. First, it was at this time that the country's "royal nationalism"—which would later be repurposed to legitimize the monarchy's resurgence and extra-constitutional status—was first conceived. Like all "official nationalisms," Thailand's royal nationalism was produced and propagated as an "anticipatory strategy" deployed by dynastic elites in an effort to stem the tide of emerging "popular nationalism," which has almost invariably given rise to demands for popular sovereignty, equal citizenship, and democracy, as well as to overcome territorial forms of resistance to centralizing reforms.[37] In Siam, state-building reforms had met with considerable resistance in peripheral territories in the country's north, south, and northeast, while "a political awakening"[38] and "a movement for popular sovereignty"[39] had taken shape in Bangkok among a small but influential group of commoners working as professionals and civil servants. From the start, Thailand's royal nationalism stressed the identification of "nation" and "king," while conceiving the nation in racial as well as in organic, hierarchical terms. Second, the causes of the coup d'état staged by the "People's Party" (Khana Ratsadon) on 24 June 1932, which replaced the absolute monarchy with the country's first constitutional regime, stemmed directly from the unintended consequences of the reforms enacted in the Fifth and Sixth Reigns, above all the creation of a civilian and military bureaucracy whose middle ranks were dominated by ambitious commoners who saw their opportunities for upward mobility stifled by the privilege still enjoyed by the "bloodsucking" nobility.[40] This new "bureaucratic bourgeoisie" proved especially receptive to liberal, popular nationalist ideas, which provided ideological content to their discontent with arbitrary royal power and privilege.[41]

King Prajadhipok, upon succeeding his brother on the throne in 1925, wasted little time before seeking the counsel of trusted advisers on the measures that might be required to prevent the monarchy from succumbing to a coup, which seemed to him imminent in light of the mounting discontent created by the profligate reign of King Vajiravudh. On the one hand, Prajadhipok believed that "the prestige of kingship in this country can hardly be lower" and that "it would be a wild goose chase to try and get back any of the old glory"—hence his determination to implement, gradually, a set of reforms that might otherwise be imposed on the monarchy through revolution.[42] At least two documents attest to the king's interest in alternatives to the absolute monarchy[43]—a skeletal draft submitted in 1926 by Francis B. Sayre, in response to the king's solicitation for advice,[44] and an outline completed by two officials in the Ministry of Foreign Affairs in March 1932.[45] Both drafts contemplated the appointment of a prime minister, to whom much of the day-to-day administration would be delegated; the 1932 outline also introduced the possibility of establishing a partially elected legislature. Conspicuously absent from both documents are any references to the concept of "popular sovereignty," or any discussion of the people's civil and political rights. On the other hand, Prajadhipok was anxious about the possibility that reforms of this sort might signal the monarchy's vulnerability, which he feared might embolden the opposition to press forward in a quest to overthrow the monarchy or enact liberal-democratic reforms for which the country was not ready.

While Prajadhipok may himself have had comparatively liberal views, his writings confessed to a great deal of skepticism about the suitability of liberal democracy to Siam. In the aforementioned exchange with Sayre, in 1926, the king offered "an emphatic No" to the question of whether the country was "ready to have some sort of representative Government."[46] A year later, in a memorandum titled "Democracy in Siam," he argued that "a parliamentary government is not suited to the racial qualities of the Siamese."[47] Indeed, while Prajadhipok would later be immortalized as the king who generously bestowed democracy on the country, there is no indication that he questioned the tenets of the "official nationalism" devised under his predecessors in defense of the absolute monarchy, including a worldview cantered on the belief in "natural inequalities."[48] Aside from his aforementioned concern for the potential that a "bad king" might ascend the throne, Prajadhipok had entertained promulgating a constitution out of a suspicion that opposing it no longer served the interests of the monarchy, the dynasty, and the country. For while "the majority of the people do not think *rationally*, but think only sentimentally,"[49] those who preyed on their credulity could make trouble if they did not get what they wanted.

If Prajadhipok's words and behavior before the advent of Siam's first constitutional regime attest to his consideration of a weak set of limitations to the monarchy's powers, the actions taken by the king and his allies upon being placed under a semi-democratic, liberal constitution would help to undermine the country's prospects of developing a stable constitutional regime for some time to come. Indeed, as easy as it was for the People's Party to seize power on 24 June 1932, the achievement of the revolution's stated goals—above all, the transition to a democratic regime that would fully actualize principles of popular sovereignty, equal citizenship, and economic opportunity—proved a different matter altogether. Unreformed royalists exploited the People's Party's conciliatory stance to sabotage the constitutional regime, on the conceit that it served as a smokescreen for the promoters' dictatorial ambitions.[50] When Prince Boworadet's rebels placed Bangkok under siege in October 1933, their propaganda not only emphasized the disrespect the promoters had shown to the king, but also featured accusations that the People's Party had betrayed the principles spelled out in the constitution, while professing their intention to establish a genuine constitutional monarchy.[51] In the aftermath of the failed rebellion, it was once again the turn of King Prajadhipok to lead the effort to undermine the government of Phraya Phahon Phonphayuhasena. The voluminous correspondence sent to the government from his self-imposed exile in England alternated between calling for democratic reforms—including the establishment of a fully elected legislature as well as the guarantee of liberal rights to speech and association—and demanding that the government restore royal prerogatives, or "strictly repress" the monarchy's critics.[52] In the terse statement with which he abdicated the throne on 2 March 1935, it was once again in the rhetoric of freedom and democracy that King Prajadhipok framed his extreme gesture. "I am willing to surrender the powers I formerly exercised to the people as a whole," the king wrote, "but I am not willing to turn them over to any individual or any group to use in an autocratic manner without heeding the voice of the people."

King Prajadhipok's abdication statement has been instrumental to the decades-old quest by Thailand's royalists to attribute the country's shift toward constitutionalism and "democracy" to the benevolence of its monarchs.[53] The promoters' actions before and, especially, *after* King Prajadhipok's abdication provided plenty of fodder for the revisionist narrative. For them, too, the defense of the constitution would increasingly serve as an excuse to betray their own principles, as evidenced in their refusal to allow the formation of political parties, the enforcement of repressive legislation such as the infamous "Act to Protect the Constitution," the reliance on a dubious Special Court to conduct proceedings that led to the imprisonment and execution of senior royalists involved in the phantom Song Suradet Rebellion in 1939, and eventually the extension of interim provisions of the constitution that delayed the election of the entire National Assembly by ten years. The rise to power of Field Marshal Plaek Phibun Songkhram coincided with the state's propagation of a virulent form of nationalism that emphasized statism and social conformity over constitutionalism and individual autonomy. As Thailand's new, self-styled "leader" (*phu nam*) consolidated his power, the word "democracy" increasingly stood for a system of government dominated by the military behind the fig leaf of a constitution and a weak legislature.

Phibun's ouster in 1944 and the defeat of the Japanese occupying force a year later provided an opportunity to place the country's democratic transition back on track. During the war, members of the royal family and other royalists had joined Pridi Banomyong's liberal/progressive supporters in the resistance against the Japanese. The alliance, however, lasted only long enough to permit the promulgation of a democratic constitution in May 1946, fracturing soon thereafter. Outclassed at the ballot box and outnumbered in parliament, the leaders of the royalist Democrat Party seized upon King Ananda Mahidol's mysterious death on 9 June 1946 to falsely accuse Pridi of regicide. Bedeviled by the allegations, Pridi resigned as prime minister shortly after the installment of Thailand's first fully elected House of Representatives in August 1946, despite having just scored an overwhelming victory at the polls. Not satisfied with Pridi's resignation, royalists hounded the government of Rear Admiral Thamrong Nawasawat with charges of corruption and republicanism, while their leaders formed an alliance with disgruntled military officers who planned to retake the country's government by force.[54] When the "Coup Group" (Khana Ratthaprahan), with Phibun as its figurehead, eventually seized power on 8 November 1947, the palace immediately sanctioned the operation, while prominent royalists praised it for heeding "the will of the people."[55] Staged on the pretext of preventing Pridi's allies from overthrowing the monarchy, the 1947 coup was followed by Pridi's permanent banishment, the appointment of Democrat Party leader Khuang Aphaiwong as prime minister, and the promulgation of a constitution complete with greatly expanded royal prerogatives. By the end of 1947, the coup was already understood to have marked a major turning point. The *Bangkok Post* described it as a counter-revolutionary measure "motivated by reactionary forces who had never accepted the revolutionary overthrow of 24 June 1932."[56]

The Extra-Constitutional Monarchy's Apogee and Decline

The cooperation between royalists and the 1947 coup-makers in the armed forces did not last long. As they grew more secure in their position, members of the Coup Group gradually rolled back their concessions to the palace, until the Radio Coup staged in 1951 abrogated the 1949 constitution and abolished most of the royal prerogatives contained therein. It was only years later that the palace found in Field Marshal Sarit, the new commander in chief of the army, an ally in its struggle for "spiritual hegemony" with Phibun.[57] Ironically, Phibun's undoing proved to be a series of liberal reforms—enacted in 1955 over the objections of rival Coup Group factions led by Sarit and Police Director-General Phao Siyanond—that lifted most restrictions to freedom of expression, assembly, association, and the press. Having entered into a pact with Sarit to overthrow the government, royalists exploited the system's liberalization to undermine the administration through lawsuits, parliamentary debates, and a press campaign that supplemented the accusations leveled against Phibun and Phao for rigging the 1957 general elections with charges of disloyalty to the monarchy.[58] When the military eventually seized power, forcing Phibun and Phao to leave the country for good, King Bhumibol gave the coup immediate legal sanction.

Field Marshal Sarit's twin seizures of power on 16 September 1957 and 20 October 1958 dealt the *coup de grâce* for the ideals in which the People's Party had grounded the removal of the absolute monarchy in 1932—popular sovereignty, equal citizenship, constitutionalism, and democracy. Having set out to overthrow every regime that had made any effort to lead the country in the direction of greater democracy since 1932, royalists finally met in the lawless military dictatorship Sarit established after the 1958 coup a system of government they could support wholeheartedly. The royalist counter-revolution was finally complete, as the state was now in the hands of military men committed to their vision of a hierarchical society led by an all-powerful government, whose legitimacy was derived from the endorsement of a re-sacralized monarchy the people were once again duty-bound to revere.[59] Sarit's "Revolutionary Council" (Khana Patiwat) introduced a bare-bones temporary charter, in 1959, doing away with the elected legislature and political parties, as well as all forms of legal opposition and dissent. Undergirding this new system of government was the revival of hierarchical, organic conceptions of the nation, founded on the premise that Thailand's prosperity and security could be achieved only if everyone knew their place, remained unified behind the government's leadership, and refrained from pressing any demand for political inclusion, economic opportunity, or social change.[60]

Field Marshal Sarit also would call his lawless military dictatorship a "democracy." Indeed, the restoration of the monarchy as the pinnacle of Thailand's social hierarchies was presented as central to the model of "Thai-style democracy" conceived by the regime's ideologues. Since World War II, palace officials such as Prince Dhani Nivas and royalist intellectuals including Phraya Anuman Rajadhon had revived Prince Damrong Rajanubhab's contention that true "Thai-style government" did not even require a constitution[61]—not so as long as the country was ruled according to the unwritten "constitution of the *thammasat*" inherited from the thirteenth-century kingdom of Sukhothai.[62] Kukrit Pramoj went so far as to argue that the absolute monarchy was more "democratic"—in substantive, if not procedural terms—than the regimes of the constitutional era.[63] Sarit's dismantlement of representative institutions received a full-throated endorsement from Kukrit and other royalists, as a means to undo the contamination of "Thainess" with the "otherness" blamed for the divisiveness of the post-1932 period.[64] Together with Luang Wichit Wathakan, who had previously been responsible for concocting "cultural" rationales for Phibun's obsession with social conformity, Kukrit's propagandistic work was crucial to the effort to cast Sarit in the role of a "Thai-style leader" (*phu nam baep thai*) wielding absolute powers for the benefit of the entire nation. The only check and balance Thailand ever needed was said to be the presence of a righteous, inviolate monarch, under whose benign reign no injustice could ever be allowed to take place.

The field marshal's death in 1963 was followed by a further increase in the monarchy's popularity and power. On this point the extant academic hagiographies of King Bhumibol[65] concur with more critical works on the subject:[66] by the late 1960s, His Majesty was once again the kingdom's most powerful political figure. The king's ascent was facilitated by the fact that Sarit's successors, Field Marshal Thanom Kittikachorn (as prime minister) and Field Marshal Praphat Charusathien (as commander in chief of the army), though almost equally corrupt, had none of Sarit's stature and charisma. It was as a result of the changing balance of power that a new, semidemocratic constitution was promulgated at the king's insistence in 1968. For the monarchy, the constitution's content was better still, as its lengthy preamble offered a re-write of recent history that placed the institution at the center of the country's "democracy," arguing that Thailand had first become a "democracy with the king as head of state" in 1932. Since 1932, the preamble stated, this particular version of "democracy" had "developed sequentially" (*dai wiwattanakan ma doi lamdap*), in a way that required many changes to the constitution so as to keep it "current" (*moh som kae kan samai*). The constitution, in essence, presented military coups as instruments of democratic development. A decade into the "hegemonic project" launched by Sarit,[67] Thai authorities now had no compunction about writing into the country's supreme legal document an idea that Khamsing Srinawk's famous short story "The Politician" had ridiculed just months before the field marshal had staged his conservative "revolution" in 1958: "They call it a 'democratic coup d'état,' see. You have to have lots of coups d'état. Otherwise it isn't a democracy."

As Thailand's monarchy approached the apogee of its status and extra-constitutional authority, the country entered an age of political instability that may be said to persist to this very day. As noted in this chapter's introduction, since the 1970s Thailand has oscillated multiple times between democracy and non-democracy (or pseudo-democracy). Indeed, the Thai monarchy under King Bhumibol has accumulated its enormous popularity and power, not through decades of totalitarian dictatorship—as is generally the case for cults of personality of this sort—but over repeated iterations of a cycle of instability that has seen the country go through, since the beginning of the Ninth Reign, ten successful coups and no less than eighteen constitutions. Once again, the establishment of a strong state and durable authoritarian regime do not feature among Bhumibol's accomplishments. Even at the height of the monarchy's power, the components of the alliance supporting Thailand's royalist order never quite mustered the wherewithal to subscribe what Dan Slater has called a "protection pact."[68] Instead, the alliance joining Thailand's state, business, and communal elites has most commonly taken the form of a "provision pact"—an agreement to divide up the spoils guaranteed by their control of the state.[69] But while intraelite divisions have been conducive to the failure of successive authoritarian regimes, Thailand's royalists have never lacked the unity of purpose required to defend their effective control of the state and its coffers, most commonly against forces seeking to exercise the powers theoretically vested in them by the constitution. Elected governments that failed to bend to the will of the royalist establishment were removed in military coups invariably justified by contrived threats to the nation and the monarchy. And, in instances where simply *referencing* such threats would likely not have sufficed for the people of Thailand to surrender their individual freedoms in exchange for the protection of their self-appointed guardians, royalists in the palace, the military, and the bureaucracy created conditions of ungovernability designed to impress upon key segments of the population— above all the urban middle class—that they could ill afford to support democratic regimes not subject to the tutelage of the royalist establishment.

As I have explained in my previous work,[70] this *modus operandi* is more reminiscent of a "protection racket" than a "protection pact." Even so, it has worked just as well to guarantee the survival of Thailand's royalist order, through the vicissitudes of the country's formal constitutional structure. Of course, an inevitable byproduct of Thailand's long series of military coups has been the enduring weakness and fragmentation of political parties and civil society organizations, not to mention a pronounced habituation to resolving disputes through extra-constitutional means. In turn, the chronic dysfunction and instability that has been the hallmark of a political system royalists have had a hand in creating, and "vested interest in preserving," has served as an additional source of legitimacy for the extra-constitutional authority exercised by unelected officials and institutions, for the contrast could not have been more stark between the staying power of the military and the monarchy and the tenuousness of Thailand's ever-changing, disposable constitutions.[71] For a time, the fact that the extra-constitutional authority wielded by Thailand's royalist establishment had actually caused the dysfunction it pretended to cure appears to have been lost on millions of ordinary citizens. So, too, have generations of academic and journalistic observers, both local and foreigner, celebrated the monarchy and its allies for their "stabilizing influence," having apparently taken no notice of the reality that royalists have only ever protected the Thai nation against threats and maladies that were entirely of their own making.

In restoring the House of Chakri's status and authority, the reign of King Bhumibol may be said to have in some ways realized the vision that his uncle and predecessor, King Prajadhipok, had begun to develop in the run-up to the events of 24 June 1932. As noted, Prajadhipok was no democrat, but he was also not terribly interested in running the country on a day-to-day basis. What he had considered experimenting with, therefore, was a system of government where the king would remain the locus of the kingdom's executive and legislative powers (hence his frequent complaints about being relegated to a similar status as the king of England[72]), but would delegate some of that authority to a prime minister. The Thai monarchy would accomplish something similar during the Ninth Reign—King Bhumibol articulated that view himself in 1989: "Nobody can do everything alone. ... The king at present does not carry the duty to run the country. He has someone else do it."[73] In essence, this is the vision put forth in Francis B. Sayre's 1926 draft constitution.

During the Ninth Reign, of course, the palace went much further than Prajadhipok had ever considered venturing in an effort to promote the monarchy's image. While Prajadhipok was skeptical of the possibility that support and respect for the monarchy could ever be restored, the cause was pursued vigorously during the Ninth Reign—through schooling and aggressive legal enforcement as well as a massive, taxpayer-funded propaganda campaign that built a cult of personality uncharacteristic of a modern society. For all the achievements, however, after years of conflict and upheaval the Thai monarchy finds itself in a predicament not unlike the one King Prajadhipok confronted before 1932. As Prince Damrong Rajanubhab predicted back in 1926, the problem with Sayre's model of limited monarchy is that the entire system might be compromised in the event of a conflict between the king and a popular prime minister.[74] In this sense, the military coups staged in 2006 and 2014—and the repressive measures unleashed in the years since Prayuth's seizure of power—may have successfully prevented the establishment of an actual "constitutional monarchy" on Thaksin's terms, but only by putting the dynasty's entire future on the line.

A Constitutional Future, or None at All

As King Bhumibol's traumatic succession loomed increasingly large on the horizon, the palace and its principals exhibited none of King Prajadhipok's foresight and self-awareness. Instead of modernizing the institution, reforming its political role, and making its survival less dependent on the talents, charisma, and good fortune of one man—as Prajadhipok at least considered doing—the decision of its supposed defenders to double down on extremism, censorship, and repression only managed to turn its preservation into an anachronism. As feared, things have only gotten worse in the Tenth Reign. For while Vajiralongkorn may have been successful in formalizing some of the monarchy's threatened extra-constitutional prerogatives, its legitimacy and popularity have suffered further as a result of the new king's grotesque behavior, to say nothing of the country's fatigue with Prayuth and the dinosaurs in his administration. The open criticism and ridicule to which Vajiralongkorn has been subjected in recent student-led demonstrations— something that would have been unthinkable only a few years ago—is only the most visible manifestation of a much deeper problem, rooted in the dubious sustainability of Thailand's "extra-constitutional" monarchy. At heart, then, the choice faced by the Thai monarchy today features the same options the People's Party had placed before King Prajadhipok on 24 June 1932—in the end, the triumphs of the intervening ninety years have served only to delay making a decision that cannot be put off indefinitely. Should the palace continue to refuse to submit to a constitutional role, it is only a matter of time before Thailand's monarchy is consigned to the refuse bin of history.

In all fairness, reforming the institution into a real constitutional monarchy may be beyond what the current reign can possibly achieve. Take, for instance, the ten reform proposals devised by the student-led pro-democracy movement in 2020, which include lifting the constitutional prohibition on filing legal complaints against the king, repealing the lèse-majesté laws and all other restrictions on criticizing the monarchy, subjecting royal spending and royal wealth to meaningful oversight, abolishing the Privy Council, stripping the king of the power to command military units, banning the king from making political statements or approving any military coups, discontinuing the taxpayer-funded royalist propaganda disseminated through the media and the educational system, and finding out the truth about the killings of people critical of (or in other ways associated with) the monarchy.[75] None of these proposals can be dismissed as unreasonable or uncalled for—indeed, most are required in order to establish a modern constitutional monarchy. However, what would be the consequence of enacting these reforms in the current context? While the students claimed that their intention was not to overthrow the monarch, it is hard to imagine any other outcome. Bluntly, Vajiralongkorn has too many skeletons in his closet to liberalize criticism of the monarchy. Even the experiment made between 2018 and 2020 with a de facto moratorium on the enforcement of the draconian lèse-majesté law—critics were still prosecuted for sedition and for violations of the 2007 Computer Crime Act—had to be discontinued in light of the anti-monarchy demonstrations held throughout 2020.[76]

Above all, the forty-four years Vajiralongkorn spent as crown prince make him too closely associated with the reign of his father for him to ever carry out the requisite "de-Bhumibolization" of Thailand. For that would entail, among other things, telling the truth about the royal family's involvement in the series of atrocities committed in its name, from the execution of the innocent men who took the fall for the accidental death of King Ananda Mahidol in 1946, to the killings of Red Shirt protesters in 2010, through everything that happened in between, such as the massacre that took place in and around the campus of Thammasat University on 6 October 1976. Simply put, there are too many such episodes[77] to guarantee that the monarchy would survive uncovering the truth about its involvement. And, for the current king, acceding to reforms of this kind is too risky to attempt, as long as the existential threats the monarchy *does* face do not present an imminent danger. Perhaps, then, the best bet for those committed to the monarchy's preservation is to ensure that Vajiralongkorn, who is over seventy years old, is succeeded by a new king who played no role in the decades-long effort made by the palace to thwart the country's democratization. Indeed, the fact that Vajiralongkorn lacks a true heir apparent may prove to be an advantage, for it presents an opportunity to enthrone someone who was not involved in, did not benefit from, and has no interest in covering up the truth about the monarchy's conduct in the Ninth and Tenth Reigns. Any of the four adult sons Vajiralongkorn disowned and banished from the kingdom upon divorcing his second wife in the 1990s might be a good choice, if the goal is to remake the monarchy into an institution that is at least compatible with the workings of a liberal democracy. Then again, the argument is of no practical relevance, as long as royalists refuse to accept that, in the long run, they cannot have it any other way.

Notes

1 Huntington, *The Third Wave*.

2 Freedom House, "Freedom in the World: Country and Territory Ratings and Statuses, 1972–2021."

3 Linz and Stepan, *Problems of Democratic Transition and Consolidation*, 6.

4 Diamond, "Facing up to the Democratic Recession."

5 Zakaria, "The Rise of Illiberal Democracy." See also Zakaria, *The Future of Freedom*.

6 Kurlantzick, *Democracy in Retreat*.

7 Riggs, *Thailand: The Modernization of a Bureaucratic Polity*.

8 Thongchai, *Prachathippatai Thi Mi Kasat Yu Nuea Kan Mueang*.

9 For a visual representation, see Streckfuss, *Truth on Trial in Thailand*, 216.

10 Thongchai, "Prawatsat Thai Baeb Rachachatniyom."

11 McCargo, "Network Monarchy and Legitimacy Crises in Thailand."

12 Parry, "The Story of Thaksin Shinawatra." Readers inclined to dismiss the comparison with North Korea as mere hyperbole might consider the meeting held by the Thai junta's minister of education with the North Korean ambassador

in November 2014, in which the former stressed the similarities between the two countries' educational systems as the basis to pursue further student exchange programs. See "Thai Education Minister: Thai Education Resembles North Korea," *Prachatai*.

13 Prajadhipok, "Democracy in Siam (1927)," 50.

14 For instance, see Marshall, *A Kingdom in Crisis*, 188.

15 For an extensive treatment, see Marshall, *A Kingdom in Crisis*.

16 Handley, *The King Never Smiles*, 17–21.

17 See "Nayok Tham Phithi Athitthan Phrachao Phichittaman," *Thai Rath*.

18 For instance, see Borwornsak and Navin, "Constitutional Drafting in Thailand."

19 Cited in "NCPO May Pick Trusted Allies," *The Nation*.

20 Thitinan, "Thailand's Stalemate and Uneasy Accommodation."

21 See "Six Changes in Constitution," *Bangkok Post*.

22 See "Thai King Takes Control of Five Palace Agencies," *AFP*.

23 See "King Vajiralongkorn Gains Two Infantry Regiments by Emergency Decree," *Prachatai*.

24 See "Thailand's King Given Full Control of Crown Property," *Reuters*.

25 "Battle Royal: Thailand's King Seeks to Bring Back Absolute Monarchy," *The Economist*.

26 Handley, *The King Never Smiles*, 116–18. See also Kobkua, *Kings, Country, and Constitutions*, 150–51.

27 Pramuan, *Phra Ratcha Amnat*.

28 Cited in Pasuk and Baker, *Thaksin*, 255–56.

29 People's Party, "The First Announcement of the People's Party."

30 For a recent analysis of the "continuous process of bricolage between Western constitutional models and Buddhist doctrines of kingship" said to define Thailand's constitutional order, see Mérieau, *Constitutional Bricolage*.

31 Slater, *Ordering Power*.

32 McCargo, "Network Monarchy and Legitimacy Crises in Thailand."

33 For an extended discussion, see Connors, "Article of Faith."

34 Connors, "Article of Faith," 151.

35 See "Six Changes in Constitution," *Bangkok Post*.

36 Nattapoll, *Kho Fan Fai Nai Fan An Luea Chuea*, 46–47.

37 Anderson, *Imagined Communities*, 101.

38 Warangkana, *Khwam Tuen Tua Thang Kan Mueang Khong Samanchon Nai Samai Ratchakan Thi Ha*. See also Nakharin, *Kan Patiwat Sayam Pho. So. 2475*.

39 Copeland, *Contested Nationalism and the 1932 Overthrow of the Absolute Monarchy in Siam*.

40 People's Party, "First Announcement."

41 Kullada, *The Rise and Decline of Thai Absolutism*, 117–25. See also Nakharin, *Kan Patiwat Sayam Pho. So. 2475*, 52–57.

42 Prajadhipok, "King Prajadhipok's Memorandum, 23 July 1926," 18.

43 The full range of reforms considered before 1932 is analyzed in Nakharin, *Kan Patiwat Sayam Pho. So. 2475*, 169–203.

44 Sayre, "Sayre's Memorandum, 27 July 1926," 34–36.

45 Stevens and Waja, "Outline of Changes in the Form of Government," 86–89.

46 Prajadhipok, "King Prajadhipok's Memorandum, 24 July 1926," 18.

47 Prajadhipok, "Democracy in Siam (1927)," 48.

48 *Khwam mai thao thiam kan yu laeo doi thammachat*, in the words of Nakharin, *Kan Patiwat Sayam Pho. So. 2475*, 38.

49 Prajadhipok, "Democracy in Siam (1927)," 48–49.

50 Ferrara, *The Political Development of Modern Thailand*, 89–99 and 101–3.

51 Reproduced in Thamrongsak, *'Kho Ang' Kan Patiwat-Ratthaprahan-Kabot Nai Mueang Thai Patchuban*, 109–13.

52 Reproduced in *Thalaengkan*, 96–99.

53 Somsak, *Prawatsat Thi Phoeng Sang*, 20–30.

54 Nattapoll, "Kan Mueang Thai Samai Ratthaban Chomphon Po," 51–59.

55 Nattapoll, *Kho Fan Fai Nai Fan An Luea Chuea*, 174–76.

56 "November 8 Coup d'État Identifies 1947 as Year of Counter Revolution," *Bangkok Post*.

57 Handley, *The King Never Smiles*, 126–31. See also Kobkua, *Thailand's Durable Premier*, 85–86.

58 Nattapoll, "The Monarchy and the Royalist Movement in Modern Thai Politics, 1932–1957," 170–71.

59 The Thai monarchy's re-sacralization is analyzed in considerable detail in Gray, "Thailand: The Soteriological State in the 1970s."

60 Thak, *Thailand: The Politics of Despotic Paternalism*, 100–105.

61 Damrong, *Laksana Kan Pokkhrong Prathet Sayam Tae Boran*, 28.

62 Dhani, "The Old Siamese Conception of the Monarchy," 91–106.

63 See Saichol, *Kan Mueang Lae Kan Sang "Khwam Pen Thai" Doi Mom Ratchawong Kukrit Pramoj*, 115–30.

64 Saichol, *Kan Mueang Lae Kan Sang "Khwam Pen Thai" Doi Mom Ratchawong Kukrit Pramoj*, 147–53.

65 Kobkua, *Kings, Country, and Constitutions*, 165. See also Nakharin, *Phra Phu Song Pokklao Prachathippatai*, 90.

66 Handley, *The King Never Smiles*, 177. See also Morell and Chai-anan, *Political Conflict in Thailand*, 68.

67 Connors, *Democracy and National Identity in Thailand*, 44–52.

68 See Slater, *Ordering Power*.

69 Slater, *Ordering Power*, 19.

70 Ferrara, "The Logic of Thailand's Royalist Coups d'État," 77.

71 McCargo, "Network Monarchy and Legitimacy Crises in Thailand," 506.

72 E.g., see the letter Prajadhipok sent from his self-imposed exile to the royal secretary in Bangkok on 27 October 1934, reproduced in *Thalaengkan*, 9–14.

73 Cited in Handley, *The King Never Smiles*, 337.

74 Damrong, "Prince Damrong's Memorandum, 1 August 1926," 39.

75 See "Klum Thammasat Lae Kan Chumnun Yuen 10 Kho Riak Rong Patirup Sathaban Kasat To Sapha," *Prachatai*.

76 See "PM Issues Lèse-majesté Warning," *Bangkok Post*.

77 For an analysis of the manner in which these abuses became "institutionalized" in the Ninth Reign as a result of the reiterated failure to hold the culprits accountable, see Haberkorn, *In Plain Sight*.

References

Anderson, Benedict. *Imagined Communities: Reflections on the Origin and Spread of Nationalism*. London: Verso, 1991.

"Battle Royal: Thailand's King Seeks to Bring Back Absolute Monarchy." *The Economist*, 16 October 2020. https://www.economist.com/briefing/2020/10/14/thailands-king-seeks-to-bring-back-absolute-monarchy, accessed 30 June 2022.

Borwornsak Uwanno and Navin Damrigan. "Constitutional Drafting in Thailand." Paper presented at the Foreign Correspondents Club of Thailand on 7 April 2015. https://www.academia.edu/12131723, accessed 30 June 2022.

Connors, Michael K. "Article of Faith: The Failure of Royal Liberalism in Thailand." *Journal of Contemporary Asia* 38.1 (2008):143–65.

———. *Democracy and National Identity in Thailand*. Copenhagen: NIAS Press, 2007.

Copeland, Matthew P. "Contested Nationalism and the 1932 Overthrow of the Absolute Monarchy in Siam." PhD diss., Australian National University, 1993.

Damrong Rajanubhab. *Laksana Kan Pokkhrong Prathet Sayam Tae Boran* [Forms of administration in Siam since ancient times]. Bangkok: Rong Phim Sophonphiphattanakon, 1927.

———. "Prince Damrong's Memorandum, August 1, 1926." In *Siam's Political Future: Documents from the End of the Absolute Monarchy*, ed. Benjamin A. Batson, 37–41. Ithaca, NY: Cornell University Southeast Asia Program, 1974.

Dhani Nivas. "The Old Siamese Conception of the Monarchy." *Journal of the Siam Society* 36.1 (1946):91–106.

Diamond, Larry. "Facing up to the Democratic Recession." *Journal of Democracy* 26.1 (2015):141–55.

Ferrara, Federico. "The Logic of Thailand's Royalist Coups d'État." In *Routledge Handbook of Contemporary Thailand*, ed. Pavin Chachavalpongpun, 71–85. London: Routledge 2020.

———. *The Political Development of Modern Thailand*. Cambridge: Cambridge University Press, 2015.

Freedom House. "Freedom in the World: Country and Territory Ratings and Statuses, 1972–2021." https://freedomhouse.org/sites/default/files/2021-02/Country_and_Territory_Ratings_and_Statuses_FIW1973-2021.xlsx, accessed 30 June 2022.

Gray, Christine. "Thailand: The Soteriological State in the 1970s." PhD diss., University of Chicago, 1986.

Haberkorn, Tyrell. *In Plain Sight: Impunity and Human Rights in Thailand*. Madison: University of Wisconsin Press, 2018.

Handley, Paul M. *The King Never Smiles: A Biography of Thailand's Bhumibol Adulyadej*. New Haven, CT: Yale University Press, 2006.

Huntington, Samuel P. *The Third Wave: Democratization in the Late Twentieth Century*. Norman: University of Oklahoma Press, 1991.

"King Vajiralongkorn Gains Two Infantry Regiments by Emergency Decree." *Prachatai*, 3 October 2019. https://prachatai.com/english/node/8230, accessed 30 June 2022.

"Klum Thammasat Lae Kan Chumnun Yuen 10 Kho Riak Rong Patirup Sathaban Kasat To Sapha" [Thammasat group, demonstrators submit to the House of Representatives 10 demands to reform the monarchy]. *Prachatai*, 26 August 2020. https://prachatai.com/journal/2020/08/89231, accessed 30 June 2022.

Kobkua Suwannathat-Pian. *Kings, Country, and Constitutions: Thailand's Political Development, 1932–2000*. London: Routledge/Curzon, 2003.

———. *Thailand's Durable Premier: Phibun through Three Decades, 1932–1957*. Oxford: Oxford University Press, 1995.

Kullada Kesboonchoo Mead. *The Rise and Decline of Thai Absolutism*. London: Routledge/Curzon, 2004.

Kurlantzick, Joshua. *Democracy in Retreat: The Revolt of the Middle Class and the Worldwide Decline of Representative Government*. New Haven, CT: Yale University Press, 2013.

Linz, Juan J., and Alfred Stepan. *Problems of Democratic Transition and Consolidation*. Baltimore, MD: Johns Hopkins University Press, 1996.

Marshall, Andrew MacGregor. *A Kingdom in Crisis: Thailand's Struggle for Democracy in the Twenty-First Century*. London: Zed Books, 2014.

McCargo, Duncan. "Network Monarchy and Legitimacy Crises in Thailand." *Pacific Review* 18.4 (2005):499–519.

Mérieau, Eugénie. *Constitutional Bricolage: Thailand's Sacred Monarchy vs. the Rule of Law*. London: Hart Publishing, 2021.

Morell, David, and Chai-anan Samudavanija. *Political Conflict in Thailand: Reform, Reaction, Revolution*. Cambridge, MA: Oelgeschlager, Gunn & Hain, 1981.

Nakharin Mektrairat. *Kan Patiwat Sayam Pho. So. 2475* [The 1932 revolution in Siam]. Bangkok: Khrongkan 60 Pi Prachathippatai, 1992.

———. *Phra Phu Song Pokklao Prachathippatai: 60 Pi Si Ratcha Sombat Kap Kan Mueang Kan Pokkhrong Thai* [The king who built democracy: The 60-year reign and Thailand's politics and government]. Bangkok: Thammasat University Press, 2006.

Nattapoll Chaiching. "Kan Mueang Thai Samai Ratthaban Chomphon Po. Phibun Songkhram Phai Tai Rabiap Lok Khong Saharat Amerika Pho.So. 2491–2500" [Thailand's politics in the era of Field Marshal Phibun Songkhram under the American world system]. PhD diss., Chulalongkorn University, 2009.

———. *Kho Fan Fai Nai Fan An Luea Chuea: Khwam Khluean Wai Khong Khabuankan Kan Pati Pak Patiwat Sayam (Pho. So. 2475–2500)* [Wanting to dream the believable dream: The movement to reverse the revolution in Siam, 1932–1957]. Nonthaburi: Fa Diao Kan, 2013.

———. "The Monarchy and the Royalist Movement in Modern Thai Politics, 1932–1957." In *Saying the Unsayable: Monarchy and Democracy in Thailand*, ed. Søren Ivarsson and Lotte Isager, 147–78. Copenhagen: NIAS Press, 2010.

"Nayok Tham Phithi Athitthan Phrachao Phichittaman" [Prime minister hosts praying ritual for Phichittaman God]. *Thai Rath*, 6 April 2015. https://www.thairath.co.th/content/491349, accessed 30 June 2022.

"NCPO May Pick Trusted Allies." *The Nation*, 25 July 2014, 1A.

"November 8 Coup d'État Identifies 1947 as Year of Counter Revolution." *Bangkok Post*, 31 December 1947, 5–6.

Parry, Richard Lloyd. "The Story of Thaksin Shinawatra." *London Review of Books* 36.12 (2014):11–12.

Pasuk Phongpaichit and Chris Baker. *Thaksin*. Chiang Mai: Silkworm Books, 2009.

People's Party (Khana Ratsadon). "The First Announcement of the People's Party." 24 June 1932.

"PM Issues Lèse-majesté Warning." *Bangkok Post*, 21 November 2020. https://www.bangkokpost.com/thailand/politics/2023103/pm-issues-lese-majeste-warning, accessed 30 June 2022.

Prajadhipok. "Democracy in Siam (1927)." *Siam's Political Future: Documents from the End of the Absolute Monarchy*, ed. Benjamin A. Batson, 48–50. Ithaca, NY: Cornell University Southeast Asia Program, 1974.

———. "King Prajadhipok's Memorandum, 23 July 1926: Problems of Siam." In *Siam's Political Future: Documents from the End of the Absolute Monarchy*, ed. Benjamin A. Batson, 13–22. Ithaca, NY: Cornell University Southeast Asia Program, 1974.

Pramuan Ruchanaseri. *Phra Ratcha Amnat* [Royal power]. Bangkok: Sumet Ruchanaseri, 2005.

Riggs, Fred. *Thailand: The Modernization of a Bureaucratic Polity*. Honolulu: University of Hawai'i Press, 1966.

Saichol Sattayanurak. *Kan Mueang Lae Kan Sang "Khwam Pen Thai" Doi Mom Ratchawong Kukrit Pramoj* [The politics and the conception of "Thainess" of M.R. Kukrit Pramoj]. Chiang Mai: Chiang Mai University, 2005.

Sayre, Francis B. "Sayre's Memorandum, 27 July 1926: Outline of Preliminary Draft." In *Siam's Political Future: Documents from the End of the Absolute Monarchy*, ed. Benjamin A. Batson, 23–36. Ithaca, NY: Cornell University Southeast Asia Program, 1974.

"Six Changes in Constitution." *Bangkok Post*, 6 April 2017. https://www.bangkokpost.com/thailand/general/1228183/six-sections-changed-in-constitution, accessed 30 June 2022.

Slater, Dan. *Ordering Power: Contentious Politics and Authoritarian Leviathans in Southeast Asia*. New York: Cambridge University Press, 2010.

Somsak Jeamteerasakul. *Prawatsat Thi Phoeng Sang: Ruam Bot Khwam Kiao Kap 14 Tula Lae 6 Tula* [History that was just made: Collected articles on 14 October and 6 October]. Bangkok: Samnak Phim 6 Tula Ram Luek, 2001.

Stevens, Raymond B., and Sri Wisarn Waja. "Outline of Changes in the Form of Government." In *Siam's Political Future: Documents from the End of the*

Absolute Monarchy, ed. Benjamin A. Batson, 86–89. Ithaca, NY: Cornell University Southeast Asia Program, 1974.

Streckfuss, David. *Truth on Trial in Thailand: Defamation, Treason, and Lèse-majesté*. Oxon: Routledge, 2011.

"Thai Education Minister: Thai Education Resembles North Korea." *Prachatai*, 17 November 2014. https://prachatai.com/english/node/4495, accessed 30 June 2022.

"Thai King Takes Control of Five Palace Agencies." *AFP*, 2 May 2017. https://www. businesstimes.com.sg/government-economy/thai-king-takes-control-of-five-palace-agencies, accessed 30 June 2022.

"Thailand's King Given Full Control of Crown Property." *Reuters*, 17 July 2017. https://jakartaglobe.id/news/thailands-king-given-full-control-crown-property/, accessed 30 June 2022.

Thak Chaloemtiarana. *Thailand: The Politics of Despotic Paternalism*. Chiang Mai: Silkworm Books, 2007.

Thalaengkan Reuang Phrabat Somdet Phra Poramintharamaha Prajadhipok Phra Pokklao Jao Yu Hua Song Sala Ratchasombat [Official report on the abdication of King Prajadhipok]. Bangkok: Rong Phim Prajant, 1935.

Thamrongsak Phetchlert-anan. *'Kho Ang' Kan Patiwat-Ratthaprahan-Kabot Nai Mueang Thai Patchuban: Bot Wikhro Lae Ekkasan* ["Reasons" given for revolutions-coups-rebellions in contemporary Thailand: Documents and analysis]. Bangkok: The Foundation for the Promotion of Social Sciences and Humanities Textbook Project, 2007.

Thitinan Pongsudhirak. "Thailand's Stalemate and Uneasy Accommodation." *Bangkok Post*, 15 February 2013. https://www.bangkokpost.com/opinion/opinion/335998/thailand-stalemate-and-uneasy-accommodation, accessed 30 June 2022.

Thongchai Winichakul. *Prachathippatai Thi Mi Kasat Yu Nuea Kan Mueang* [Democracy with the king above politics]. Nonthaburi: Fa Diao Kan, 2013.

———. "Prawatsat Thai Baeb Rachachatniyom" [Thailand's royal nationalist history]. *Sinlapa Watthanatham* 23 (2001):56–65.

Warangkana Niyomrit. *Khwam Tuen Tua Thang Kan Mueang Khong Samanchon Nai Samai Ratchakan Thi Ha* [The political awakening of commoners in the Fifth Reign]. MA thesis, Ramkhamhaeng University, 2003.

Zakaria, Fareed. *The Future of Freedom: Illiberal Democracy at Home and Abroad*. New York: W.W. Norton, 2007.

———. "The Rise of Illiberal Democracy." *Foreign Affairs*, Nov./Dec. 1997.

3

Reining in Reigning Monarchs: The Problematic Legal Status of Kings in Thailand

DAVID STRECKFUSS

I. Introduction: Unbridled Monarchy as a 70-Year-Old Model Collapses

IT WAS ALWAYS LIKELY that the reign of King Vajiralongkorn, or Rama X, would be a difficult one.[1] His father, Bhumibol Adulyadej (r. 1946–2016), had reigned for seven decades and had largely come to define Thailand's monarchy. Bhumibol was portrayed as a thrifty, humble, concerned monarch. Around him was built a royalist ideology that was expressed in a semilegal way as the centerpiece of "the democratic regime with the king as head of state." His inviolable and sacred status was cited as justification for a vigorous application of the draconian lèse-majesté law. This monarchical model was under attack in the last decade of his reign, leading to a massive use (and abuse) of the lèse-majesté law against perceived critics. Vajiralongkorn had been seen in a very different way as the crown prince, especially among the staunchest Bhumibolists. He seemed unsuited for the throne, yet his 1972 designation as heir apparent locked him into the position.[2]

As crown prince, Vajiralongkorn lived a lavish lifestyle filled with endless scandal. In 2013, the then–crown prince stripped his wife of her titles and divorced her, and seven members of her family were jailed for lèse-majesté. One family member apparently jumped to his death from a building (and was quickly cremated before an autopsy could be performed or a full

81

investigation could be carried out.[3] In late 2015, in connection to the newly consecrated monuments to Thai kings, Rajabhakti Park, and the "Bike for Dad" and "Bike for Mom" activities for the ailing king and queen, led by Vajiralongkorn, three were arrested for raising illicit funds: two died in custody—one from hanging himself and the other from reported blood poisoning—and the third, a personal bodyguard of the prince, was stripped of his titles for having committed "grave evils" and disappeared, now presumed dead. Two other military officers charged with lèse-majesté also disappeared from sight.[4]

The military's anxiety over succession was cited as a pretext for carrying out the 2014 coup that toppled the democratically elected government; there was a short period when the military government seemed to hesitate in naming Vajiralongkorn as king.[5] Vajiralongkorn has since been covered by the constitutional provision of inviolability, and after becoming crown prince he has been protected by the lèse-majesté law. Thus, the monarchy was shielded from criticism, at least until mid-2020. Despite the continuous and vociferous claims that the monarchy is "above politics," Vajiralongkorn has not hesitated to interfere in politics. After five years of dictatorial rule by Thailand's military, elections were held in March 2019. As campaigning heated up in February, the king's sister Ubolratana, who had previously been stripped of her royal title, was nominated to become prime minister by the Thai Raksa Chart Party. Within hours, the king issued a royal decree saying that the nomination of a member of the royal family was "extremely inappropriate" and "unconstitutional."[6] The military-appointed Constitutional Court concurred and ordered the disbandment of the party that had nominated her. Just before the elections, the king issued a widely televised statement saying that people should vote for "good people," a reference understood to back the military junta's candidates. In 2020 when protests against the monarchy were erupting throughout the country, the king said encouragingly to a pro-monarchy protester: "Very brave. Very good. Thank you."[7]

Moreover, Vajiralongkorn has essentially ordered the government to make his bidding "legal." The military rulers had gone through all the trouble of legitimizing a new, authoritarian constitution with a referendum only to have the new king make unilateral changes to a number of provisions afterward.[8] Although relieving some tension when instructing the government to stop lèse-majesté prosecutions in early 2018, the king did not have the constitutional power to order that any law not be observed.[9] The king had the military-appointed legislature in secret sessions change laws that left the king as the sole owner of crown properties, and issued royal decrees to form a sort of private, personal military force at the taxpayers' expense. The king has even given himself the prerogative of appointing the supreme patriarch of Thai Buddhism, the de facto state religion. After the 2019 elections, these royal orders were opened up to debate in a semielected parliament. A rare challenge to royal power was launched by the most vocal opposition party, the Future Forward Party (FFP). The issue was portrayed as an abuse of power by the prime minister. The FFP noted that such decrees could be passed only when "urgent." What was so urgent about this?[10]

While generally uninterested in royal duties, Vajiralongkorn is devoted to ceremony exalting his royal person. His coronation, scheduled after elections in 2019 so it could be carried out under "democracy," cost one billion baht (US$33 million).[11] Despite willingness to use state funds for the coronation, the Chakri family has been rated as one of the richest royal families, indeed one of the richest families, on the planet, with one publication estimating its worth at US$60 billion.[12] Despite this, the institution receives a more-than-generous cut of the national budget. As a comparison, of the total 2020 national budgets of Thailand and Spain, the Thai monarchy received US$989 million (29.7 billion baht)—0.93 percent—while Spain's monarchy got only 0.0017. In nominal terms, the Thai monarchy gets 547 times more than its Spanish counterpart.[13]

The king's actual power—financial, constitutional, sacral—is incomparable. To ensure the monarchy's place, there has emerged a set of interlinking cultural, legal, and constitutional laws and mechanisms designed to undermine the credibility of critics and to imprison them if necessary. According to Kevin Hewison, the result of the institution's repositioning, abetted by the military, is that "the monarch now holds more formal power than any king since 1932"—the year that Siam/Thailand became a nominal constitutional monarchy.[14]

The record of Thai kings under "democracy" since 1932 has been poor; more often than not they engaged in activities designed to frustrate popular sovereignty. King Prajadhipok (1925–35) connived with royalist factions to undermine and overthrow democratic upstarts, and he fantasized about executing the rebels and displaying their severed heads outside the palace.[15] Bhumibol consented to the design of coup-makers first in 1947, and he continued endorsing coups against governments, both democratically elected and otherwise, time and time again: 1951, 1957, 1958, 1971, 1973, 1976, 1977, 1991, 2006, and 2014.[16] It is not unreasonable to argue that Thailand never made a democratic transition; better said, it has remained an absolute monarchy with democratic aberrations. Comments Patrick Jory: "A superficially modernised Thai monarchy continues to carry within itself the essence of an ancient theory of political authority that is alien to modern concepts of political legitimacy."[17]

Most monarchies in Europe capitulated to the rise of democracy and granted constitutions to their subjects in the nineteenth century. The most intransigent absolute monarchies—Russia and Persia—granted constitutions in the first decade of the twentieth century. The absolute monarchy in Siam was an outlier: only decades later was its monarchy forced to grant a constitution. The People's Party, flushed by its overthrow of the absolute monarchy, read out a public declaration on 24 June 1932.[18] The scathing indictment of the monarchy pointed out five instances of the "the king above the law" or the king's "power above the law."

The People's Party invited the king to be head of state, but with a condition: "he must be under the law of the constitution for governing the country, and cannot do anything independently without the approval of the assembly of people's representatives." If the king refuses "for the selfish reason that his power will be reduced, it will be regarded as treason to the nation, and it will be necessary for the country to have a republican form of government." The statement also says: "You, all of the people, should know that our country belongs to the people—not to the king." The People's Party, through the parliament, would be the instrument by which popular sovereignty would be defended.

The original agenda of those overthrowing the absolute monarchy was to bring Siam into the modern world; this held for a few months. Remarkably, the People Party's declaration was the first—and last—systematic critique of the monarchy ever to be aired in Thailand. The monarchy and its supporters worked methodically to claw back the privileges and prerogatives the People Party threatened to take away. Somewhere along the way, despite the student movement of the 1970s, the anti-dictatorship movement of 1992, and the various social movements of the 1990s, the "network monarchy" had somehow so successfully taken control of the discourse that its clearly anti-democratic agenda was passed off as democratic. It had constructed a narrative that placed the monarchy at the center of the so-called fight for democracy, but ever framed as one thwarted by corrupt politicians who selfishly put their self-interest ahead of the nation's.[19]

Whatever the failings of the People's Party might have been, the declaration of 24 June 1932 is a clear-sighted critique of absolute monarchy but one that dimmed over time and has been largely forgotten. It might have stayed that way had a youth movement not arisen and brought the statement back to the public's attention. On 10 August 2020, student protesters publicly made ten demands on the monarchy that were quite similar in tone to the 1932 declaration. Their statement called for the monarchy to be stripped of its sacred and inviolable status, for the lèse-majesté law to be abolished, and for those in jail for the crime to be released. It called on parliament to investigate any possible wrongdoing of the king, in particular the murder and disappearance of the institution's critics. It said that assets presently held by the monarchy should be clearly delineated between property of the Crown and personal expenses, that the annual budget allotment for the monarchy should be reduced, and that donations to royal charities should be frozen and audited. It called for the elimination of all government bodies connected to the monarchy, such as the Privy Council. The statement called for an end to the propaganda of the monarchy in education and in the media. Finally, it said the royal family should be banned from publicly expressing any statement on politics and that the king be barred from endorsing coups.[20]

There were three key precipitating factors to the ten demands: the 2014 coup had set a tone of illegitimacy, the elections of 2019 were undemocratic and the results managed to allow the military more or less to stay in power, and the rise and dissolution of the Future Forward Party. There has always been an expectation, never disappointed by Thai courts, that the amnesty Thai coup-makers give themselves would eternally save them from prosecution for overthrowing the government and that Thai people would let the question of the coup's legitimacy fade into the past. But the stench of the 2014 coup carried out by General Prayuth Chan-ocha and his associates did not dissipate as expected. The upstart FFP laid out a social democratic vision of Thailand and saw the problematic roles the military and the monarchy played as obstacles to realizing it. Its base was the youth in particular, but the FFP's political positions also appealed to disgruntled followers of the Pheu Thai Party (that had been closely connected to former prime minister Thaksin Shinawatra), activists, and progressives. The success of the party in the 2019 elections had spooked the conservative establishment and forced it to come up with creative ways to manipulate the results of the election to its side. That the pro-military parties were barely able to cobble together (with a lot of money) a ruling majority in the House of Representatives made the FFP such a perceived threat to the military that the military immediately sought ways to eliminate it. After suffering months of embarrassing FFP challenges in parliament, the Constitutional Court (whose judges had previously been appointed by the military government) finally ordered the party's dissolution in late February 2020. The government had seriously misjudged the effect of this, as suddenly student protests sprung up across the country. After the COVID-19 crisis let up somewhat in June, the protests continued. Most notable were protests on 24 June, the anniversary of the overthrow of the absolute monarchy. In July and August, student protests began making more direct references to the monarchy.[21]

Public opinion polls showed that Thai society had changed—or perhaps for the first time people felt brave enough to speak honestly. A poll held shortly after the 10 August event showed that 63 versus 25 percent of those surveyed agreed with the student demand for revision of the constitution. Most remarkable was that there was a question about the monarchy at all: 59 percent said students were "making demands as allowed in democracy," while only 42 percent said students "must not infringe on the monarchy." Thailand appeared to be a truly changed place.[22]

The sharp, public criticism of the monarchy, especially on 10 August, outraged and shook the upper echelons of Thai society. But rather than attempting to manage changes to the institution, the authoritarian government responded using apparently the only way it knew: repression. It revived use of the lèse-majesté law in late November and picked off student leaders one by one. By mid-December, more than 30 activists, mostly youths, had been charged with the crime. By May 2021, 50 more were facing such charges.[23]

A peculiar legal moment

A particular moment, a clash between the old and new, that communicates the state of sovereignty in Thailand is a royal edict announced in October 2020 that "Royal Noble Consort" Sineenat Wongvajirapakdi was to be demoted in military rank and stripped of her titles. The edict said the royal consort had "committed offenses against royal customs and of disloyalty to the King" and "violated royal authority." The conflict, said the royal announcement, "affected the institution and public of the nation." She had acted "to derive direct personal benefit" and "not actually for the public [good]." It concluded that dishonorable actions created "misunderstanding among the people" and "undermined the nation and the institution."[24]

The language of the edict is reminiscent of treason trials of the seventeenth century that are colored darkly by various shades of sedition, treason, and betrayal. The language of the edict is completely incongruous with the legalese of the otherwise staid, official *Royal Gazette*. Her subordination likely landed her in a secretive military court, and she was sent to prison.[25] Ten months later, the royal consort's incarceration ended, and her position was restored. A royal edict declared that "Sineenat Wongvajirapakdi is not tarnished" and henceforth "it will be as if she had never been stripped of her military ranks or royal decorations."[26]

Did anyone for a moment think this palace tempest "affected the institution and public of the nation," or that there was something in the affair that involved "the public good," or that it had such gravity and weight that it "undermined the nation?" What did it mean that this view could even come to the mind of the king? How absurd would it be for a nation if such a petty incident could be seen as capable of undermining it?

More than that—indeed, this being the precise point—is that this is a statement of royal sovereignty, of sovereignty over the state: I have the power to pronounce this; there are no constraints on my power to make such a pronouncement; there is no competing claim to sovereignty to check my ability to do this when and how I choose. I have the power to pronounce against persons I choose. I have the power to say that the effects of my actions now are absolute and unassailable and correct; that later those actions may be expunged, the facts revised, and that I may pronounce a new reality.

Legal status of king and commoners

The current king has made at best dubious, at least questionable legal demands on the state: his "divorces" culminated in house arrests and throwing entire families into jail; he issued royal edicts to take control over the state's budget, personnel, and crown property, to change the constitution after a referendum, and to ban his sister from standing as candidate for prime minister; and he ordered a government body to not follow the law and made statements that indicated support for one political faction over another.[27]

As a constitutional monarch, the legal status (and power) of the king is not clearly demarcated. If the king did overstep his constitutional power, what could the parliament, or the courts, or the common citizen do? Within his personal realm—if indeed monarchs can really be said to have a personal life—can the king do no wrong? If the king had been a commoner, it is doubtful that many of his actions would or should have been ignored by the law. Can citizens question royal actions that would otherwise be criminal? Can any unit of the government do such a thing? Or is it criminal for anyone or any government body to point out the crimes of a king who is legally shielded from all accusation?

II. Sacredness of Monarchies in Rome and Western Europe

Where did this phrase—"The person of the king is inviolable and sacred"—originate? Was it an idea common to law under absolute monarchies, or did it appear only when the legality of the monarch was put into question? In approaching an answer, the history of three interrelated concepts has to be examined, however briefly: inviolability and sacredness (can a monarch be tried?); sovereignty (who makes the decision?); and lèse-majesté (how is the entire edifice of monarchy protected?). The monarch makes the decision; the lèse-majesté law makes the monarchy (and the monarch that made it) inscrutable and free of any criticism; the monarch cannot be held liable and to even suggest so borders on heresy.

Curiously, it seems it was under the Roman Republic that "majesty" was first used. To commit a crime against the majesty of the Roman people was treason, something Cicero called "a lessening of the dignity of the people or … authority" given by the people."[28] Later, Roman emperors became the head of the state religion and occasionally deified themselves, making lèse-majesté a crime against both the state and religion. By the beginning of the third century, Ulpianus observes, "The crime of *lese majesty* may closely resemble that of sacrilege."[29] Under Diocletian (CE 286–305), the eminent scholar of Roman law, Floyd Seyward Lear, asserts, "The emperor's powers became supernatural and sacred, and the emperor himself became the incarnation of God on earth."[30] Lèse-majesté had become a "most dreadful feature of the age" that "infected" society, making it impossible to "distinguish between aliens and kinsfolk, between friends and strangers."[31] Treason was no longer an offense against the Roman people, or government, or state, but "the safety of the Emperor."[32] The jurist Modestinus warned that judges should not use lèse-majesté trials "as an opportunity to show their veneration for the majesty of the Emperor" and should prescribe lower punishment for what might have been a "slip of the tongue."[33] A contemporary observer said: "False suspicions of *lèse-majesté* have always been a common scourge." He reports that "if the head of a household, in the seclusion of his private apartments, with no confidential servant present, had whispered something in the ear of his wife, the emperor learned it on the following day."[34] By the fourth century CE, advisers to the emperor said that in cases of lèse-majesté, "suspicion is equivalent to proof," which "supposes the intention of mischief." Perceived intention was equivalent to the act itself, and such person "no longer deserves to live, if his life may threaten the safety, or disturb the repose of his sovereign."[35] It was decreed that the lèse-majesté law would cover not only the emperor, but anyone in his service: "Illustrious men who are members of Our Council and Consistory, and of the Senate (as they form part of Our Government), or finally, of anyone else who is in Our Service."[36]

Rough-and-tumble political struggles of those below the throne served to strengthen the emperor but they also made "political instability the dominant characteristic of Roman imperial history."[37] Argues Paul Veyne, there was no sense that usurpers had "illegally" seized power, nor any concept of a "legitimate ruler." An act of tyranny was a "perfectly legal decision." In reality, the emperor "alone held real power while pretending to be a responsible servant of the state, and this ambivalence was the very essence of the system."[38]

As Christianity became the state religion, emperors fashioned an empire that made heresy, blasphemy, and sacrilege new kinds of violations against *majestas*. Boyd writes that starting in CE 381, "Theodosius made the violation of divine law equivalent to sacrilege, and such violations involved the loss of certain rights of Roman citizenship."[39] An imperial decree of CE 384 makes discussion of public affairs sacred: "The conduct of the Emperor should not be discussed, for it is the same as sacrilege to doubt whether he whom the sovereign selects for an office is worthy or not."[40]

It was under empire that Rome developed the key elements of absolute monarchy. Veyne, though, argues that the Roman emperors were in fact loved by the people. It was not an "unthinking enthusiasm" that brought people to have "genuine affection" for their ruler. Considered as a "disinterested father" or "member of the family," even the most mediocre emperor was "honored as a divine being." As such, "everything an emperor did was seen as a blessing, including the most banal administrative formality." Says Veyne: "He was not a god by virtue of his personal merit, he was a god because he was the emperor."[41]

The Roman Empire laid out a model. Scott writes that "the embodiment and concentration of the authority of the entire mass of citizens in the occupant of the Imperial throne ... gave rise to the doctrine of laesa majestas." The law would later serve as "an indispensable concomitant of all monarchic institutions, extended and magnified in subsequent ages."[42]

In thirteenth-century England, though, Anglo-Saxon law, serving as the foundation of common law, was focused on "wrongs" and the procedures to settle them: combat, writs, and oaths, and judgment by one's peers. The social hierarchy was held together by a descending system of oaths lower-ranking people made to their superiors; at the apex of which was perched the king. Henry de Bracton writes:

> The king has no equal within his realm. Subjects cannot be the equals of the ruler, because he would thereby lose his rule, since equal can have no authority over equal nor [over] a superior, because he would then be subject to those subjected to him. The king must not be under man but under God and under the law.[43]

For Bracton, since "law makes the king," the king should "bestow upon the law what the law bestows upon him, namely, rule and power." A king can only rule where "will" is subordinated to the law. If the king were to let "his power remain unbridled," there would be no remedy as "no writ runs against him." Only a petition for redress could be submitted in which the king could "correct and amend his act." But, it depended on the pleasure of the king. If he did not take heed of complaints submitted in petition, there was no recourse and "it is punishment enough for him that he awaits God's vengeance." In actual practice, though, such a petition is hard to imagine; as Bracton also says: "No one may presume to question his acts, much less contravene them." It was not that no one could sue the king so much as it was a legal impossibility, for the question came down to who could judge the case. According to Bracton: "It is clear that it cannot be the king himself in his own suit, for he would thus be both actor and judge." Neither could it be "a justice since in judicial matters he represents the person of the king whose deputy he is." Bracton asks: "Who then shall judge when the king himself must be the actor at the trial?"[44]

Frederic Pollock and Frederic Maitland point out there was "no established orderly method" to try a king. The king might be under the law, but he was at the time "below no man and below no court of law." No one has the right to restrain "an erring king," and "the law has no means of punishing him, and no direct means of compelling him to make redress for the wrongs that he has done." The king was not sacred: he was just a man at the top of the hierarchy, and there was no one higher to judge him. Pollock and Maitland cheekily suggest: "If Henry III had been capable of being sued, he would have passed his life as a defendant."[45]

There was one modest restraint on monarchs: the oath. Before being consecrated with holy oil and becoming "sacred and inviolable," many European kings made an oath.[46] In England, kings made an oath to observe the fundamental laws and protect the people. William Blackstone mentions the importance of "the old Gothic constitution" of the coronation oath by which monarchs bind themselves to "the public," which is "an invisible body" that "has delegated all it's [sic] power and rights, with regard to the execution of the law, to one visible magistrate" through its own oath to their monarch.[47]

The embracing of Roman law in the late Middle Ages played a key role in expanding the purview of the lèse-majesté law and bringing the concept of divine right into bolder relief. In turn, the areas defined as under the king by the lèse-majesté law helped to unify polities into centralized kingdoms and bestowed upon kings an imprimatur of sacredness. In France, for instance, Jean Brissaud argues the absolute monarchs, with "concentration of all public authority," enjoyed "unlimited power." The marriage of secular and sacred power, founded on "a tradition that royal authority came from God," endowed absolute monarchs with sacred status: "The person of the king was sacred; he was accountable only to God; his subjects had no more rights against him than the creature against its creator," but embracing religious obligations "enjoined the king to devote himself to his subjects and it forbade him to oppress them."[48]

Absolutist theorists such as Jean Bodin equated "majesté" with "sovereignty"—monarchs became "the incarnation of the State" with "all the attributes of supreme power." Bodin avers the scope of absolutist monarchs "had no legal limits."[49] He cites "Jewish theologians" as the originators of the idea that kings "should be regarded by their subjects as sacred and inviolable." He also argues that even if a king "has committed all the evil, impious, and cruel deeds imaginable, … [n]o process of law is possible, for the subject has no jurisdiction over his prince, for all power and authority to command derives from him." Bodin continues: "It is not allowable for the subject to pass judgement on his prince, the vassal on his lord, the servant on his master." The subject could never resist the prince, no matter how tyrannical. He could only "fail to obey him in any commands contrary to the law of God and of nature." For Bodin, all civil bodies were beholden to the king, whose "mere presence suspends the powers of all magistrates, corporations, colleges, estates, and communities."[50]

There is no better account of divine right and absolute monarchy than what James I himself penned in 1609. He wrote: "The state of monarchy is the supremest thing upon earth; for kings are not only God's lieutenants upon earth, and sit upon God's throne, but even by God himself are called gods." He continued that kings are "justly called gods" because "they exercise a manner or resemblance of divine power upon earth." Just as God can rule at his pleasure, kings can "make and unmake their subjects, they have power of raising and casting down, of life and of death, judges over all their subjects and in all causes and yet accountable to none but God only." To "dispute" what God does is blasphemy, so too it is "sedition" for "subjects to dispute what a king may do." He warns his subjects not to "meddle with the main points of government; that is my craft." The king will not "be taught my office." Neither should subjects question his right to rule, as "I would be loath to be quarreled in my ancient rights and possessions." Finally, as "all novelties are dangerous" in politics, the people should "beware to exhibit for grievance anything that is established by a settled law" and should not "press their king."[51]

While the sacred role of the monarch was never formalized in law in England, it was in France. One jurist of the eighteenth century writes that lèse-majesté was primarily for maintaining "public peace" and "the tranquility of all the subjects of the Prince." Lèse-majesté was heinous as "it is committed directly against the sacred person of the sovereign, who is the living image of God on earth" as ordained by "Divine providence." As such, a crime against the king was an act of sacrilege.[52] It was typical of French jurists to discriminate between divine and human lèse-majesté, between offenses committed "against God or against the Sovereign Powers," but with no clear-cut boundary demarcating treason, blasphemy, impiety, sacrilege, or heresy.[53]

III. "The King Can Do No Wrong"—But What If He Does?

Only 40 years after James I's musings on divine right, his son Charles I was executed by order of parliament in 1649. But there was the earlier case of the Earl of Strafford (Thomas Wentworth) in 1641 that reveals key dynamics by which a king could be impugned. At one point, Charles I dispensed with parliament altogether and initiated "personal rule." Strafford, appointed by the king as lord deputy of Ireland from 1632 to 1640, served Charles I well, raising the fortunes of the crown. Strafford returned to England in 1639 and became one of the king's principal advisers, advising that Irish troops be used to suppress Scottish rebels. Needing to levy funds for war, Charles I recalled parliament and, as one of its first acts, impeached Strafford for "subverting the fundamental rights" and raising an army against England. Strafford argued that it was impossible for him to be found guilty of treason as he had been acting under the king's orders. For charges against him, Strafford produced the king's letter of authorization. The House of Commons issued a "bill of attainder" which, without a trial, simply declared Strafford guilty of treason and sentenced him to death. With mobs threatening the palace, the king assented to the attainder, and Strafford was executed on 12 May 1641.

Strafford was not found guilty of treason for being or acting disloyally to the monarch. He was found guilty precisely for remaining loyal to Charles I, who was the real target of the proceeding. But the king could not be tried. So instead, the House of Commons pretended that the king "had been led astray by wicked counsel." Strafford had aided the king in his designs for "arbitrary government" and attempting "to place the king above the law." The House of Commons thought by condemning the king's "wicked" adviser, "no other minister would be found daring enough to carry out the orders of a king who was bent upon reducing parliament to subjection."[54]

But there was a deeper issue beneath the specific charges. What the parliament meant in "subversion of fundamental laws" brought up the questions of what law was and who or what had the authority to create it: a question of sovereignty, prompting a new understanding of what "reason" meant. One judge and member of the House of Commons, York, argued, in a more traditional way and ignoring Strafford's claim that he was working under the king's orders, that "a levying of war to subvert the laws was necessarily a war against the king as the king was the fountain of the law and bound to maintain it."[55] It might be that Strafford's greatest crime was being a devout monarchist and following his king too well. York said that however authoritarian Strafford might have acted, "his offense was not one which could by any straining of language be included in the limits of high treason." Strafford believed that England "could only proceed with the increase of the power of the executive, not of the parliament, with a government controlled by the king and not by the people."[56]

There was also the question of treason not against the king, but against the people, the public, and the public interest. One commenter at the time wrote that it was true that Strafford had not acted against "the king's sacred person" but rather "against the king's people. ... [T]hough it be the homicide of a mean subject, it is against the king's crown and dignity because it is against the protection and safety of that man that is the king's subject."[57] The conflict was also over sovereignty between the parliament and the king. In this context, it was argued "that the law was the 'soul' of the political body by which the king held his crown and to destroy it was to destroy also the king and his kingdom along with it," leading to a "redefinition of treason, not simply as a crime against the king's person, but against the state," at a time when the idea of the "state" was not entirely "divorced from the person or persons of any individual."[58] In early 1649, the House of Commons declared itself "the supreme power" of the land and could legislate law without recourse to the House of Lords or the monarch.[59] It then established a special "High Court of Justice," and Charles I was accused of acting "out of a wicked design to erect and uphold in himself an unlimited and tyrannical power to rule according to his will, and to overthrow the rights and liberties of the people," which voided "the fundamental constitutions of this kingdom."[60]

Charles I rejected the legitimacy of "this pretended court" and claimed "no earthly power can justly call me ... in question as a delinquent." He invoked the maxim that "the king can do no wrong," and "that no learned lawyer will affirm that an impeachment can lie against the king." He also pointed out that the majority of his subjects, who were not consulted, would not countenance the proceeding. He said it was the House of Commons itself that was subverting the fundamental laws.[61] The judgment against Charles found him guilty of high treason "as a tyrant, traitor, murderer, and public enemy to the good people of this nation." The trial and execution of the king was in part the result of a new way of understanding the relationship between monarchs and the public. The prosecutor argued that not every contingency could be predicted. They had to turn to "general reasons of state" and act "for the good of the community." The king may reign by divine right, but his prosecution for failing his office was "god's and the kingdom's errand," whereby the people resumed the people's sovereignty.[62] The king had failed his coronation oath, which was "a Contract and Bargain made betwixt the King and his People." The king was obliged to guarantee the safety and protection of the people in exchange for the people's allegiance.[63] Alan Orr argues that the people had become "a corporation (universitas), a single, abstract, juristic person." It was not the "immorality of the kingly dignity" that "lent continuity to the constitutional order," but rather "the whole people."[64] If treason was defined as acting against the king, it would have been impossible for the king to commit treason. But in the conviction, treason was now defined as acts against "the common good, whether that was conceived of as the public interest, the public good, or, more traditionally, the commonwealth." In the judgment, the "fiction that the king could do no wrong was utterly abandoned." The king could do wrong, and, if he did, if he worked against the public good, then engaged citizens had the obligation to remove him.[65]

The Stuarts were restored to the throne in 1660, but were dethroned in 1688 by the Glorious Revolution when the primacy of the parliament was confirmed, thereby affirming citizen rights and creating the first major so-called constitutional monarchy of Europe. It is probably then that a coronation oath was made law, one that made automatic abdication for "attempt to overthrow the constitution, violation of the fundamental pact, [and] abandonment of the kingdom."[66] Decades later, Blackstone says King James II had "invaded the fundamental constitution of the realm." A "new settlement of the crown" was established that serves as a warning to any future monarch who "should endeavor to subvert the constitution by breaking the original contract between king and people" or "should violate the fundamental laws." Nonetheless, these extraordinary circumstances could not be solved through the law. Future generations, "whenever necessity and the safety of the whole shall require it," would have to depend on "the exertion of those inherent (though latent) powers of society, which no climate, no time, no constitution, no contract, can ever destroy or diminish."[67]

Blackstone hedges on the maxim "The king can do no wrong." He writes that it did not mean that all actions of the king were never wrong and beyond "remedy." It would be a "great weakness and absurdity in any system of ... law," he says, "to define any possible wrong, without any possible redress." Blackstone affirms that parliament has "the right of remonstrating and complaining to the king even of those acts of royalty ... such as messages signed by himself, and speeches delivered from the throne." The king can do no wrong but neither can parliament: "The supposition of *law* that neither the king nor either house of parliament (collectively taken) is capable of doing any wrong."[68] Blackstone infers that interfering with elections is a kind of treason, "for in a democracy there can be no exercise of sovereignty but by suffrage, which is the declaration of the people's will. In all democracies therefore it is of the utmost importance to regulate by whom, and in what manner, the suffrages are to be given." Athenians held as high treason "usurping those rights of sovereignty." It is for this reason that he writes, in contrast somewhat to what he wrote of the monarch, that parliament is "in truth the sovereign power, is always of equal, always of absolute authority: It acknowledges no superior upon earth."[69]

Blackstone makes the case that the king was incapable of doing "any injury" because the crown was a power "created for the benefit of the people." If perchance the exertion of the royal prerogative was "manifestly to the grievance or dishonor of the kingdom," the king's advisers would be called by parliament "to a just and severe account." If a prerogative "be abused to the public detriment," then it is "unconstitutional." The crown could not be accused of negligence as "the law intends that the king is always busied for the public good."[70] The law "will not make any accusation of the king," as he is incapable "of intentionally disregarding his trust." No act can be attributed to the king that "might lessen him in the eyes of his subjects." It would thus be "rendered void."[71]

It can be understood from Blackstone that the public good can be a factor in measuring acts and prerogatives of monarchs. They cannot cause national dishonor, public detriment, or be prejudicial to the commonwealth. They also cannot interfere with elections, which served as the wellspring of parliamentary sovereignty. For Blackstone, the monarchy cannot in the "ordinary course" of law act against the commonwealth, except by virtue of bad royal advisers. He does speculate, through inference, that a king could at least theoretically act treasonously against the commonwealth or parliamentary sovereignty.

In the case of France, the revolution of 1789 overthrew the absolute monarchy. Two years later, Louis XVI apparently attempted to flee the country. The incident sparked a furor in the constituent assembly. It responded by suspending some of the king's powers, confining the royal family, and debating the role of the king. Conservative members protested, saying that such measures "were contrary to the constitution and a direct attack upon the inviolability of the sacred person of the king." The virtual imprisonment of the king and stripping him of prerogatives "perpetually exposed" the king to insults: "The monarchy had been destroyed, the very appearance of royalty obliterated."[72]

The incident also led to one of the greatest debates on inviolability of the monarch.[73] Space constraints make it impossible to give justice to the subtlety and sophistication of the debate here. Though involving a certain degree of invective, the three-day presentation of positions provides a model of reasoned, enlightened, and inspired rhetorical contestation.[74] A committee established by the assembly had concluded that the king had been kidnapped and therefore committed no wrong. The conservative position was that the king's inviolability was itself inviolable. In any case, the king would be bound by the oath in the new constitution to come into effect some weeks later.[75] What follows are summaries of some of the positions taken by representatives in the assembly.

LA ROCHEFOUCAULD-LIANCOURT: "A non-inviolable king," he says, "would be neither a hereditary king, nor a king for life, but a king for a day." A king is inviolable to put himself "outside the circle of factions." The king's scepter "is like the lever" of ruling and "inviolability is its only fulcrum." The principle of inviolability was established to safeguard the constitution and public peace, "and against factions." Without inviolability, "how would royalty be lasting" or would there even be a royalty? A monarch without inviolability would be "frightful" as it would be overwhelmed by slanders and suits. It would "be as easy to debase as to dethrone." For monarchy to be durable, it can allow no exemptions to inviolability.

MARC-GUILLAUME-ALEXIS VADIER: The king has made a "voluntary and culpable abdication." He is "a perjurer and fugitive king, a king who cowardly deserts his post to paralyze the government, to deliver us to all the horrors of civil war and anarchy ... who is going to throw himself into the arms of a traitor ... a monster who wanted to sprinkle blood on the hospitable land which satiated him with his favors; a king who ... dared to tear up your constitution." Inviolability would "be a monstrous fiction to give this astonishing prerogative" to "a crowned brigand" who can "with impunity kill, set fire to, conspire, call the foreign satellites onto our frontiers, spread desolation and carnage everywhere." "Such a monstrosity" as inviolability "in our laws would be a real poison, a pestilential germ." The king "is a man like any other, and a man cannot be above, nor more, than the law."

JOSEPH PRUGNON: In his actions, the king has "not ceased to be inviolable, because he has not forfeited the constitution." As a principle, "Inviolability is not purely relative; it is absolute." While not wanting to "establish here a royal superstition," still, inviolability "cannot be subjected either to analysis or to exceptions. ... [R]elative inviolability would be illusory." The king can do nothing without a government minister's countersignature. "Would it not be ridiculous to declare that he who can do nothing is not a guarantor and that he is inviolable for what he does not do or for what he is, [for what he is] not supposed to do? ... [T]he person of the king is indivisible, and being necessarily sacred in one respect, it must be so in all." The royalty "is a unique and supreme magistracy which is beyond all comparison, and which in this respect makes an exception to all your rules ... a part of the nation is holding on to the monarchy out of civility, in principle. The position in which France finds itself, the very character of the French, their very virtues, require a leader. And if religion, according to Montesquieu, has its root in the hearts of those who inhabit the empire, the nation needs a constitutional monarchy just as it needs a gospel."

MAXIMILIEN ROBESPIERRE: Inviolability "is in itself a revolting monstrosity in the social order, or rather it is the absolute overthrow of the social order." If a king robs a widow, steals a man's vineyard, buys off a judge—"will the law say to him, 'Sire, you have done it without crime ....

Sire, you are using your right; we have allowed you everything!'" Would you call this state of affairs "establishing public order?" But instead, you say that inviolability is "the unchanging basis of social order!" Is inviolability to mean that the king should have the privilege of committing crimes? "The king is inviolable!" If so, "would not the people be inviolable as well?" Monarchy creates an intolerable system, "for, first of all, by raising a man above the law, by assuring him the power to be criminal with impunity, he is pushed, by an irresistible slope, into all speed and excess; he is made the most base and, consequently, the most unhappy of men." Now France suffers under "the bizarre and disastrous assumption of a nation that would be ruled by a criminal king of lèse-nation!" Monarchy is maintained by factionalism and weak government.

ADRIEN DUPORT: There must be a clearly defined balance of powers. The assembly may be "the expression of the will of the representatives" and is "the point where the general will is formed." Nonetheless, it takes time for people to "be enlightened, and public opinion, generally consulted and slowly formed." In the meantime, it is "necessary to place a brake on the legislative body, a means of preventing its too rapid and too arbitrary action." This brake can come in [the form of] a monarchy in which the monarch can slow the motion of the legislature and allow new laws to become known to the people and for the legislature to listen to public opinion and make corrections as necessary. As the constituent assembly chose monarchy, the only form that "suits our Empire, our customs and our position," then "it is absolutely necessary" that the monarch "be absolutely inviolable." Otherwise, the legislative body "would be a real despotism" that as the single sovereign power would be "not only as dangerous, but a hundred times more fatal than that which would be exercised by a single individual." If the power of the king were dependent on a legislative body, "the latter could destroy its own brake." A brake that is dependent is "useless" and only serves as "a vain obstacle, which would even irritate the legislative body." In such a state, liberty is lost. If the king can be accused, then anyone can accuse him; "then the king is dependent on all; and there is no one in the 25 million men who make up the empire who cannot accuse him."

PIERRE-VICTOR MALOUËT: Louis XVI is the first king in history born to absolute power who then renounced it. The people had expressed their "general will" when they elected representatives to the assembly in 1789.

They had agreed to certain principles that would permit no exception: the king would respect the rights of the people and in turn the people ensured his inviolability. Under monarchy, "sovereignty and law have a perpetual representative." The legislature can act as it likes, but it can only act "without undermining the independence of the throne, without altering the essence of the monarchical government." Now there are those in the assembly claiming an exception to these core principles, and it is one that "endangers the whole of society … for, if you admit a single exception, the independence of the throne, the safety of the monarch, are at the mercy of each dominant faction."[76]

The king's attempt to flee the country and the debate saw the first outpouring of republican sentiment in France. A demonstration for republicanism occurred a day after the assembly debate ended, resulting in the Champs de Mars Massacre. The new constitution came into effect, but the king vetoed a number of democratic measures. Then in August 1792, demonstrators stormed the king's palace and public opinion turned sharply against monarchy. A new election with full male suffrage was called. The new convention convened and sidestepped the issue of inviolability by essentially dethroning the king by declaring France a republic on 21 September 1792. The convention debated for a few months on whether it could try citizen Louis Caput, but without the sophistication of the debate from the year before.[77]

The last appeal for inviolability was made by Louis's lead lawyer, Raymond Desèze.[78] Desèze argued the constituent assembly in 1789 discussed "all the doubts, all the objections, all the difficulties" and settled on what constituted constitutional monarchy. Representatives may now wish to allow themselves to "change the intention of the law, or to disguise it." We cannot somehow return to what is clear in the constitution and somehow "restrict the absolute inviolability that it pronounces to a relative or modified inviolability." But we must respect the fact that the nation accepted the constitution and it cannot now "allow any more objections" after the king took an oath to it. Legally and morally, the constitution provided inviolability and the consequences the king faced in three separate instances leading to abdication. These did not obtain, and so the provisions of the constitution, as a manifestation of the general will, must be upheld. But even "if you deprive Louis of the inviolability of king, you owe him at least the rights of a citizen;

because you cannot make Louis cease to be king when you declare that you want to judge him, and that he becomes king again at the time of this judgment that you want to render." Looking out to the members of the convention, Desèze said: "I am looking for judges among you, and I see only accusers. You want to pronounce on the fate of Louis; and it is you yourselves who accuse him! You want to pronounce on the fate of Louis; and you have already made your wish!" He concluded, "Louis will therefore be the only French for whom there will be no law or form. He will have neither the rights of a citizen nor the prerogatives of a king. He will enjoy neither his old condition nor the new one. What a strange and inconceivable destiny!" Remember, he said, that history "will judge your judgment and that it will be that of the centuries." By a razor-thin vote, Louis Caput was sentenced to death in January 1793 and executed.

The French Revolution did not quite have the effects that its proponents might have hoped. Within a little more than a decade, a French monarchy was to be re-established under Napoleon, and by 1815 the Bourbon dynasty was back in power. The continuation of the Bourbons severely limited suffrage, gave the king veto power, and brought lèse-majesté back.[79] However, European kings generally were put on notice that changes needed to be made. European monarchies begrudgingly or not (in the words of the Persian ruler, in "Our gracious benevolence") "granted" constitutions to their subjects. These constitutions as a whole are highly uneven, but they all demarcate in one way or another new power arrangements between the monarch and elected bodies and citizens. One peculiar permutation in many of these constitutions reflects the uneasy relationship between the central thrust of these constitutions that focuses on equality, on the one hand, and the elevated status of the monarch, on the other. The question of royal versus popular sovereignty, the proposition that all are equal before the law, and the exceptional status of the monarchy were all addressed in one way or another by nearly all constitutions in Europe in the nineteenth and early twentieth centuries.[80] Even with such advance notice, many regimes did not adjust to the new reality and were soon abolished.[81]

Returning specifically to the status of the monarch, which underpins and in many ways determines the spirit of these constitutions, the phrase on the sacred and inviolable status of the king is repeated in many constitutions: Norway (1814), Italy (1848), Liechtenstein (1862), Austria (1867), Spain (1876), Japan (1889), Montenegro (1905), and the Ottoman Empire (1908).[82]

It was no easy matter to put monarchs under the laws they were often seen as the fount of or under judges who held court in their names. Even after constitutional monarchy theoretically placed monarchs under the law, there was still no practical way to actually make a monarchy legally accountable in normal law, not to mention that monarchs, as heads of state, were also almost universally granted sovereign immunity. So while anti-monarchical political movements sought to make every citizen equal in the eyes of law, constitutional provisions provided exceptions. It was only through extraordinary and questionable legal means that a monarch could conceivably be tried.

In some instances in European history there have been efforts to bring monarchs to account, despite life-long inviolability. In Belgium, for example, the atrocities committed in Leopold II's private venture in the Congo were stopped only when the Belgian parliament purchased the private colony from the king. His actions made even the most vociferous colonialist blush: Leopold had brutalized and terrorized the population to get rubber. The first call had come from a Black American who, in his protest letter to Leopold in 1890, coined the term "crimes against humanity."[83] Millions lost their lives under the brutal regime, which even brought disfavor from Belgians, many of whom booed at Leopold's funeral procession in 1909.[84] A more recent instance comes from Spain. King Juan Carlos had once been seen as a champion of democracy. But in 2012, he had been pictured shooting wildlife in Africa with his mistress, causing outrage back home. A poll in 2013 showed that two-thirds of those surveyed thought the king should step down.[85] Juan Carlos obliged but it was not the end of his woes. In 2018, a Spanish newspaper published a transcript of a 2012 phone call in which his mistress alluded to the king's money laundering and said, "The king has no concept of what is legal and what isn't." The transcript sparked interest by Swiss prosecutors who discovered a US$100 million "gift" the king had received from the Saudi king in 2008, possibly a kickback for a Saudi Arabian rail link project won by a Spanish consortium. In June 2020, the Spanish Supreme Court took up the case. A month later, Juan Carlos had fled Spain, angering many in that country. The prime minister said the matter was "disturbing" and that Spain had "no room for impunity." Right-wing political parties showed unconditional support for the former king. Despite a lèse-majesté law that occasionally levied fines and imprisonment, left-leaning parties issued a joint statement, saying, "we have no king" and that the monarchy is an "anachronistic institution."[86] While the prime minister resisted calls to make a formal inquiry into the alleged crimes of the former king, he did concede that it might be time to revise the "inviolability" clause in the 1978 constitution that makes the reigning king as head of state immune from accusation or prosecution. Leftist parties argue, though, that the king was and is not immune from "parliamentary investigations or those of the media." Their efforts to initiate a parliamentary investigation failed four times.[87]

IV. Royal Sovereignty and Inviolability in Siam/Thailand

It is likely that the clash over royal versus popular sovereignty will frame and perhaps come to define the reign of Rama X. Popular sovereignty has had a hard time of it in Thailand. The People's Party's overthrow of the absolute monarchy in 1932 was so sharp and immediate, the criticism of the monarchy so pointed, and the demand against royal power so forceful, that it was truly revolutionary. It was a liminal moment for the revolutionaries, as they delivered their demands and waited to see what the reaction might be one of the most obstinate absolute monarchies in the world at the time, that power be given to the people. The new constitution was singularly unambiguous. In the modest preamble, the king states that one of the demands was that he be placed "under the constitution" (hence, making Siam a "constitutional monarchy"). Sovereignty was in the hands of the people and not the king. The king could in certain instances be held accountable by the law.[88] It was, though, a six-month victory for popular sovereignty. The rest of Thai modern history, especially after 1947, has seen the erosion of popular sovereignty.[89] The royalty was able to regain control over "its" property and ideologically and culturally was able, in association with the military, to re-create the monarchy. In a more concrete form, there were no laws concerning the king that were revised in the criminal law code in 1957 despite the overthrow of the absolute monarchy. From the 1950s to 1970s, threats to the government and monarchical sovereignty were fended off with anti-communist laws. The punishment for lèse-majesté was imprisonment of up to seven years. Importantly, after the military coup of 1976, the law was amended, setting up a minimum sentence of three years and increasing the maximum to 15 years. The lèse-majesté was used to a certain degree through the 1980s and 1990s, but when royal powers were under threat in the mid-2000s, the law's use skyrocketed. Cases were tried in civilian courts at first, and then were placed under military court after the coup in 2014.

Sovereignty has effectively been shared between the military and the monarchy: the military overthrows governments, the monarchy signs off on the action—without any serious reference to the role of parliament, which has never, until recently, contested the power of the king or played any sort of role as repository of popular sovereignty. In fact, the most common impulse of the parliament has been to join the military and monarchy against popular sovereignty. One might even hazard that the very organization of the Thai state since 1932, its most base impulse, has been to suppress the specter of popular sovereignty. Royalist supporters pretend to be democratic, but they cannot compete in a fair fight. So they have devoted themselves to running a rigged game: coups when elections do not go their way (2006, 2014); dissolving political parties of adversaries through court order (2007, 2008, 2020); having the constitutional court remove prime ministers and its greatest rivals, and drawing up new constitutions to change the rules of the game (2007, 2017); having a constitutional referendum but criminalizing debate or criticism (2016); using government organizations such as the Election Commission to remove challengers, gerrymandering, and loading up the senate with appointees (2019); playing with the math post-election to gain control of parliament (2019); and bringing charges of lèse-majesté against all critics.

Royal sovereignty has always shrouded itself behind a variety of democratic-sounding euphemisms, celebrating in the same breath that the monarchy in Thailand is unique while saying that "the democratic regime with the king as head of state" is true democracy where the king is "above politics" by social consensus.[90] The most prominent instance of ambiguity in language is found in the peculiar phrasing that is sometimes, and wrongly, translated as "constitutional monarchy" in Thai: "rabop prachathipatai an mi phramahakasat pen pramuk" (awkwardly rendered into English as "the democratic regime of government with the king as head of state"). This "form" does not really clearly communicate anything, as the king (or queen) of all current monarchical forms of government, whether democratic or otherwise, serves as head of state.[91] Adherents call it Thai-style democracy, royal democracy, Thai democracy, Buddhist democracy, and the like, and invariably affirm that the monarchy is "above politics." They call for governance with a strong executive (if military), highly limited elections, an appointed senate, a limited, even a largely symbolic representative body where the public will is kept safely in the minority and away from power. Its critics call it authoritarianism, aristocracy (or oligarchy), dictatorship, and so on. First used in the 1949 constitution, the phrase is endlessly invoked and has inspired a vast body of obeisant commentary, but no clear definition, legally or otherwise.[92] Yet, it is embedded in law and constitution, and being perceived as working against it incurs serious legal, political, and social opprobrium. Though undefined, the concept has increasingly infused Thai constitutions.[93]

Royalist politicians used provisions prohibiting laws contrary to "the democratic regime of government with the king as head of state" to destabilize the ruling coalition by having the matter adjudicated in the Constitutional Court, such as in late 2013 when the House of Representatives passed a law that would have amended the constitution so that the senate could be fully elected. The 1997 constitution also has liberal use of the phrase, even in the "coup-proof" provision Section 63 that prohibited (unsuccessfully it turns out) anyone to "overthrow the 'democratic regime of government with the king as head of state' under this constitution or to acquire the power to rule the country by any means which is not in accordance with the modes provided in this constitution."[94]

Unimaginative politicians have done little to hide the true nature of sovereignty. Junta leader and prime minister General Prayuth, for instance, brazenly announced before parliament:

> In the name of His Majesty the King who presented his royal power to us, today who among us thinks of this? From the point of view of the government, you are using the three powers [ie. legislative, executive and judicial power] which belong to him. The power does not belong to you. You do not receive this power when you are elected. It is power that comes from His Majesty the King. His Majesty presented this power to us to form the government. Today, the power that I have was presented to me by the king.

It is ironic that while the 2017 constitution reiterates "Sovereign power belongs to the people," the content is dependably undemocratic and quite clearly indicates that the people are anything but sovereign.[95] When Prayuth and his cabinet as head of the new "democratically elected" government took their oaths to office before the king in July 2019, as stipulated by the constitution, they pledged their loyalty to the king and to "faithfully perform" their duties "in the interests of the country and of the people forever." They omitted to say, ironically, "I will also uphold and observe the constitution of the kingdom of Thailand in every respect." The omission erupted into a controversy that went on for months. One opposition politician suggested that the omission violated the lèse-majesté law. A student brought a complaint before the Constitutional Court, then the king sent a letter to the cabinet, saying, "I want to take this occasion to wish you encouragement, confidence, and determination to do your duty in line with your oath for the benefit, happiness, and security of the country and the people." Some read this letter to mean the king felt the original oath in its shortened form was acceptable. A law instructor opined that the letter of encouragement might be seen as official as "at times the king's advice takes the form of law in Thailand," but sometimes a royal announcement is "against the principle of the constitutional monarchy." The Constitutional Court threw out the case, rejecting the concern of the complainant that the omission might be later used by the cabinet to overthrow the government.[96]

V. Monarchy Called to Account by a New Generation

And so it was perhaps appropriate that the student movement cut through all the empty constructs of "Thai-style democracy" and went back to the beginning, to the People Party's clear calls for popular sovereignty in 1932. If a single element can be found in the ideology behind the student movement's attacks on the undemocratic constitution, the power-hungry military, and the monarchy's attempt to return to absolutism, it is their adherence to the doctrine of popular sovereignty. The movement is not so much anti-monarchy or anti-military as it is pro–popular sovereignty, for it is these two institutions whose very existences have been dedicated to stifling, demeaning, and destroying any threat to their own claims over sovereignty. In the spirit of that notion, protesters are calling the military and the monarchy to account. But it is their call for reform of the monarchy that has attracted so much attention, which is understandable given that the demand has not been articulated so publicly and persistently in Thailand since 1932.

The student critique might be summed up here: the king is wealthy beyond imagination and still demands nearly 1 percent of annual government expenditures. If he were a commoner, his behavior—toward his former wives, their families, his consort, palace officials, and activists—would invite criminal investigation. He has ordered constitutional amendments that increase his constitutional powers and assembled his own "private" military force. And all these abuses—both alleged and apparent—are shielded by the lèse-majesté law. The students have made 10 demands regarding reform of the monarchy. But it might be argued that many of the demands would be more easily addressed after the more elemental aspect of the king's status has been resolved.[97] The four demands directly related to the legal status of the king are: (1) remove the king's constitutional inviolability; (2) allow parliament to investigate any alleged wrongdoing; (3) revoke the lèse-majesté law; and (4) prohibit the king from endorsing coups.

Does this historical overview of the legal status of monarchs provide any clues to how these abuses associated with monarchs might be addressed? Can the king's legal status be challenged? What legal mechanisms might be used? What might be the cultural considerations? Do any of these have to do with notions associated with popular sovereignty: assent, consent, general will, parliamentary supremacy?

Inviolability

While inviolability of kings, linked to divine right, was something commonly understood but perhaps not actually put into law, certainly the legal status of monarchs and their inviolability became enshrined in constitutions that were the key element of constitutional monarchies. The mystique of kingship and the sacred touch of divine right no doubt remained with monarchies to some extent, but constitutions also grounded monarchs to this human world. All current constitutional monarchies are given the status of inviolability (except Japan), and some are even given a sacred status. From our discussion here on the case of France, royalists argued that inviolability was necessary for any sovereign power (like members of the assembly or a president) because the possibility of endless accusations while serving in office could prove unmanageable and paralyze the sovereign. Others argued that as the executive in a lifetime position, inviolability was necessary so the king could freely act for the best interests of his people.

We also saw the case of England where a sitting king was tried in 1649. There did not seem to be much discussion in parliament on Charles's inviolability. Charles for his part did not recognize the jurisdiction of the high court that tried him partly because he felt he was not answerable for his actions as king and was certainly not answerable to a special court. Nonetheless, he was executed while theoretically still inviolable, and the monarchy came to an end. In the French case, the question of inviolability was discussed intensely and in some detail in July 1791. In declaring France a republic in September 1792, Louis was not so much dethroned so another could take his place, as his throne was removed from beneath him. Because he had not abdicated as specified in the constitution, there was also some doubt whether he might still retain inviolable status. The question was now whether the actions he took as king and while still inviolable yet applied. After discussion in November and early December, the assembly determined that the king could be tried by the assembly itself—and not by a special tribunal, a normal court, or a popular referendum.

In Thailand, the king is protected by Section 6 of the current constitution, which reads: "The king shall be enthroned in a position of revered worship and shall not be violated. No person shall expose the king to any sort of accusation or action." The student movement has demanded that this provision be revoked, perhaps because this provision is linked to the lèse-majesté law. If the king did not have a special status, then the need for such a severe law might no longer be necessary (see more on this below).

There is no necessary link between sacred status and use of the lèse-majesté law or the degree of its punishment. The king of Norway is given a constitutionally sacred status and yet the law is very rarely used, its punishment is up to five years imprisonment, and the king himself is made accountable for deciding whether a charge of lèse-majesté is to move forward or not. At the same time, though, the king of Norway is not enormously wealthy, he does not act or speak in ways that are unconstitutional, he does not commit acts that would warrant arrest or at least investigation if he were a commoner, and he does not endorse criminal acts, like overthrowing the government. In other words, neither he nor the monarchy as an institution acts in any way that might draw justified criticism. In addition, an institution can still be revered as sacred without compelling the population, as in the case of Japan. The constitution does not give the emperor sacred status or inviolability, and there is no lèse-majesté law. And yet many Japanese show a natural (meaning not forced) affection and respect for the institution.

Therefore, the demand of the students to revoke Section 6 may not be necessary if other conditions are met in terms of the lèse-majesté law. Students have said that the sacred status of the monarch might be tied to the section of the criminal code where the lèse-majesté law is placed—national security offenses. But the constitution of the Netherlands, for instance, does not give the monarch any special status or inviolability, and its lèse-majesté law is not under its national security section.[98]

Another aspect often related to inviolability is whether a monarch can be made criminally accountable. At present, there is no mechanism constitutionally or in Thai law that would allow the king to be accused or tried. The legal argument is an old one that we saw in the case of England and France and then later in many constitutions: The king is not responsible; his ministers or agents are. We also saw in the case of France that it was argued that it is not possible to separate the role of the king from his personal life. There was also an argument made that if the king hired a bunch of thugs to beat someone up, the king would not be accountable, but his thugs would be.

Could the king order the arrest and imprisonment of someone and not be held accountable? Could the king, as in Spain, take kickbacks from a company for securing a contract? The answer seems to be no. From a legal standpoint within the confines of a nation's sovereign laws, the king is covered by inviolability. However, those actually carrying out such alleged crimes would be liable. That the king ordered a crime to be committed would not be a defense. But the inviolability clause does not extinguish crimes committed before becoming king, nor does it extend after abdication when the king would have the status of a common citizen.

Are there no exceptions? What if a king raised an army against parliament, as in England, or if the French king had raised an army to fight a civil war? What if the king acted to eradicate the sovereign power of the parliament (where popular sovereignty resides) or to destroy the constitution (another repository of sovereignty)? In England, it was decided by what remained of parliament that no court could competently try such an extraordinary case. So through an act of parliament, a special court, a special tribunal, was established. In France, the assembly made itself the prosecutor and judge after voting in a new constitution. In Thailand's case, a special court was in fact established by parliament specifically to try reactionary forces who rebelled against the democratic government in the 1930s, many of them members of the royal family. If, under the circumstances described earlier, the Thai parliament did in fact establish a special tribunal that would be tried by parliament itself or a special court established for this specific purpose, no doubt Thailand's Constitutional Court would deem it unconstitutional. But then that would mean that a court whose judges were appointed by a military dictatorship would have sovereignty over parliament (which, in practice, it does). But it would be a different matter in most constitutional monarchies. The parliament could also amend the existing constitution or draft a new one that changed the inviolability of the king or made the king legally liable under certain conditions. But again, opponents would argue that the current constitution prohibits any measure that counters or even attempts to revise "the democratic regime of government with the king as head of state" designation.

As a final point on inviolability, the constitutional provision prohibits accusations of any kind. But note that in 1932 the constitution specifically made the king civilly liable, and any cases against him would be tried by the parliament itself. A rationale for this provision was no doubt connected to the enormous wealth of the king, one that at the time involved huge land holdings. If not liable civilly, the king could have acted without any mechanisms for accountability. If it was true then, it is even more so today when "Thailand's largest financial empire," as Hewison calls it, not only owns large swaths of land, but has significant influence over commercial banking and industry.[99] When a large part of that wealth was partly managed by the ministry of finance before 2018, there was at least a nominal level of transparency. But now that the king has claimed it all as his personal assets, and there is no mechanism in law to ensure accountability, the situation is considerably more serious. It is for this reason that students listed as a demand that the 2018 law be rescinded and the wealth of the Crown Property Bureau and the personal wealth of the king be clearly defined.

Lèse-majesté and Thai courts

In the case of Thailand, inviolability itself protects a monarch only from being civilly or criminally tried. Theoretically, suspected crimes could be investigated and perhaps even the king could be compelled to give testimony, something that has happened very occasionally in constitutional monarchies. This would at least give priority to truth. But the second part of the provision, "No person shall expose the king to any sort of accusation or action," could easily create obstacles to the facts of a matter coming out. If "no person" could make an accusation, could parliament?

One of the core features of the Thai lèse-majesté law is that it is designed specifically to suppress facts, in particular, and the truth in a larger sense. Although it appears like a simple defamation law, it actually operates to suppress re-envisioning of Thai politics and society. It overshadows the core of the Thai public sphere, and it casts a pall over the political imaginings that would have otherwise invigorated the democratic body politics. Many student leaders have been jailed for lèse-majesté and sedition. Many are unable to get bail, bringing in the question of whether judges are equipped with a view of justice that can transcend the boundaries of strict legalism. Duncan McCargo's recent work does not give much hope.[100] He writes that as judges "[s]ee their legitimacy as deriving from an exalted position in the Thai social hierarchy, proximate to the throne, they are often disinclined to see themselves as dispensing justice on behalf of the nation, let alone for the people. Rather they exercise justice in the name of the king, and for the sake of the land."

Without training or awareness of "progressive social or political stances" and a willingness to "work with military regimes," judges have a "limited worldview" and lack "empathy and imagination," which leads to an "inability to understand the role of the courts in a democratic order." Judges see themselves as part of "virtue rule" that legitimates "royalism, militarism, and Buddhism" and "privileges select groups" (like judges) who have special access to virtue. Drawing on Benedict Anderson, who calls royalism "a curiously antique form in contemporary Siam," McCargo argues that virtuous rule serves as "the primary source of legitimacy for the Thai state" where "a benevolent ruler, or *dhammaraja* ... embodies notions of Buddhist kingship," and a royal family is in "an active quest for real power in the political system." As such, the Thai legal system as a whole "is primarily dedicated to the preservation of peace and order, rather than ... promoting right-based justice." Court decisions in the past 15 years have "led perversely to a decline of peace and order" and have caused many to believe that the courts are more interested in maintaining authoritarianism than being a locus of justice.

This phenomenon is clearest in the realm of lèse-majesté. McCargo writes, "Thai judges tend to equate serving the king with performing justice" and "believe their highest loyalty is to the crown rather than the public interest." Lèse-majesté is seen as tantamount to cultural treason, a betrayal of "Thainess." Critics of the monarchy are seen as "undermining a shared sense of nationhood and collective identity." So what is perceived as lèse-majesté often triggers an emotional, rabid, and sometimes hysterical response entirely antithetical to democratic pluralism. McCargo recounts a judge's attitude toward critics of the monarchy: "If you cannot accept it then it is not hard at all. You do not have to stay in Thailand and you can find somewhere else to stay. ... [In] Thai society, we uphold loyalty and treat it with the utmost importance .... As for those who really do it [defame the monarchy] intentionally, I would say they are mentally and spiritually dysfunctional."

The students are well aware that their chances of prevailing in the court on charges of lèse-majesté are slim. They have spoken out against the monarchy knowing full well that they might be arrested, and even with the hope that a mass of charges and jailing of young people will work against the royalists, tip public opinion, and lead to action against the regime and its ideology.

A number of years ago, one of the more sophisticated defenses of the lèse-majesté law was written by Borwornsak Uwanno, ironically, perhaps, the principal drafter of the 1997 "People's Constitution."[101] He argues that under the "paternalistic governance" of Thailand, if "the Thai king is unfairly criticized, most Thais feel like their own parent is being attacked" and this criticism is "comparable to ingratitude towards one's own father," and they "cannot accept it." The lèse-majesté law, he says, does not harm only the king, but it is harmful "to Thai society, ethics and culture." Implied in what he says is that the punishment would be determined by that society. So it would follow that the people of Spain have a consensus of some sort in setting the maximum punishment for lèse-majesté at two years. For Sweden, it is six years, the Netherlands and Norway at five, and Belgium three.[102] In Borwornsak's logic, these societies do not see the harm on society as great, or they do not value their monarchies as highly.[103]

Interestingly, Borwornsak takes the risk of tying the lèse-majesté law to popular sovereignty when he introduces the piece with the following: "The first principle is that the ultimate power to govern lies with the people. The government must come from the consent of the people." The people, he says, "exercise such power themselves (direct democracy), or elect representatives to exercise the power on their behalf (indirect democracy)." Such a society, he says, "should have the right to self-determination" regarding its own laws. Borwornsak places Thailand right along with Belgium, the Netherlands, Norway, and Spain. He assumes, over-romantically, that the government in Thailand and its laws have all come "from the consent of the people." But how could he? There is no sense of consent to the coups of 1958, 1971, 1976, 1991, 2006, or 2014—especially the one in 2006 where the majority of voters had just voted the year before for the government the military overthrew. Coups, and the laws the junta impose, are the very extra-legal expression of compulsion, the perfect opposite of "consent." Take in point the very laws he uses to make his argument: the defamation laws. The punishment for the lèse-majesté law was changed by the coup makers in 1976 from up to seven years' imprisonment to up to 15; this was not an expression of "consent of the people." But he says societies have the right to legislate law to match "the cultural and moral norms of the majority of their peoples." Did the Thai people, through their elected representatives, determine that harm? Or was it military leaders deciding for them and imposing it? Borwornsak, like many Thai royalists, absurdly imagines Thailand's monarchy to be based on the British model. He places Thailand among those democratic constitutional monarchies where the king "reigns but does not rule, and acts upon the advice of a government which is elected by the people and has the power to govern." But Thailand is nothing like these other constitutional monarchies.

Coups and oaths

Most monarchs are constitutionally required to make an oath, typically in front of parliament, to uphold the constitution. In Thailand, there is no such requirement. There have not been any words provided for Thai monarchs to use in making an oath upon coming to the throne. Rama X made an oath based on what his father had pledged in 1946: "I shall continue, preserve, and build upon the royal legacy and shall reign with righteousness for the benefit and happiness of the people forever."[104] There is no mention of parliament, the repository of popular sovereignty, or the constitution. Is there any moral or legal obligation inferred in the oath? Is there any point where the populace could say that certain actions hazarded breaking the oath? Could it be interpreted by some Thais that endorsing coups or dictating certain laws worked against the "benefit and happiness" of the people?

As we have seen, people understood there was some sort of pact between the king and them. For England, the implicit pact was that the king would not subvert the "fundamental law." In France, the 1791 constitution obliged Louis to make an oath to the assembly, as representatives of the people. Refusing to do so was an assumed abdication. The oath created a pact: The king vows to respect the constitution and in return the people take an oath of loyalty to the king. But like any pact, it was conditional. If the king broke his oath and, say, headed up an army to overthrow the assembly, then the people had a right to rise up against him. The constitution provided for this by saying if the king did so, he would be assumed to have abdicated the throne.

Borwornsak draws on the perceived character of King Bhumibol as a virtuous king. But in this way he also lays bare the fatal weakness of his argument that becomes apparent only in the current reign. He singles out the Thai monarchy as unique, based on the perceived image of Bhumibol, because in doing so, the main thrust of this argument is lost when his son Vajiralongkorn came to the throne with none of the same caché of virtue. He says that the Thai monarchy "has a long history dating back to ancient times, has an exalted religious and social status as well as strict royal traditions, but has close bonds with the people, who love and respect them for the monarch's contributions to their well-being." Bhumibol and the queen were often seen "sitting on the ground and conversing in plain language with ordinary people in remote, harsh areas of the country where no one wanted to go," indicating "monarchy's closeness to the people." Borwornsak claims that Thai kings adhere to Buddhist principles and are examples of a *dhammaraja*, one "who rules with righteous principles." Thai kings are "'the people's choice' or 'one whom the public acclaims as their leader'" or "who brings happiness or contentment to others." The king, he says, "attains such a position by his 'virtues,' not his 'vices.'" Bhumibol, through "his tireless dedication in alleviating socio-economic problems faced by Thai people" and solving political crises, has "transformed the Thai monarchy from a 'dignified political institution'" into "an 'efficient social institution'"; he is not someone who is "unreachable and cloaked in mystique but rather a 'father,' as Thais call him, whom Thai people love and respect."[105]

Putting the hagiographic elements aside, what is implied here is that it is through his virtue that a man becomes a king, that virtue precedes his enthronement. There is a sort of agreement here: If a king acts virtuously, then the people will show respect to him. So what happens if a Thai king does not adhere to the Buddhist principles? Could that be interpreted, at least culturally, as a kind of violation of oath, or at least a violation of a behavioral expectation? What, indeed, can we expect of someone like Borwornsak, who fashions himself an expert on the model of Thai kingship, if he were to face the sobering reality of a Thai king whose position was not attained by virtue?

VI. Conclusion

The question in this chapter is common to all modern states: What are the privileges of the executive power? The heads of state enjoy some level of immunity from prosecution, for many of the same reasons given for monarchs in constitutional monarchies. However, monarchs have a very special kind of life-long immunity. It is precisely because of their absolute inviolability that monarchists argue that monarchs are the perfect reservoir to ensure the viability of the state and the eternal recognition and defense of rights of citizens.

But the question here has been a simple one: Maybe "the king can do no wrong," but what if he does? Historically, has there been any way to bring a monarch to account? We saw that there did not seem to be any ordinary way to legally try a monarch. The example of England showed that only through a special tribunal could a monarch be tried and punishment meted out, but the special tribunal was extraordinary and strained the sense that "rule of law" was strictly observed. In the Glorious Revolution, the new settlement saved the king from getting into too much mischief, ensuring an institutional basis for monarchy in democracy. In France, the monarchists made a compelling case for the king's inviolability in 1791, but after a turbulent year and with conservatives in retreat, the national convention dethroned the king by ending the monarchy. The king was tried, although the king's attorney made debatably the better case in arguing for the king's inviolability. Political circumstances and the misguided revolutionary logic of the time, though, rushed ahead of reason into the Reign of Terror.

Most monarchies made begrudging allowances to democratic forces in the nineteenth and early twentieth centuries. European monarchs had to reposition themselves to new political configurations and popular expectations. Those that did not do so put the institution's future at peril. Germany's Wilhelm II had reigned over one of the most vigorous lèse-majesté regimes in Europe, which did nothing to endear the population to the institution. Although Wilhelm II stepped in to stop lèse-majesté prosecutions in 1904, the institution was unable to survive the German Revolution in 1918.[106] He was given the courtesy of abdicating hours before Germany was declared a republic. Italy's monarchy snuggled up too closely with Mussolini in World War II. In 1946, 54 percent of citizens ended the monarchy in a national referendum. More recently, Gyanendra of Nepal was thrust upon the throne after the Nepali Royal Family Massacre. He took on more powers before establishing absolute monarchy in 2005. He relinquished power only in 2007 when a coalition of political parties agreed upon a role for the monarchy in the future. The political scene shifted, and a provisional parliament ended the 240-year-old monarchy in 2008.[107]

Most modern-day monarchies (with any pretention to democracy) have found ways to make this supreme symbol of inequality and undeserved privilege more appealing. They have opened up budgets to public scrutiny, responded to the many public opinion polls carried out by the media, not provoked the ire of republican groups, and limited the use and severity of lèse-majesté prosecutions. In short, they have made the monarchy respected and popular within normal social and political discourse.

Thailand would not fit into this group of monarchies. Instead, it would be grouped with those monarchies strongly steered by authoritarian impulses and where other accoutrements of democracy are decidedly weak: poor adherence to guarantees of freedom of the press and human rights, weak legislative bodies, and so on. In terms of democracy and freedom, Thailand is nowhere near the types of monarchies that Thai monarchists presume to compare with Thailand's. Freedom House's 2021 global ratings give "Free" scores to Belgium (96), Sweden (100), Norway (100), The Netherlands (98), Japan (96), Spain (90), and the United Kingdom (93). Thailand is even considerably lower than "Partly Free" Bhutan (61), Malaysia (51), or Morocco (37). Rather, Thailand (30) is more in line with "Not Free" Jordan (34), Brunei (25), and Cambodia (24). In terms of "political freedom," in fact, Thailand is on the level of absolute monarchies such as the United Arab Emirates (5 out of 40).[108]

Inviolability is specified for monarchs to save them, and heads of state, from being inundated with suits. In most republics, presidents or heads of state are granted temporary inviolability while in office for the same reason.

In either case, it is not necessary for them to have sacred status. In and of itself, the sacred status given to monarchs in some regimes does not seem to have any direct legal effect. All current constitutional monarchies are given the status of inviolability (except Japan), and some are even given a sacred status. It would be uncommon if not unheard of to have a head of state who was not immune from accusation and prosecution.

The king's sacred status as provided in the constitution, though, does have implications, especially for the lèse-majesté law. The sacred status and the fact that the law is in the section of national security offenses makes any infraction seem more serious, and conditions surrounding prosecution, such as bail, more severe. Repealing the law completely, again, would make Thailand an outlier. But other kinds of revisions could bring Thailand back into the fold of constitutional monarchies: Substantially reducing the penalty of the lèse-majesté law, creating brakes concerning its use, putting lèse-majesté into its own section, and creating new standards for those charged with the crime.

While inviolability would make it impossible to make any legal accusations against the monarch, it does not mean that the parliament could not launch an investigation to find out the truth behind missing activists or other acts alleged to the palace. While there may exist certain laws (immunity, inviolability) that may bar any legal action, it might be possible to suggest, as in the case of Spain, being able to investigate the truth of matters.

Another socio-legal aspect that constitutional monarchies depend on is the coronation oath. Most monarchs when crowned are required constitutionally to take an oath to, among other things, to uphold the constitution. The implicit meaning is that if such monarch were to ever act against the constitution, it would be perceived as violation of the oath and perhaps as presumed abdication. Constitutional monarchs do not act at their own pleasure, but within the confines of the constitution. As we have reviewed here, treason in modern constitutional monarchies is not based on loyalty to the throne only, but also, and perhaps more importantly, on the public good, the commonwealth, and so on. Thus, it is possible under this view of treason to be loyal to the throne but nonetheless act against the public good, in the same way that a monarch perceived as acting against the public good could be grounds for questioning their legitimacy.

In the Thai context, it is difficult to depend on any particular constitutional provision as constitutions are so often the first victim of coups. Not so, though, for the provisions concerning the monarchy. A coronation oath to the laws and constitution, if instituted, might hold over successive constitutions. If the king endorses a coup, it would be perceived as breaking his oath. Thus, if the parliament made a legal provision or added an oath to the constitution (and Rama x takes this new, revised oath), the final demand of the students could be satisfied.

For this to happen, it would be necessary for the parliament to make amendments to the lèse-majesté law and to the 2017 constitution. But the current power structure of Thailand is held by the Bangkok elite, which lacks any interest in making Thailand more democratic. It is this group that has granted itself the prerogative to define the national interest. It has insisted on its own power, which in many ways works against the long-term interests of either democracy or the monarchy. Thailand's ruling elite has nothing of the sophistication of the French monarchists in the 1790s. It is singularly unable to make a rational case for monarchy and instead is given to excesses of puerile emotionalism on the one hand, and accusations, threats, and thuggery on the other.[109] The Bangkok elite is willing to crush the best and brightest of the new generation; it is equally unwilling to allow Thailand anything other than an endless, authoritarian future.

The reign of Rama x has already been historic. Two forces, broadly speaking, are in conflict. One side represents decay and decline, but in its shrinking space conservative forces have become more desperate and dangerous. These are the champions of "Thainess," of a narrow, Bangkok-centric, xenophobic world clinging to an outdated and increasingly infeasible model of governance, bereft of political imagination and utterly incapable of fashioning accommodation—and yet armed with all the violence the force of law and the courts can afford against its perceived enemies. The other side, representing popular sovereignty, appears greatly out-armed. Except for moral support from the Move Forward Party, which has represented some of the student movement's positions, the students lack support from the political establishment. Based on student activists, this camp seems to lack traditional allies. What it does have is a penetrating intellect, an acerbic tongue, and its ideals. Its members are willing to sacrifice their freedom and futures to make Thailand more democratic. This camp has adopted a "more inclusive and deliberative politics" that has drawn in many other groups who have not found a political space in the current political scene: the Assembly of the Poor, red shirts, Malay Muslims, feminists, and the LGBTQ community.

The movement has been able to grow because it has eschewed Thainess and extended the boundaries of what defines the citizen. It rejects the old model and discourse and has instead adopted "humanness." Pasit says that this movement "could be the first nationwide political movement to incorporate 'humanness' into its core discourse," what constitutes, he says, "quite a phenomenal development for Thai politics." Promoting hashtags like "Decrease Thainess, Increase Humanness," the movement has transformed the traditional way of gauging patriotism via the question "Are you Thai or not?" by asking, "Are you still human or not?"[110]

The success or failure of the reign of Rama X will depend on whether and how the monarchy decides to place the fate of both the institution and the country. Does the king have any interest in coming down on the side of popular sovereignty, and, if he does, does he have sufficient charisma to move the intransigent Bangkok elite to rethink the national project? Will Thailand come to embrace equality, pluralism, and humanism and come to reject Thai exceptionalism? If Vajiralongkorn is so moved to come down on the side of democracy, his reign will be even more historic than his father's. If not, Thailand will continue into the political morass that has defined it for the last few decades.

Notes

1 This chapter was submitted on 13 February 2021, with minor changes in the editing process.

2 Streckfuss, "The Future of the Monarchy in Thailand."

3 "What's Behind the Downfall of Thailand's Princess Srirasmi?," *BBC News*.

4 Head, "Thai Park Exposes Corruption Claims and Murky Politics."

5 Streckfuss, "Thailand's Peculiar Interregnum."

6 Reuters, "Thailand's King Calls His Sister's Candidacy for PM 'Inappropriate.'"

7 "'Support Good People to Rule this Country,'" *Prachatai*; "Concern over Standpoint of the Monarchy as King Thanks a Pro-Monarchy Protester," *Prachatai*.

8 Mérieau, "Seeking More Power."

9 Pavin, "Thai Royalty Attack on Exiled Critic."

10 "Protkhlao ph.r.k. on kamlang phon-ngop praman bang suan khawng krom thahan rap thi 1-rap 11 pai pen khawng nuai banchakan thawai khwam plawtphai raksa phraong," *BBC News*; "Decree Sees Royal Guard Bolstered," *Bangkok Post*; Aekarach, "House Passes Royal Security Decree in Face of FFP Proposition."

11 Prior to the coronation, the king quickly married his newest consort, Suthida
Tidjai, so there could be a proper "queen." In the three-day event dedicated to
extravagance, the king was transported, ceremonially but also actually, in a royal
palanquin: once requiring 343 people to carry the palanquin, and once to carry
the palanquin in the royal procession over a 7-kilometer route, requiring 16
carriers for every 500 meters before being replaced with a new team. Thousands
were involved, and foreign dignitaries and heads of state were expected to attend.
"Thailand Rehearses Elaborate $31 Million Coronation for King," *Reuters*.

12 It is curious that estimates of the world's wealthiest and the world's richest royal
families often do not overlap. One publication puts King Vajiralongkorn as the
sixth richest royal individual and family, which would have placed the Chakri
family at sixth in the world's richest families, but he does not place at all in
Forbes's list. See "The World's Richest Royal Families Ranked," *Lovemoney*; Ang,
"Ranked: The World's Richest Families"; "The Richest in 2020," *Forbes*.

13 To provide perspective, the Spanish monarchy costs US$0.21 per capita, as
compared to US$14.16 for Thailand. Looking at each country's minimum wage,
it takes a Spaniard at minimum wage to work for about a minute and a half to
pay for his/her monarchy. It takes a comparable Thai minimum-wage worker 10
hours to do the same. Roughly, the Thai annual budget is US$106 billion and the
monarchy receives US$989 million. The Spanish annual budget is US$571 billion
and its monarchy costs US$9.7 million. The minimum wage per hour in Spain
is US$7.58. At the high end, the Thai minimum wage per hour, if based on an
8-hour work day, is US$1.40. "Poet ngop praman pi 2563 suan thi kieowkap
sathaban phramahakasat 2.9 moenlan baht," *Prachatai*; Kottasová and Khaliq,
"Here's How Much Europe's Royal Families Really Cost"; Castro, "El Presupuesto
de la Casa del Rey Crece un 0,9% para 2018."

14 Hewison, "The Monarchy and Succession," 125–27.

15 Nattapoll, "The Monarchy and the Royalist Movement in Modern Thai Politics,
1932–1957," 146.

16 Ferrara counts all but the 1951 and 1977 coups as royalist. See Ferrara, "The Logic
of Thailand's Royalist Coups d'État," 81.

17 Jory, *Thailand's Theory of Monarchy*, 22.

18 "Read the Declaration that Heralded the Democratic Revolt 85 Years Ago Today,"
Khaosod English.

19 McCargo, "Network Monarchy and Legitimacy Crises in Thailand," 499–519.

20 "[Full statement] The Demonstration at Thammasat Proposes Monarchy Reform," *Prachatai*.

21 Hathairat and Streckfuss, "The Ten Demands that Shook Thailand."

22 "Majority Agree with Free People Group's Demands: Poll," *Bangkok Post*.

23 "32 People Now Charged under Section 112," *Prachatai*.

24 "Prakat: Ruang hai kharatchakan nai phraong fai thahan phan jak tamnaeng
thawt thanadornsak lae yot thahan talawt jon riak khoen khruang ratchais-
ariyaphorn thuk chantrai," *Ratchakitjanubeksa*.

25 Political Prisoners in Thailand, "Further Updated: Sineenat's Travels."

26 "Thailand's King Reinstates His Consort after Her Fall from Grace," *BBC News*; "Thai Prince Said to Trigger Police Purge," *Asia Sentinel*.

27 Journalist Andrew MacGregor Marshall has said: "The concubines give a lot— with the hope of winning big. Some are happy to join and are hoping for riches and success for themselves and their families. Others give in to the king's pressure to join over fear of the consequences if they refuse." Article 3 of the UN protocol on human trafficking defines "trafficking in persons" to mean "the recruitment, transportation, transfer, harboring or receipt of persons, by means of the threat or use of force or other forms of coercion, of abduction, of fraud, of deception, of the abuse of power or of a position of vulnerability." It includes "the exploitation of the prostitution of others or other forms of sexual exploitation, forced labor or services, slavery or practices similar to slavery, servitude." United Nations, General Assembly Resolution 55/25; Holloway, "Inside Luxury Hotel Where Thai King, 67, Is in Coronavirus Lockdown with 20 Girlfriends in 'Pleasure Room.'"

28 Smith, *A Dictionary of Greek and Roman Antiquities*; Chilton, "The Roman Law of Treason under the Early Principate," 73–74.

29 Ulpianus, "On the Duties of Proconsul."

30 Lear, "The Idea of Majesty in Roman Political Thought," 66.

31 Church, *The Annals*; Robinson, *Ancient Roman Statutes*, 274; Smith, *A Dictionary of Greek and Roman Antiquities*, 114.

32 Scott, "The Enactments of Justinian."

33 Scott, "Code of Justinian."

34 Marcellinus, "The Cruelty of Gallus Caesar."

35 Advisers to Valens (CE 364–78), in Gibbon and Smith, *The History of the Decline and Fall of the Roman Empire*, 190.

36 Code of Justinian 9, "Title 8. On the *Lex Julia* Relating to Treason," in Scott, "Code of Justinian."

37 Veyne, "What Was a Roman Emperor?," 7–11.

38 Veyne, "What Was a Roman Emperor?," 3–7.

39 Boyd, *The Ecclesiastical Edicts of the Theodosian Code*, 51.

40 Code of Justinian, "Book IX:29:3," in Scott, "Code of Justinian."

41 Veyne, "What Was a Roman Emperor?," 9, 12–15.

42 "Note 1," in Scott, "Code of Justinian."

43 Bracton, *Bracton on the Laws and Customs of England*, Vol. 2, 33.

44 Bracton, *Bracton on the Laws and Customs of England*, 33, 35–37.

45 Pollock and Maitland say that redress for a king whose crimes were so great was not a court of law but rather invoked, vaguely, "A right of revolution, a right to defy a faithless lord and to make war upon him" (*The History of English Law before the Time of Edward I*, 182–83, 515–16).

46 Brissaud, *History of French Public Law*, 345–46.

47 It is in light of this obligation to the public, Blackstone says, that the royal prerogative to pardon is limited. When a public official has acted "against the public" and then been impeached, the monarch should let it stand. It is only the public, as represented by parliament, that "should have the power of forgiving"— and not the monarch. Blackstone, *Laws of England*, 258–59.

48 Brissaud, *History of French Public Law*, 333–34.

49 Brissaud, *History of French Public Law*, 337–38.

50 Bodin, *Six Works of the Commonwealth Abridged*, 67–69.

51 King James I, "On the Divine Right of Kings."

52 de Ferriere, *Nouvelle Introduction a la Pratique*, 181.

53 Maillane, *Dictionnaire de Droit Canonique et de Pratique Bénéficiale*, 467; Brillon, *Dictionnaire des Arrêts*, 98.

54 Gardiner, *The Constitutional Document of the Puritan Revolution*, xxix–xxx, 156–57.

55 Orr, *Treason and the State*, 99.

56 York, "Strafford, Thomas Wentworth, Earl of," 978–80.

57 Orr, *Treason and the State*, 88.

58 Orr, *Treason and the State*, 95–99.

59 Orr, *Treason and the State*, 173.

60 Gardiner, *The Constitutional Document of the Puritan Revolution, 1625–1660*, 357–58, 371–74.

61 Gardiner, *The Constitutional Document of the Puritan Revolution, 1625–1660*, 374–76.

62 Orr, *Treason and the State*, 195–97, 200.

63 Orr, *Treason and the State*, 193, 202–3.

64 Orr, *Treason and the State*, 171.

65 Orr, *Treason and the State*, 198.

66 Brissaud, *History of French Public Law*, 345–46.

67 Blackstone, *Laws of England, Book the First*, 237–38.

68 Blackstone, *Laws of England, Book the First*, 237, 239–40, 243. But for members of parliament, Blackstone warns, "the objections must be proposed with the utmost respect and deference." When one member failed to show sufficient deference when he said the king had used "high words, to fright the members out of 'their duty,'" the king obliged and had him thrown into the Tower of London.

69 Blackstone, *Laws of England, Book the First*, 90, 164–65.

70 Blackstone, *Laws of England, Book the First*, 239, 244.

71 Blackstone, *Laws of England, Book the First*, 239.

72 Craik and Farland, *The Pictorial History of England*, 660.

73 This debate was much richer than the series of debates in November and December of 1792 when the fate of the king was all but a foregone conclusion. See Pugh, "Historical Approach to the Doctrine of Sovereign Immunity," 476–94; Hayworth, "Inviolability Controversy in the Trial of Louis XVI."

74 To show some generosity of spirit in that period, Emmanuel-Joseph Sieyès thought monarchy the best form but saw the value of debate. He said he would gladly engage republicans with reasoned debate: "I hope to be able to prove, not that monarchy is preferable in this or that circumstance, but that, on every hypothesis, men are more free under it than under a republic." He said he would not attack republicans merely on their belief: "I will not oppose them with cries of impiety and anathema; I will make use of no injurious expressions." But for monarchy to work, it had to be free of "corrupting and conspiring." If uncontrolled, such qualities are "more likely to spoil it and destroy it. A public allowance of thirty millions of lives is very contrary to liberty, and, as I understand it, very anti-monarchical" (Craik and Farland, *The Pictorial History of England*, 661–62).

75 The five following accounts are in an online archive: *Archives Parlementaires de 1787 à 1860, Première Série (1787 à 1799), Tome XXVIII du 6 Juillet au 28 Juillet 1791, Archives Parlementaires de Louis XVI, Assemblée Nationale, Présidence de M. Charles de Lameth.*

76 Malouët, "Opinion de M. Malouët sur Cette Question: Le Roi Peut-il être Mis en Jugement?," 274–78.

77 There are a few moments that deserve notice here. Antoine Saint-Just said, "[W]hat legal relationship is there between humanity and a king? A king should be tried not for the crimes of his administration, but for that of having been king." Robespierre famously said, "The tyrant must die so the fatherland can live .... [P]eople don't judge in the same way as judicial courts. They don't issue sentences; they cast lightning bolts. They don't condemn kings; they cast them back into the void." See Hayworth, "Inviolability Controversy," 112, 114; Jaurès, "The Trial of the King."

78 *Archives Parlementaires de 1787 à 1860, Première Série (1787 à 1799), Tome LV du 11 Décembre 1792 au 27 Décembre 1792, au Soir, Archives Parlementaires République Française Convention Nationale, Le Président*, 617–35.

79 Where the Bourbons end came the Orleans, followed by a Bonaparte. It was 78 years after France ended absolute monarchy before it finally freed itself of monarchy in 1870. Bouveresse, *Histoire des Institutions de la Vie Politique et de la Société Françaises de 1789 à 1945*, 123–48.

80 A more conservative interpretation of constitutional monarchy is seen in the 1887 constitution of Bulgaria. It starts with the king's status—"The person of the king is sacred and inviolable"—and makes no attempt at approaching popular sovereignty. All legislative, military, and executive power "belongs" to the king, while "[t]he judicial power belongs entirely to the authorities and persons vested with judicial powers, who act in the name of the king." A more liberal combination of these items is found in Belgium's 1831 constitution. Article 6 says, "There shall

be no distinction of classes in the state" and that "[a]ll Belgians are equal before the law," but then adds there may be some distinctions for "civil and military offices." Articles 25 and 26 say, "All powers emanate from the people [and] shall be exercised in the manner established by the constitution [and] exercised collectively by the king, the House of Representatives and the senate." Article 63 does not grant the king sacred status: "The person of the king is inviolable; his ministers are responsible" and requires of him a "solemnly taken" oath "before the united houses." Wright, *The Constitutions of the States at War, 1914–1918*, 88–89, 127, 135.

81 A clear example is Russia. The 1906 Fundamental Law of Russia focused on the majesty of the emperor. Chapter 1, Article 4 says, "The emperor of all the Russians wields the supreme autocratic power. To obey his authority, not only through fear, but for the sake of conscience, is ordered by God himself." Article 5 repeated the familiar formulation: "The person of the emperor is sacred and inviolable." While many monarchs settled on a 50–50 split in sovereign power, Article 7 granted popular sovereignty only a third share: "The emperor is vested with the legislative power jointly with the Imperial Council and the Imperial Duma." The law does not explicitly guarantee equality of all; instead, there is equal obligation in terms of respecting the law and carrying out one's duty. Articles 42 and 43 state: "The Russian empire shall be governed in accordance with the immutable principal [sic] of law" and "[t]he laws are binding upon all Russian subjects without exception and upon all foreigners residing in Russia." Article 28 states, "The defense of the throne and of the country is the sacred duty of every Russian subject." Under the Fundamental Law, the emperor took no oath to the law. Wright, *The Constitutions of the States at War, 1914–1918*, 538, 541–42. The oath was not merely a formality. It was important enough that the Ottoman Constitution added the following in its 1909 amendment (590): "On his accession the Sultan shall swear before Parliament ... to respect the provisions of the Sheri and the constitution, and to be loyal to the country and the nation."

82 Wright, *The Constitutions of the States at War, 1914–1918*, 23, 338, 352, 375, 408, 590. It is noteworthy that Persia shied away from constitutionally designating its shah as sacred (494), stating only in its 1907 Supplementary Constitutional Law that "the king is absolved from all responsibility." The German empire did not give its emperor any special constitutional status in 1871 (210–38). Also see the Constitución de la Monarquía Española (30 de Junio de 1876), as laid down on 17 May 1814 by the constituent assembly at Eidsvoll and subsequently amended, most recently on 20 February 2007.

83 Williams, "An Open Letter to His Serene Majesty Leopold II."

84 Jalata, "Colonial Terrorism, Global Capitalism and African Underdevelopment," 23–25.

85 Kassam, "Spain's King Juan Carlos to Abdicate."

86 Nayer, "Is Spain's Royal Family Finished?"

87 Peláez, "Spain: Felipe VI and the Corruption of the Monarchy!"

88 "Phraratchabanyat thammanun kanpokkhrawng phaendin sayam chua khrao."

89 See Nattapoll, "The Monarchy and the Royalist Movement in Modern Thai Politics, 1932–1957," 155–63.

90 Borwornsak provides one of the most sophisticated takes on this notion, but it is ubiquitous in the far-right expressions of right-wing and far-right groups, such as the 2006 coup group, the Council for National Security, which initially called itself the "Reform Council in the Democratic Regime with the King as Head of State" (but which was officially translated into English only as "Council for Democratic Reform"). The People's Democratic Reform Committee, set up in 2013 to create chaos and spark the 2014 coup, originally called itself the "People's Committee for Absolute Democracy with the King as Head of State." Neeranuit and Rujira write that the coup leader of the NCPO instituted in 2014 "core values" that were to be recited by children every morning. Some of these core values, separated into different "categories of ideology," "derived from feudalism," such as "being respectful of lows, elders and seniority." More modern, apparently, was that the values would engender "understanding the true essence of democratic ideals with King as Head of State, being conscious and mindful of action in line with the King's royal statements, and upholding the monarchy as one of the three main pillars of the country are examples of the monarchy ideology." Neeranuit and Rujira, "Ideologies in Thai Politics," 424; Borwornsak, "The Law of Inviolability in Thailand."

91 The Spanish constitution of 1978 helpfully first defines its essence: "Spain constitutes itself into a social and democratic state of law which advocates liberty, justice, equality, and political pluralism as the superior values of its legal order." It then defines its "political form" simply as a "parliamentary Monarchy." See "Constitution of Spain of 1978."

92 The phrase is used with some randomness—see an example by Dr. Okat Tephalakun, chairman of the National Economic and Social Advisory Council and drafter of the 2007 constitution. In his 20-page paper, "On the Democratic Regime of Government with the King as Head of State," Okat begins with a very competent overview of democracy and popular sovereignty. The second section lays out the constitutional role of the king, and the last section is dedicated to the good deeds of King Bhumibol. Nowhere is there any explanation or definition of the actual system itself. The paper is undated but was written around 2006. Okat, "Ruang kanpokkhrawng rapop prachathipatai an mi phramahakasat song pen pramuk."

93 The concept might be called the heart of royal sovereignty, and it forms the core of Thai constitutions. Thailand's 2017 constitution, for instance, declares in Section 5 that when no provision "is applicable to any case," such provision "shall be made in accordance with the constitutional conventions of Thailand under the democratic regime of government with the king as head of state" (hereafter, DRKHS). Section 45 allows people to form political parties "under the DRKHS." Section 49 says, "No person shall exercise the rights or liberties to overthrow the DRKHS." Section 50 prescribes as the duty of Thai citizens "to protect and uphold the nation, religions, the king, and the DRKHS." Section 78 instructs that the state "should promote the correct knowledge and understanding of the public and communities regarding the DRKHS." The oath judges are to make, according to Section 191, is to rule in the name of the king and to "uphold and

observe the DRKHS, the constitution of the kingdom of Thailand and the law in every respect." Section 255 prohibits amendments "that amount to changing the DRKHS or changing the form of the State." Section 257 orders that policies of national reform must ensure that "the people are happy, have good quality of life, and participate in development of the country and DRKHS." In political reform, there must be ways of ensuring that people have correct knowledge and understanding on the DRKHS," as well as "a mechanism to resolve political conflicts by peaceful means in accordance with the DRKHS," Constitution of the Kingdom of Thailand of 2017.

94 "Constitution of the Kingdom of Thailand of 1997."

95 Hewison, "Thailand: Contestation over Elections, Sovereignty and Representation."

96 Thammachart, "Oath Error: Recapping Case that Shakes Government." It should be noted that progressive politician and former law instructor Piyabutr Saengkanokkul did hear the youth's concerns and attempted an explanation of DRKHS, arguing that the primary part of the concept is democracy and the secondary is the king. As such, the king can do nothing on his own. The people and the king, he argued, must respect and defend the constitution, "so the military does not carry out a coup, abolish the constitution, and then force the king to endorse the coup." There were demands to reform the monarchy, a process that can move forward only through public discussions. Common solutions had to be found to maintain the monarchy that's aligned with democracy. See Newtv18, "'Piyabut' chi 5 laksana kanpokkhrawng nai rabop p.ch.t. an mi phramahakasat pen pramuk."

97 Many of the students' demands involved the financial status of the king (designating personal assets of the king, returning assets to the government, reducing the national budget allocation to the palace, auditing royal charities). Others have to do with prerogatives (the king speaking in public, abolishing royal offices). And others involve "cultural" items such as demanding the end of royalist propaganda (including the evening television programming on the movements of the royals, educational treatment of the royalty, and compelling people to show respect during the playing of the royal anthem). "[Full statement] The Demonstration at Thammasat Proposes Monarchy Reform."

98 Netherlands, Penal Code, https://wetten.overheid.nl/BWBR0001854/2012-05-09/1.

99 Hewison, "The Monarchy and Succession," 127.

100 McCargo, *Fighting for Virtue.*

101 Borwornsak, "The Law of Inviolability in Thailand."

102 Spain, http://www.ub.edu/dpenal/CP_vigente_31_01_2011.pdf; Sweden, https://legislationline.org/sites/default/files/documents/98/Sweden_CC.pdf; Netherlands, http://wetten.overheid.nl/BWBR0001854/TweedeBoek/geldigheidsdatum_03-06-2012; Norway, http://www.un.org/Depts/los/LEGISLATIONANDTREATIES/PDFFILES/NOR_penal_code.pdf; Belgium, https://www.constituteproject.org/constitution/Belgium_2014.pdf?lang=en.

103 Another peculiar reading of the long sentence for lèse-majesté is that it is an opportunity for the king to show his "mercy and compassion." The punishment can remain high so that those punished for the crime can realize their wrong, confess their infraction, and then ask the king for a pardon. Most confess immediately because there is a 93 percent conviction rate combined with a frighteningly long sentence. Of course, the compassion of the pardon is generally only given to those who affirm their loyalty to the institution.

104 Upon his brother's death and his being declared king, Bhumibol is reported to have said (but not before parliament or the people as such): "We shall reign with righteousness, for the benefit and happiness of the Siamese people." See Anand, "Forward," 11; Patpicha and Panarat, "'I Shall Reign with Righteousness.'"

105 In the inverse world of ethics that Borwornsak inhabits and describes, Thailand is unique because it has such a unique expression of kingship. He appeals to a variant of popular sovereignty to make his case, saying that the lèse-majesté law is an expression of "the needs and consensus of the majority" of Thailand. If anyone—another country, the United Nations—tries to pressure Thailand on the issue of lèse-majesté, such person is "an ethical despot." Instead, the world should leave autocratic Thailand completely alone. There should be a "recognition of ethical and cultural diversity based on the concept of ethical pluralism that is democratic and open-minded because it appreciates the right to self-determination of each society." Borwornsak, "The Law of Inviolability in Thailand."

106 Streckfuss, "The Intricacies of Lèse-majesté," 119.

107 Sen, "A Reflection on Nepal's Path to a Republic."

108 "Global Freedom Scores," *Freedom House*. It is telling that despite the pretence of elections and a return to democracy, Thailand's ranking in the World Press Freedom Index remained in the bottom quarter of the 180 countries rated. It was ranked 140th in 2018 under "dictatorship" and had the same ranking in 2020 with "elected government." "World Press Freedom Index," *Reporters without Borders*.

109 These defenders of this model of monarchy in Thailand have for decades and decades more or less monopolized official media, education, and so on. See the upcoming publication of Connors and Ukrist, "Introduction: The Bhumibol Era," *Thai Politics in Translation*.

110 Pasit, "From 'Being Thai' to 'Being Human.'"

References (Western Languages)

"32 People Now Charged under Section 112." *Prachatai*, 16 December 2020. https://prachatai.com/english/node/8973, accessed 16 December 2020.

Aekarach Sattaburuth. "House Passes Royal Security Decree in Face of FFP Opposition." *Bangkok Post*, 17 October 2019. https://www.bangkokpost.com/

thailand/politics/1774084/house-passes-royal-security-decree-in-face-of-ffp-opposition, accessed 15 August 2020.

Ananda Panyarachun. "Forward." In *King Bhumibol Adulyadej: A Life's Work*, ed. Nicholas Grossman and Dominic Faulder, 11. Singapore: Editions Didier Millet, 2011.

Ang, Carmen. "Ranked: The World's Richest Families." *Visualcapitalist.com*, 3 September 2020. https://www.visualcapitalist.com/the-worlds-richest-families-2020/, accessed 15 November 2020.

Archives Parlementaires de 1787 à 1860, Première Série (1787 à 1799), Tome XXVIII du 6 Juillet au 28 Juillet 1791, Archives Parlementaires de Louis XVI, Assemblée Nationale, Présidence de M. Charles de Lameth, 255–66. https://sul-philologic. stanford.edu/philologic/archparl/navigate/28/0/0/0/0/0/0/0/263/, accessed 12 December 2020.

———. *Archives Parlementaires de 1787 à 1860, Première Série (1787 à 1799), Tome LV du 11 Décembre 1792 au 27 Décembre 1792, au Soir, Archives Parlementaires République Française Convention Nationale, Le Président*, 617–35. https://sul-philologic.stanford.edu/philologic/archparl/navigate/55/2/?byte=3927935, accessed 11 December 2020.

Blackstone, William. *Laws of England, Book the First*. Oxford: The Clarendon Press, 1763.

Bodin, Jean. *Six Works of the Commonwealth Abridged and Translated by M.J. Tooley*. Oxford: The Alden Press, 1955.

Bouveresse, Jacques. *Histoire des Institutions de la Vie Politique et de la Société Françaises de 1789 à 1945*. Mont-Saint-Aignan: Presses Universitaires de Rouen et du Havre, 2012.

Borwornsak Uwanno. "The Law of Inviolability in Thailand / Thai Laws Reflecting Thai Culture and Ethics/Lèse-majesté: Abuse and Benevolence," 3 November 2013. https://dvifa.mfa.go.th/th/content/40461-the-law-of-inviolability-in-thailand-thai-laws-reflecting-thai-culture-and-ethics-lese-majeste:-abuse-and-benevolence-(by-prof-dr-borwornsak-uwanno)?cate =5f206717170d9008ea136ad1, accessed 21 December 2020.

Boyd, William K. *The Ecclesiastical Edicts of the Theodosian Code*. New York: Columbia University Press, 1905.

Bracton, Henry. *Bracton on the Laws and Customs of England*. Bracton Online. https://amesfoundation.law.harvard.edu/Bracton/index.html, accessed on 15 January 2021.

Brillon, Pierre-Jacque. *Dictionnaire des Arrêts, ou Jurisprudence Universelle des Parlements de France, et Autres Tribunaux: Contenant par Ordre Alphabétique les Matières Bénéficiales, Civiles et Criminelles, les Maximes du Droit Ecclési-*

astique, du droit Romain, du Droit public, des Coûtumes, Ordonnances, Édits et Déclarations. Vol. 4. Chez Guillaume Cavelier, 1777.

Brissaud, Jean. *History of French Public Law.* Trans. James W. Garner. Boston: Little, Brown and Company, 1915.

Castro, Irene. "El Presupuesto de la Casa del Rey Crece un 0.9% para 2018." *elDiario.es*, 3 April 2018. https://www.eldiario.es/politica/presupuesto-casa-real-encadena-incremento_1_2196826.html, accessed 21 December 2020.

Chilton, C.W. "The Roman Law of Treason Under the Early Principate." *The Journal of Roman Studies* 45:1 and 2 (1955):73–81.

Church, Alfred John, et al., eds. *The Annals*, Tacit. Ann. I. 72, 74, VI. 7 (n/a). http://www.perseus.tufts.edu/hopper/text?doc=Perseus:text:1999.02.0078, accessed 28 December 2020.

"Concern over Standpoint of the Monarchy as King Thanks a Pro-Monarchy Protester." *Prachatai*, 24 October 2020. https://prachatai.com/english/node/8951, accessed 11 November 2020.

Connors, Michael K., and Ukrist Pathmanand. "Understanding Thai Conservatism." In *Thai Politics in Translation: Monarchy, Democracy and the Supra-constitution*, ed. Michael K. Connors and Ukrist Pathmanand,18–39. Copenhagen: NAIS Press, 2021.

Craik, George Lillie, and Charles Mac Farland. *The Pictorial History of England: Being a History of the People, as well as a History of the Kingdom.* Vol. 6. London: Charles Knight, 1849.

de Ferriere, Claude-Joseph. *Nouvelle Introduction à la Pratique, ou Dictionnaire des Termes.* Vol. 2. Paris: Chez Claude Prudhomme, 1734.

"De Quaestionibus." *Codicis Domini Nostri Iustiniani.* http://droitromain.upmf-grenoble.fr/. date n/a, accessed 3 November 2021.

"Decree Sees Royal Guard Bolstered." *Bangkok Post*, 1 October 2019. https://www.bangkokpost.com/thailand/general/1761984, accessed 27 November 2020.

Ferrara, Federico. "The Logic of Thailand's Royalist Coups d'État." In *Routledge Handbook of Contemporary Thailand*, ed. Pavin Chachavalpongpun, 71–85. London: Routledge, 2020.

"[Full statement] The Demonstration at Thammasat Proposes Monarchy Reform." *Prachatai*, 11 August 2020. https://prachatai.com/english/node/8709, accessed 20 August 2020.

Gardiner, Samuel R., ed. *The Constitutional Document of the Puritan Revolution, 1625–1660.* 3rd ed. Oxford: Oxford University Press, 1906.

Gibbon, Edward, and William George Smith. *The History of the Decline and Fall of the Roman Empire.* New York: Harper & Brothers, 1857.

"Global Freedom Scores." *Freedom House*, date n/a. https://freedomhouse.org/countries/freedom-world/scores, accessed 5 February 2021.

Hathairat Phaholtap and David Streckfuss. "The Ten Demands that Shook Thailand." *New Mandala*, 2 September 2020. https://www.newmandala.org/the-ten-demands-that-shook-thailand/, accessed 1 November 2020.

Hayworth, Ronald L. "Inviolability Controversy in the Trial of Louis XVI." *Journal of the Arkansas Academy of Science* 20 (1966):111–17.

Head, Jonathan. "Thai Park Exposes Corruption Claims and Murky Politics." *BBC News*, 11 December 2015, https://www.bbc.com/news/world-asia-35069188, accessed on 15 August 2020.

Hewison, Kevin. "The Monarchy and Succession." In *Routledge Handbook of Contemporary Thailand*, ed. Pavin Chachavalpongpun, 118–33. London: Routledge, 2020.

_____. "Thailand: Contestation over Elections, Sovereignty and Representation." *Murdoch Research Repository* 51:1 (2015):1–23. http://researchrepository.murdoch.edu.au/27060, accessed on 3 December 2020.

Holloway, Henry. "Inside Luxury Hotel Where Thai King, 67, is in Coronavirus Lockdown with 20 Girlfriends in 'Pleasure Room.'" *The Sun*, 7 May 2020. https://www.thesun.co.uk/news/11570696/inside-hotel-thailand-king-coroanvirus-lockdown-20-girlfriends/, accessed 21 November 2020.

Jalata, Asafa. "Colonial Terrorism, Global Capitalism and African Underdevelopment: Five Hundred Years of Crimes Against African Peoples." *The Journal of Pan African Studies* 5:9 (March 2013):1–47.

Jaurès, Jean. "The Trial of the King." In *Histoire Socialiste de la Révolution Française*. Paris: Éditions Sociales, 1968, https://www.marxists.org/archive/jaures/1901/history/trial-king.htm, accessed 23 January 2021.

Johnson, Allan Chester, et al., eds. *Ancient Roman Statutes: A Translation with Introduction,*

Commentary, Glossary, and Index. Austen: University of Texas Press, 1961.

Jory, Patrick. *Thailand's Theory of Monarchy: The Vessantara Jataka and the Idea of the Perfect Man.* Albany: State University of New York Press, 2016.

Kassam, Ashifa. "Spain's King Juan Carlos to Abdicate." *The Guardian*, 2 June 2014, https://www.theguardian.com/world/2014/jun/02/spains-king-juan-carlos-to-abdicate, accessed 12 December 2020.

King James I. "On the Divine Right of Kings." 1609. In *Works*, chap. 20. W.W. Norton, 1997. https://wwnorton.com/college/history/ralph/workbook/ralprs20.htm, accessed 7 July 2022.

Kottasová, Ivana, and Aleesha Khaliq. "Here's How Much Europe's Royal Families Really Cost." *CNN*, 19 March 2020. https://www.cnn.com/2020/03/14/

europe/european-royal-families-intl/index.html, accessed 17 December 2020.

Lear, Floyd Seyward. "The Idea of Majesty in Roman Political Thought." In *Treason in Roman and Germanic Law: Collected Papers*, 49–72. Austin: University of Texas Press, 1965.

Maillane, Pierre Toussaint Durand. *Dictionnaire de Droit Canonique et de Pratique Bénéficiale: Conféré avec les Maximes et la Jurisprudence de la France*. Vol. 3. Lyon: Chez Joseph Duplain, 1775.

"Majority Agree with Free People Group's Demands: Poll." *Bangkok Post*, 23 August 2020. https://www.bangkokpost.com/thailand/politics/1973067/majority-agree-with-free-people-groups-demands-poll, accessed 24 August 2020.

Malouët, Pierre-Victor. "Opinion de M. Malouët sur Cette Question: Le Roi Peut-il être Mis en Jugement?" *Archives Parlementaires de 1787 à 1860, Première Série (1787 à 1799), Tome XXVIII du 6 Juillet au 28 Juillet 1791, Archives Parlementaires de Louis XVI, Assemblée Nationale. Présidence de M. Charles de Lameth. Deuxième Annexe*. 14 July 1791. Stanford University Libraries. https://sul-philologic.stanford.edu/philologic/archparl/navigate/28/0/0/0/0/0/0/279/, accessed 7 July 2022.

Marcellinus, Ammianus. "The Cruelty of Gallus Caesar." In *Roman Antiquities*, Book XIV, 1:7, date unknown. http://www.perseus.tufts.edu/hopper/text?doc=Amm.%2014.1&lang=original, accessed 15 January 2021.

McCargo, Duncan. *Fighting for Virtue: Justice and Politics in Thailand*. Ithaca, NY: Cornell University Press, 2019.

———. "Network Monarchy and Legitimacy Crises in Thailand." *The Pacific Review* 18:4 (2005):499–519.

Mérieau, Eugénie. "Seeking More Power, Thailand's New King Is Moving the Country away from Being a Constitutional Monarchy." *The Conversation*, 3 February 2017. https://theconversation.com/seeking-more-power-thailands-new-king-is-moving-the-country-away-from-being-a-constitutional-monarchy-71637, accessed 12 December 2020.

Nattapoll Chaiching. "The Monarchy and the Royalist Movement in Modern Thai Politics, 1932–1957." In *Saying the Unsayable: Monarchy and Democracy in Thailand*, ed. Søren Ivarsson and Lotte Isager, 147–78. Copenhagen: Nordic Institute of Asian Studies Press, 2011.

Nayer, Mark. "Is Spain's Royal Family Finished?" *Foreign Policy*, 13 August 2020. https://foreignpolicy.com/2020/08/13/is-spanish-spain-juan-carlos-corruption-royal-family-finished/, accessed 12 December 2020.

Neeranuit Traijakvanich and Rujira Rojjanaprapayon. "Ideologies in Thai Politics." Master's thesis, School of Language and Communication, National Institute of Development Administration, 1977. https://s004.tci-thaijo.org/index.php/svittj/article/download/241211/166909/, accessed 21 December 2020.

Orr, D. Alan. *Treason and the State: Law, Politics and Ideology in the English Civil War.* Cambridge: Cambridge University Press, 2007.

Pasit Wongngamdee. "From 'Being Thai' to 'Being Human': Thailand's Protests and Redefining the Nation." *New Mandala*, 26 November 2020. https://www.newmandala.org/from-being-thai-to-being-human-thailands-protests-and-redefining-the-nation/, accessed 13 December 2020.

Patpicha Tanakasempipat and Panarat Thepgumpanat. "'I Shall Reign with Righteousness': Thailand Crowns King in Ornate Ceremonies." *Reuters*, 4 March 2019. https://www.reuters.com/article/us-thailand-king-coronation/i-shall-reign-with-righteousness-thailand-crowns-king-in-ornate-ceremonies-idUSKCN1S924H, accessed 8 January 2021.

Pavin Chachavalpongpun. "Thai Royalty Attack on Exiled Critic." *Asia Sentinel*, 2 December 2020. https://www.asiasentinel.com/p/thai-royalty-attack-on-exiled-critic, accessed 20 January 2021.

Peláez, Juanjo V. "Spain: Felipe VI and the Corruption of the Monarchy–for the Third Republic and Socialism!" 20 April 2020. https://www.marxist.com/spain-felipe-vi-and-the-corruption-of-the-monarchy-for-the-third-republic-and-socialism.htm, accessed 13 December 2020.

Political Prisoners in Thailand. "Further Updated: Sineenat's Travels." *Political Prisoners in Thailand*, 28 October 2019. https://thaipoliticalprisoners.wordpress.com/2020/08/28/sineenats-travels/, accessed 20 November 2019.

Pollock, Frederick, and Frederic W. Maitland. *The History of English Law before the Time of Edward I.* Vol. 1, 2nd ed. Boston: Little, Brown, & Company, 1903.

Pugh, George W. "Historical Approach to the Doctrine of Sovereign Immunity." *Louisiana Law Review* 13:3/5 (1953):476–94.

"Read the Declaration that Heralded the Democratic Revolt 85 Years Ago Today." *Khaosod English*, 24 June 2017. https://www.khaosodenglish.com/news/2017/06/24/read-declaration-heralded-democratic-revolt-85-years-ago-today/, accessed on 22 October 2020.

Reuters. "Thailand's King Calls His Sister's Candidacy for PM 'Inappropriate.'" *Reuters*, 8 February 2019. https://www.reuters.com/article/uk-thailand-election-king-sister/thailands-king-calls-his-sisters-candidacy-for-pm-inappropriate-idUKKCN1PX1RF (*Note:* The original source is Channel News Asia: "Thai King Says Sister's Candidacy for Prime Minister is 'Inappropriate,' 'Unconstitutional': Palace Statement," 8 February 2019. https://www.channelnewsasia.com/news/asia/thai-king-sister-princess-ubonratana-pm-candidacy-inappropriate-11224338. The story, accessible on 20 November 2020, while still appearing in a search, leads to a dead link.)

Scott, S.P. "Code of Justinian, Title 4, Book xlviii, on the Julian Law Relating to the Crime of Lèse-majesté." In *The Digest, The Enactments of Justinian*, ed. S.P. Scott, "The Civil Law, xi." Cincinnati, 1932. https://droitromain.univ-grenoble-alpes.fr/Anglica/D48_Scott.htm#IV, accessed 5 November 2020.

———. "The Enactments of Justinian: Title 41. Concerning Torture. 1. The Emperors Severus and Antoninus to Antiana, Published on the *Kalends* of January, During the Consulate of Fuscus, Consul for the Second Time, and Dexter." In *The Civil Law, IX*. Cincinnati, 1932. https://droitromain.univ-grenoble-alpes.fr/Anglica/CJ9_Scott.gr.htm#41, accessed 23 December 2020.

Sen, Pawan K. "A Reflection on Nepal's Path to a Republic." *East Asia Forum*, 15 August 2020. https://www.eastasiaforum.org/2020/08/15/a-reflection-on-nepals-path-to-a-republic/, accessed 18 January 2021.

Smith, William. *A Dictionary of Greek and Roman Antiquities*. London: John Murray, 1875.

————— et al., eds. *A Dictionary of Greek and Roman Antiquities*. London: J. Murray, 1891.

Streckfuss, David. "The Intricacies of Lèse-majesté: A Comparative Study of Imperial Germany and Modern Thailand." In *Saying the Unsayable: Monarchy and Democracy in Thailand*, ed. Søren Ivarsson and Lotte Isager, 105–44. Copenhagen: Nordic Institute of Asian Studies Press, 2011.

———. "The Future of the Monarchy in Thailand." *Kyoto Review of Southeast Asia* 13 (March 2013). https://kyotoreview.org/issue-13/the-future-of-the-monarchy-in-thailand/, accessed 29 December 2020.

———. "Thailand's Peculiar Interregnum." *New Mandala*, 20 October 2016. https://www.newmandala.org/just-formality-thailands-peculiar-interregnum/, accessed 18 November 2020.

"'Support Good People to Rule This Country,' Says King of Thailand on Eve of Election." *Prachatai*, 24 March 2019. https://prachatai.com/english/node/7990, accessed 12 June 2019.

"Thai Prince Said to Trigger Police Purge." *Asia Sentinel*, 24 November 2014. https://www.asiasentinel.com/p/thailand-prince-said-to-trigger-police-purge, accessed 17 November 2019.

"Thailand Rehearses Elaborate $31 Million Coronation for King." *Reuters*, 28 April 2019. https://www.reuters.com/article/us-thailand-king-coronation-rehearsal-idUSKCN1S40H4, accessed 23 September 2020.

"Thailand's King Reinstates His Consort after Her Fall from Grace." *BBC News*, 2 September 2020. https://www.bbc.com/news/world-asia-53994198, accessed 1 November 2020.

Thammachart Kri-aksorn. "Oath Error: Recapping Case that Shakes Government." *Prachatai*, 13 September 2019. https://prachatai.com/english/node/8212, accessed 22 December 2020.

"The Richest in 2020." *Forbes*, 18 March 2020. https://www.forbes.com/billionaires/, accessed 15 November 2020.

"The World's Richest Royal Families Ranked." *Lovemoney*, date unknown. https://www.lovemoney.com/gallerylist/71850/richest-royal-families-world-ranked, accessed 15 November 2020.

Ulpianus. "On the Duties of Proconsul." In *The Civil Law*, *Book VII*, Title IV: On the Julian Law Relating to the Crime of Lèse-majesté, date unknown. https://droitromain.univ-grenoble-alpes.fr/Anglica/D48_Scott.htm#IV, accessed 29 December 2020.

United Nations. General Assembly Resolution 55/25. "Protocol to Prevent, Suppress and Punish Trafficking in Persons Especially Women and Children, Supplementing the United Nations Convention against Transnational Organized Crime," 15 November 2000. https://www.ohchr.org/EN/ProfessionalInterest/Pages/ProtocolTraffickingInPersons.aspx, accessed 1 December 2020.

"What's Behind the Downfall of Thailand's Princess Srirasmi?" *BBC News*, 1 December 2014. https://www.bbc.com/news/world-asia-30275513, accessed 20 November 2020.

Williams, George W. "An Open Letter to His Serene Majesty Leopold II, King of the Belgians and Sovereign of the Independent State of Congo By Colonel, the Honourable George W. Williams, of the United States of America." *Blackpast*, 20 August 2009. https://www.blackpast.org/global-african-history/primary-documents-global-african-history/george-washington-williams-open-letter-king-leopold-congo-1890/, accessed 15 February 2021.

"World Press Freedom Index." *Reporters without Borders*, date unknown. https://rsf.org/en/ranking/2020, accessed 7 July 2022.

Wright, Herbert Francis. *The Constitutions of the States at War, 1914–1918.* Washington, DC: US Government Printing Office, 1919.

Veyne, Paul. "What Was a Roman Emperor? Emperor, Therefore a God." *Diogenes* 50:3 (2003):3–21.

York, Philip Chasney. "Strafford, Thomas Wentworth, Earl of." *Encyclopedia Britannica* 25, ed. Hugh Chisholm, 11th ed. Cambridge: Cambridge University Press, 1911.

References (Thai)

Newtv18. "'Piyabut' chi 5 laksana kanpokkhrawng nai rabop p.ch.t. an mi phramahakasat pen pramuk" ["Piyabutr" (Saengkanokkul) point out five characteristics of the democratic regime with the king as head of state]. *Newtv18*, 2020. https://www.newtv.co.th/news/62641, accessed 14 January 2021.

Okat Tephalakun. "Ruang kanpokkhrawng rapop prachathipatai an mi phramahakasat song pen pramuk" [On the democratic regime of government with the king as head of state] Part of the "Rule of Law for Democracy Course No. 2," Constitution College, Office of the Constitutional Court, date unknown. https://www.constitutionalcourt.or.th/occ_web/ewt_dl_link.php?nid=1354, accessed 18 December 2020.

"Phraratchabanyat thammanun kanpokkhrawng phaendin sayam chua khrao" [Temporary Constitution of 1932]. http://lad.correct.go.th/main/wp-content/uploads/2018/08/พรบการปกครอง2475.pdf, accessed 7 July 2022.

"Poet ngop praman pi 2563 suan thi kieowkap sathaban phramahakasat 2.9 moenlan baht" ["Revealing the 2020 budget for the monarchy, 29 billion baht"], *Prachatai*, 12 March 2563 [2020]. https://prachatai.com/journal/2020/03/86761, accessed 17 December 2020.

"Prakat: Ruang hai kharatchakan nai phraong fai thahan phan jak tamnaeng thawt thanadornsak lae yot thahan talawt jon riak khoen khruang ratchais-ariyaphorn thuk chantrai" [Announcement: Regarding the removal of military officials from positions of honor and military ranks, as well as the revoking of all insignia and ranks]. *Ratchakitjanubeksa*, 21 October 2562 [2019], Vol. 1136, Part 55, B, p. 1. http://www.ratchakitcha.soc.go.th/DATA/PDF/2562/B/055/T_0001.PDF, accessed 19 October 2019.

"Protkhlao ph.r.k. on kamlang phon-ngop praman bang suan khawng krom thahan rap thi 1-rap 11 pai pen khawng nuai banchakan thawai khwam plawtphai raksa phraong" ["His Majesty orders transfer of some personnel and budget of the 1st Infantry Regiment/the 11th Infantry Regiment to the Royal Security Command"]. *BBC News*, 30 September 2562 [2019]. https://www.bbc.com/thai/thailand-49880897, accessed 30 November 2020.

Constitutions and Criminal Codes

[Belgium] Constitution of 1831 with Amendments through 2014. https://www.constituteproject.org/constitution/Belgium_2014.pdf?lang=en, accessed 7 July 2022.

[Denmark] Constitution. https://www.constituteproject.org/constitution/Denmark_1953?lang=en

———. The Criminal Code. https://www.globalwps.org/data/DNK/files/Danish%20Criminal%20Code.pdf, accessed 7 July 2022.

[The Netherlands] Constitution. http://www.servat.unibe.ch/icl/nl00000_.html.

———. Penal Code. https://wetten.overheid.nl/BWBR0001854/2012-05-09/1, accessed 7 July 2022.

[Norway] Constitution as Laid down on 17 May 1814 by the Constituent Assembly at Eidsvoll and Subsequently Amended, Most Recently on 20 February 2007. https://web.archive.org/web/20110829055430/http://www.stortinget.no/en/In-English/About-the-Storting/The-Constitution/The-Constitution/, accessed 7 July 2022.

———. General Civil Criminal Code. https://www.un.org/Depts/los/LEGISLATIONANDTREATIES/PDFFILES/NOR_penal_code.pdf, accessed 7 July 2022.

[Spain] Constitution de la Monarquía Española (30 de junio de 1876). http://www.dircost.unito.it/cs/docs/CONST%201876.htm, accessed 7 July 2022.

———. Constitution of Spain of 1978. https://www.servat.unibe.ch/icl/sp00000_.html, accessed 7 July 2022.

———. Criminal Code. https://www.mjusticia.gob.es/es/AreaTematica/DocumentacionPublicaciones/Documents/Criminal_Code_2016.pdf, accessed 7 July 2022.

[Sweden] Instrument of Government. https://www.servat.unibe.ch/icl/sw00000_.html.

———. The Swedish Criminal Code. https://www.government.se/contentassets/7a2dcae0787e465e9a2431554b5eab03/the-swedish-criminal-code.pdf, accessed 7 July 2022.

[Thailand] Constitution of the Kingdom of Thailand of 1997. http://www.asianlii.org/th/legis/const/1997/1.html, accessed 22 December 2020.

———. Constitution of the Kingdom of Thailand of 2017. https://www.constituteproject.org/constitution/Thailand_2017.pdf?lang=en, accessed 15 December 2021.

4

Friends Close and Enemies Closer: Rama X and the Thai Military

GREGORY V. RAYMOND

> I was sick almost to the point of death. There was no one person I could
> trust to save me ... and there were enemies whose intentions were openly
> bared against me, both inside [the palace] and outside, both within the capital
> and abroad.
>
> — King Chulalongkorn, as quoted in Battye,
> *The Military, Government and Society in Siam, 1868–1910*

PERPETUAL INSECURITY is the curse of Thai monarchs. King Mongkut, or
Rama IV, spent years in the monkhood to avoid a succession conflict. King
Chulalongkorn, or Rama V, began his reign when sizeable private armies
abounded, like that of the so-called Second King Prince Wichaichan and,
separately, his uncle Pin Klao. That these threatened the security of his rule
was made abundantly clear in the 1875 Wang Na (Front Palace) incident,
when open conflict between the forces of Chulalongkorn and Wichaichan
was a distinct possibility. King Prajadhipok, or Rama VII, was removed from
power by modernizing revolutionaries. The anxieties of Vajiralongkorn,
tenth monarch of Thailand's Chakri dynasty, were initially more about his
personal status than the security of the monarchical institution. Becoming
king late in life is never easy, and the adulation accorded to his father,
Bhumibol Adulyadej, or Rama IX (1946–2016), added unfavorable compar-
isons to the task. But since 2020, Vajiralongkorn's problems have become
more serious. Confronted by a vibrant youth protest movement committed
to removing the vestiges of feudalism from Thai political culture,

Vajiralongkorn is fighting to preserve monarchical privilege. In this struggle, there is no ally more important than the Thai military.

In this chapter I argue that Thailand's durable monarchical-military partnership may have strengthened in the face of a new democracy movement but is not without its cracks and tensions. Outwardly, the fundamental bargain whereby the monarchy legitimizes the military's role in politics in exchange for its support remains extant, even if a decline in monarchical charisma is eroding its efficacy. Internally, the dynamics within the partnership are very different in this reign from the previous one. Vajiralongkorn is aggressively personalizing control of the military in a way that Bhumibol never did. In this endeavor, he is advantaged by his own professional background as a soldier, including his own network of trusted aides and his significant knowledge of the inner workings of military organizations. Confident in his own military training, he is very directly affecting the structure, training, and image of the Thai military, including by transferring regiments of the King's Guard from the mainstream army to the Royal Security Command (RSC) in 2019. He is also stamping his own preferences on military promotions, a policy, that when resulting in some factions feeling disenfranchised, has in Thai history carried the risk of a backlash.

Vajiralongkorn has taken out insurance to hedge against the risk of military disloyalty. The strongest evidence for this hypothesis is the RSC itself, in essence a new army directly under his personal command. The RSC was established prior to the accession in 2017 but since then has been strengthened. Other indications include the 2017 founding of a new unarmed public volunteer force, the Volunteer Spirit (Jit Arsa), and the 2018 movement of key units of the Thai army out of metropolitan Bangkok. The latter was ostensibly to alleviate traffic problems, but it has also made a military coup without royal approval significantly riskier.

In unpacking this murky game of thrones, I begin with a sketch of the historical relationship between Thailand's monarchs and the modern military, before considering Vajiralongkorn's own upbringing and vocation as a professional soldier. I then examine the establishment and rapid development of Vajiralongkorn's Royal Security Command, and changes to Vajiralongkorn's relationship with the Thai armed forces. I look particularly at their renewed partnership of illiberalism, but also at the effect the new monarch is having on the military, and the evidence of lingering distrust at deeper levels of the relationship.

Monarchs and Militaries in Thailand

Most Southeast Asian militaries—for example, Indonesia's Tentara Nasional Indonesia and Burma's Tatmadaw—formed in wars of national liberation. In contrast, Thailand's King Chulalongkorn created the modern Thai military as a personal bodyguard. The Royal Pages Bodyguard was modeled on European lines, providing the template of a professional military, which could be applied to other military and paramilitary units. Professionalizing—paying a regular salary, housing in barracks, and training in modern drill and weapons—was as much to centralize control over the dispersed fragments of military force as it was to increase the capability of the Thai armed forces.[1] The 1875 Wang Na incident was a turning point. Chulalongkorn, after the incident was resolved in his favor, took over control of rival forces and steadily brought the Thai army and navy under the control of a single ministry. He then commenced a practice of sending trusted family members abroad for training in European military schools and, on their return, appointing them to leadership positions. His son Vajiravudh, later Rama VI (1910–25), was the first Thai monarch to receive military training in Europe, at Sandhurst, the training college of the British army.

Vajiravudh and Prajadhipok (1925–35) were both trained soldiers and active supreme commanders of the Thai military. Vajiravudh took a strong interest in military affairs, raising public funds for the purchase of a new warship and actively managing Thailand's wartime diplomacy in World War I, first as a neutral state and then as a belligerent on the side of the Allied Powers. Prajadhipok trained abroad at Britain's Royal Military College in Woolwich and the École de Guerre in France, later commenting that he would have been happy with a military career if fate had not intervened to force him onto the throne.[2] He, like Vajiravudh before him, was seriously interested in the structure and organization of the military. But Prajadhipok was faced with the consequences of the Great Depression and decided to impose deep cuts on the military to preserve the kingdom's financial position. This was one factor that led to the 1932 revolution.[3]

Bhumibol differed from his predecessors in his knowledge of military matters. A graduate in law, and interested in science, engineering, and music, Bhumibol recognized the importance of the military only after he became king. He became convinced that a strong military was needed as a bulwark against the threat from communist forces within and outside the country's borders. As the military held the upper hand in the early years of the military-monarchical partnership, developing close relationships with Thai generals was also a matter of survival. Nonetheless, he was never as intimately acquainted with matters of military doctrine, equipment, tactics, and command as his two predecessors. He also differed from his son Vajiralongkorn, who displayed an interest in a military career from his early teens.

Still, under Bhumibol's reign, the military-monarchy relationship changed significantly. It became increasingly a fundamental component of so-called Thai-style democracy (TSD).[4] As a rule, militaries in Asia have frequently supported authoritarianism in the name of development and, as part of this, cemented a role for themselves in public life.[5] In Thailand, TSD has facilitated authoritarianism and the Thai military's claim to a political role. Saichon has explained that this is because Thai middle classes, far from being a vanguard of democratization, have been avid consumers of TSD's paternalistic conception of Thais being best served by the leadership of "good persons."[6] This conception implicitly condones the military-monarchy partnership, and a role for the monarch far less constrained by law than in Western-style constitutional democracies. The Thai military, for its part, has readily expounded its own version of civil-military relations under TSD. In 2006, just months before the 19 September coup against Thaksin Shinawatra, Prem Tinsulanonda, Bhumibol's closest adviser and intermediary between himself and the military, summed up civil-military relations under Thai-style democracy through his horse analogy. If the military was a horse, the former prime minister and army general stated, the monarch was its owner and the government merely its jockey.[7]

The Making of a Military King: Vajiralongkorn, Maturing, and the Royal Military College Duntroon

Vajiralongkorn grew up in the Cold War with the military ever present and his father deeply concerned with threats to Thailand. Bhumibol saw a threat from China, stating that "they are an expansive people," and calling for Thailand to remain wary of "communist trickery."[8] When Vajiralongkorn was thirteen, he was appointed to the *mahadlek* royal guards and given sublieutenant ranks and uniforms for the army, navy, and air force.[9] The youth thereafter frequently visited the royal bodyguard units in the palace, reportedly asking them about their duties. Although Vajiralongkorn was sent to boarding school in Britain, during his holidays he would visit Border Patrol Police and army camps in uniform and began to undertake basic military training including in weapons.[10]

In July 1970, Bhumibol announced that the prince would study in Australia, first at King's School in the Sydney suburb of Parramatta, and then at the Royal Military College, Duntroon, in Australia's capital, Canberra.[11] The eighteen-year-old arrived in Sydney in September of that year.[12] At Duntroon, Vajiralongkorn pursued a Bachelor of Arts in military studies, a course consisting of both military and academic study taken over four years.[13] The course aimed at achieving the "best balance between the short-term requirements of a junior regimental officer and the broader foundation necessary for those wishing to progress to the higher ranks of the Army."[14] The academic subjects, delivered by the University of New South Wales, included Western systems of government, international politics, European and American history, and Western literature.[15] The military components included drill and ceremonial, infantry minor tactics, intelligence, leadership, methods of instruction, and military engineering. The course was structured to bring the cadets firstly to the standard of a trained soldier, then an infantry section commander, and finally a platoon commander. Military training was conducted in the field and, in the final year, at the Australian Defence Force's Jungle Training Centre at Canungra in the northern state of Queensland.[16] The final year also included visits to several other Australian army bases across the country.

At Duntroon, Vajiralongkorn was called Mr. Mahidol and allegedly treated as other cadets were, as was another enrolled Southeast Asian royal, Tuan Syed Zainal Rashid Putra, the Malaysian sultan of Perlis.[17] Mr. Mahidol's academic file is today unavailable, and so we cannot be sure of his level of achievement.[18] Of the 66 cadets to graduate in 1975, Mr. Mahidol was not among the prize winners (while the Queen's Medal went to another foreign student, H.K. Tan of Singapore, the Sword of Honor went to one A.J. Miles of Queensland[19]). Moreover, the College Handbook records that "Val" (his apparent nickname) had "a lack of interest in accas [meaning academic study] and nil work and enjoyment of a full social life."[20] He did however participate in sport, including swimming, cross-country running, and swimming.

Training and drill were matters of both pain and pride for the young Vajiralongkorn during his time in Australia. After watching Australians commemorate ANZAC Day, which remembers especially those who died attempting to land at Gallipoli in Turkey in the First World War, the prince put pen to paper and wrote a poem in Thai.[21] The translation of a few lines reads:

> I go and quietly listen and watch,
> And see the orderly glorious tradition
> Dressed in beautiful uniforms both men and women
> Together in body and heart remembering the young
>   warriors
> If our nation had a day like this, it would be very good
> People who sacrifice and endure suffering getting honor
> To be an example to do good
> A nation of many popular heroes.[22]

At the same time, Vajiralongkorn suffered. Another poem, written for his mother in 1972, describes how he felt "very upset" in the first five weeks of being a cadet.[23] He describes his dislike of the early hours and his bitterness at being made to clean the toilets or other sundry punishments "whenever he did something wrong." He was punished for misunderstanding drill instructions and weapons use. Inspections and tests of endurance were constants at Duntroon:

> In the Military College every morning.
> There was an examination of cadet's uniform.
> Health, hair, manner, and clothing,
> The poise of walking to and from.
> Those who did something wrong
> Would always lose some score.
> Included, some punishment more.
>
> The field exercise and weapons training were difficult
> We were supposed to escape from the enemy.
> And had to hide in the mud,
> To be attacked by thorns and to feel wearily.
> To escape from those enemies getting close every minute.

> We did not have anything to eat.
> In two or three days we had to beware of the beat.

While there is no evidence he was bullied, one of his aides, Major General Samroeng Chaiyong, later wrote that senior students denied Vajiralongkorn a chance to display his soccer talents:

> In the evening after the school had finished, the Prince would practice sport, mostly football. He played as a back either left or right. At the beginning when he went to a school to prepare for being a cadet, he played very well, was a star of the school, got an historic number of goals. But when he went to study at cadet school, the older group coerced (*bip*) him. He had no opportunities to kick goals and he was sent to the weakest team. This was because the older group didn't want him to be a star.[24]

We know little about what other indignities or harsh treatment from other cadets Vajiralongkorn might have experienced while at Duntroon. What is well documented, however, is that the culture among the cadets was similar to that of an English boarding school, with chronic bullying of younger recruits by their seniors. Each cadet belonged to a company headed by a first-class cadet (a student in his final year), underscoring the hierarchical nature of the college. In 1970 an official inquiry known as the Fox Report concluded that "the class structure, with its particular emphasis on the inferiority of the Fourth Class, has long been a part of College life."[25] The inquiry further noted that the class structure "had contributed to the excesses of Fourth Class training ('bastardization')."[26] Known elsewhere as "hazing," the term "bastardization" denotes gross bullying behavior by older classes toward new recruits. It is plausible that Vajiralongkorn witnessed, and possibly even experienced, "bastardization."

The Fox Report recommended changes to the class structure to reduce the practice of bastardization, but it was not easily excised. A 2012 investigation into sexual and other abuse in the Australian Defence Force received a submission from a former Duntroon cadet who described a photograph of one ritual:

> Here shown is a cadet being held down by his hands and feet by several other cadets. His groin has been forcefully smothered with Metsal (a liniment ointment similar to Dencorub, it causes excruciating burning pain when applied to genitals). The cadet subject of the activity is being bucketed with a concoction comprising human excrement and a multitude of other things

(coffee, vegemite, sour milk, and the like). This is but just one of the types of conditioning activities cadets were subjected to on a daily basis.[27]

The former cadet concluded by stating that he was still tormented by the memory of the physical and mental abuse years later.

Vajiralongkorn's time at Duntroon, traumatic or not, finished in 1975 with Australian Governor-General Sir John Kerr commissioning him as a captain in the Thai army. In concession of his regal status, he was given a position in the graduation ceremony to allow his mother, Queen Sirikit, a better view.[28] After graduating, Vajiralongkorn undertook parachute and commando training with Australia's elite Special Air Service (SAS) at their headquarters in Swanbourne near Perth in Western Australia. There, between January and October 1976, he studied irregular operations, advanced navigation, and patrol.[29] In recent times, the reputation of Australia's SAS and commando regiments has been tarnished by reports of war crimes. In November 2020, an internal investigation of Australia's Special Forces actions, while on deployment in Afghanistan from 2005 to 2016, found allegations of 39 unlawful killings by or involving ADF members. The alleged crimes did not occur during the heat of battle and the alleged victims were non-combatants or prisoners.[30]

On returning to Thailand, Vajiralongkorn became involved in the Thai military's efforts to counter a home-grown communist insurgency. A substantial number of villages were under Communist Party of Thailand (CPT) control or influence.[31] With Cambodia, Laos, and South Vietnam all having fallen under communist control in 1975, fear of communism was running high. Relations between the CPT and Thai royal family were particularly venomous. In 1977, communist insurgents shot down a helicopter carrying queen's aide M.C. Vibhavadi Rangsit, killing the minor royal. Accusations and name-calling flew back and forth. The CPT attacked the royal family for its indulgent lifestyle and criticized the prince as "uncontrollably violent."[32]

On 13 February 1977 Vajiralongkorn himself experienced a clash with communist forces in the Khao Kor area of Petchabun Province of northern Thailand. His assailants were most likely Hmong communists, who had resisted Thai military operations in Petchabun for many years.[33] The Hmong were adept at guerrilla warfare and in 1972 had defeated a much larger force of 12,000 Thai soldiers of the First Division.[34] In fact the insurgents were not defeated until the Thai military employed four hundred former Kuomintang soldiers, who had previously been granted refuge in northern Thailand, as mercenaries.[35] Vajiralongkorn was traveling in an armored personnel carrier (APC) when it was ambushed.[36] Two helicopter gunships received fire from insurgents. Vajiralongkorn remained on the scene to call in mortar and artillery fire in a counterattack. He was authorized to leave the APC to eliminate the adversaries. This he did "shoulder to shoulder" (*kiang ba kiang lai*) with the other soldiers. The two damaged helicopters were able to land safely, and Vajiralongkorn returned to Chiang Mai the same day.[37]

This incident is now publicized frequently, cultivating Rama x's image as a heroic soldier king, prepared to endure hardships alongside the common people. For example, in October 2019, army chief General Apirat Kongsompong gave a public speech in which he described the king's actions during the deployment, saying that they showed that "the monarchy, the military, and the people cannot be separated."[38]

As crown prince, Vajiralongkorn continued to travel overseas for military training. After completing the Thai Army's Command and Staff College regular course 1977–78 (class 56), he traveled to the United States.[39] There, between January and May 1980, he studied six weapons and tactics courses, including counterinsurgency, special operations, and air transport.[40] In 1981 he met with Australian defense officials to talk on army aviation and infantry issues, and flew Australian army tactical aircraft.[41] He also visited Australia in 1985 and 1987. On the latter occasion he stayed several days in Canberra, at the residence of the Australian governor-general.[42]

As Bhumibol's long reign stretched into the 1990s and 2000s, Vajiralongkorn took an interest in the air force. In 1980 he studied to become a helicopter pilot, and from about 1987 flying became a major pursuit. By 1997, he had accumulated 2,000 hours of flying time, meaning he had spent many days on military bases.[43] In 2004 he passed a commercial flying test allowing him to captain a Boeing 737-400.[44] He later combined his flying skills with charity work, raising money for hospitals in the three southern border provinces by captaining a special Thai Airways flight between Chiang Mai and Bangkok.[45] Today he has accumulated a private air wing of some 38 jets and helicopters, eight of which are combat aircraft, including the Russian Sukhoi Superjet 100.[46] At the same time that he pursued his flying, he continued to play a role in palace security. In 1984, he became a commander of the King's Guard Ratchawallop, and in 1992 became the commander of the Royal Security Command.[47] Since Vajiralongkorn ascended the throne following his father's death in October 2016, it is the Royal Security Command that has been Vajiralongkorn's signature military reform.

The Royal Security Command and the Volunteer Spirit

Vajiralongkorn started to transform the palace guard while still crown prince. In November 2013, Thailand was in crisis, as former Democrat politician Suthep Thaugsuban's royalist protest movement sought to bring down Prime Minister Yingluck Shinawatra. While Bhumibol retained power as monarch, he was ailing. Against this backdrop, Crown Prince Vajiralongkorn greatly enlarged his role as an operational military commander. Via a royal command, he amended Article 10 of the Defense Administration Act, giving a legal basis to the Royal Security Command (*nuai banchakan thawai khwam plod phai raksa phra-ong*). The Royal Security Command was in effect made equal in status to the office of the minister of defense, the office of the permanent secretary of defense, the royal aide-de-camp, and the Royal Thai Armed Forces.[48]

The Royal Security Command was also large and clearly more than a mere household security detail, such as might be provided for a Western leader's personal protection. Containing six battalions, each between three hundred and eight hundred soldiers, the RSC amounted to a force of several thousand soldiers.[49] Personnel would be recruited directly from the population and given opportunities for specialist training such as parachuting and ranger training, similar to that provided to commandos or special forces.[50] The RSC was effectively a private army answering directly to the then crown prince, even if its official duties remained looking after the royal family's security and managing the palace's administrative affairs.

After Vajiralongkorn became king, the National Legislative Assembly passed more legislation revealing the scope and structure of the Royal Security Command. It would contain a command office, staff wing, a police wing, a special operations unit, and a command unit for the King's Guard Ratchawallop. It would operate anywhere in the country where royal safety needed to be assured, and in the event that plans with other state agencies were inconsistent, the plans of the Royal Security Command would hold sway.[51] Vajiralongkorn has continued to refine the new apparatus. He relaxed the eligibility rules for the *mahadlek*, with the first generation of female *mahadlek* recruited in 2014.[52] The female recruits now provide the same protective services as male members, as well as service to the broader population in times of natural disaster. Conditions for both selection and service are strict. Women must be above 165 cm in height and aged between twenty and twenty-eight. Once selected they must complete 10 years of service, during which time they are not permitted to marry or have relationships, and they are not allowed to resign or seek transfer to other units. Vajiralongkorn also severed the connections of six palace agencies—the Office of the Principal Private Secretary, the Royal Household Bureau, the Royal Aide-de-Camp Department, the Royal Security Command, and the Royal Court Police—to the police, government, and mainstream military and placed them solely under his own control. The legislation made these agencies, according to one commentary, "independent of government laws" and "run only by the King."[53]

Further and deeper changes were made in 2019. In January, the Special Service Division Special Operation and Safety Unit within the Royal Security Command was renamed the King's Guard 904.[54] The King's Guard 904 would have a nationwide structure with subunits assigned geographical areas of responsibility, as well as a special unit with nationwide responsibility for "special tools" and "news analysis."

Vajiralongkorn still has his network of King's Guard units within the mainstream Thai armed forces; the Royal Security Command is in addition to these. These 69 King's Guard units all pledge a special oath of loyalty and are distributed across the three services. The majority (42) are in the army.[55] Within the Thai army itself there are King's Guard battalions in the infantry corps, the cavalry (tank) corps, the artillery corps, and even the engineering, signals, and transport corps. By far, the most well-known of these are the infantry units, especially the 1st and 11th King's Guard departments (*krom*) of the 1st Division and the 21st King's Guard department of the 2nd Division, usually known as the Queen's Guard. The Thai air force has five King's Guard units and the navy seven, including four marines departments. In April 2019, Vajiralongkorn relieved a large number of mainstream military units of their palace-related duties, such as parades on the previous king's birthday, 5 December.[56] Some 64 army units, 8 navy units, and 15 air force units were affected by the command. The command, which first removed many of the units from royal duties, and then reappointed them, may have been to ensure that the units were under an order signed by him rather than his father,

Bhumibol. Most controversially, in September 2019, Vajiralongkorn transferred all personnel and associated budgets of the red-uniformed 1st Infantry Regiment King's Guard and the blue-uniformed 11th Infantry Regiment King's Guard from the Royal Thai Army to the Royal Security Command.[57] For the first time, this reform attracted public opposition, although carefully framed as criticism of Prime Minister Prayuth rather than the king.[58]

The establishment of the Royal Security Command is Vajiralongkorn's most significant reform in the sphere of defense and security, but not the only one. It is paralleled by Vajiralongkorn's creation of a new volunteer force, the Jit Arsa (Volunteer Spirit), in 2017. Although unarmed, the Jit Arsa is managed through the King's Guard 904 and provides Vajiralongkorn with a massive workforce under his direct control. There are now a reported four million members, across the country and social strata.[59] The Jit Arsa program resembles previous Cold War schemes to involve citizens for security and nation-building purposes, in particular the Village Scouts. Bhumibol founded the Village Scouts in 1971 as a new "mass rural patriotic organization."[60] Initiates underwent ideological training and were instructed that the preservation of the nation-king-religion trinity was essential for survival against the threat from Vietnam and China. The scouts had no links to government and were funded by middle-class donations. The king and queen personally handed out scarves during initiation ceremonies. Vajiralongkorn himself promoted the Village Scouts during the late 1990s, attending Village Scout events across the country. While unarmed, the Village Scouts were capable of vigilantism and were involved in the attacks on students at Thammasat University in 1976. Vajiralongkorn met an assembly of the Village Scouts at this time.[61]

The similarities between the Village Scouts and the Jit Arsa are striking. Initiates to the Jit Arsa are identifiable by their light blue scarves. The Village Scouts were also presented with scarves. Of these Handley writes, "like holy amulets, the kerchiefs gave each scout a sense of proximity to the throne."[62] The Jit Arsa perform community work, such as cleaning streets and rivers, as well as disaster relief, and commence each task by saluting a portrait of the king. In July 2019, all 1,798 staff and executives of the Siam Commercial Bank pledged loyalty to the scheme, citing the importance of the "four major institutions of the country: Nation, Religion, Monarchy, and People."[63] The king has also founded a further volunteer unit, the Volunteers Unit 904, made up of the military and police. They go to university campuses to extol the achievements of the Chakri dynasty, including in keeping Thailand independent during the colonial period.[64]

Vajiralongkorn's Partnership with the Regular Military

What kind of country do the military and monarchy wish to achieve through their partnership? In June 2018, Vajiralongkorn stated that he wished Thailand to be a "disciplined country where people are instilled with a sense of voluntary sacrifice."[65] But it has been acts and gestures rather than words, omissions more than explicit ideology, which have told the deeper story of their imagined future Thailand, one that appears to allocate a marginal place for constitutional democracy.[66] First, Vajiralongkorn made changes to the Thai constitution after its approval by referendum, ignoring any notion of consent of the governed.[67] Then, when former Thai general, coup-maker, and junta leader General Prayuth Chan-ocha and his cabinet swore an oath of loyalty to Vajiralongkorn following the 26 March 2019 election, they omitted a pledge to "uphold and observe the Constitution of the Kingdom of Thailand in every respect."[68] The omission, likely to have been deliberate, was never rectified, and the Constitutional Court refused to accept a case on its unconstitutionality.

The military and monarchy also appear united in efforts to alter Thailand's memoryscape to downplay the significance of the 1932 revolution and, conversely, celebrate efforts by royalists to defeat the revolution. Contestation over Thailand's history is not new; there is abundant evidence, for example, that the Thai military and the monarchy have long prevented significant public commemoration role of the Seri Thai movement in World War II because it raises questions about the military's wartime actions.[69] The new revisionism seeks to erase the historical traces of Thailand's original democracy movement, the Khana Ratsadon. In 2017, the plaque commemorating the 1932 revolution disappeared from Sanam Luang and was replaced with one praising the monarchy. In 2018 the Constitution Defense Monument, which stood at the Laksi Intersection in northern Bangkok, was dismantled. The monument had commemorated the suppression of the 1933 Boworadet royalist rebellion.[70] Although the palace has not publicly claimed responsibility, neither did Vajiralongkorn suggest that he opposed these highly symbolic actions. In 2019 the Thai army staged its own commemoration of the Boworadet royalist rebellion on 24 June, on the very day previously reserved for commemorating the 1932 revolution.[71]

In this revisionist history endeavor, the Thai military is even prepared to repudiate its own. Statues and tributes to one of the Thai army's most formidable and important leaders, Field Marshal Plaek Phibun Songkhram, are also being removed, presumably because of Phibun's well-known dislike of the monarchy and role in the 1932 revolution. In 2015, I observed a prominent statue of Phibun at the Royal Thai Armed Forces National Defense Studies Institute in Bangkok, which praised his contributions to Thai defense studies (*phu-mi-khunupakan kansueksa witthaya kanpongkan prathet*). In January 2020, Thai dissident Somsak Jeamteerasakul reported that the statue had been removed. He also revealed "before" and "after" photographs of a sign in front of a history center. These showed that information informing the public that the building had been a former holiday house of Phibun had been removed.[72]

In 2019 and 2020, it became starkly apparent that Thailand's younger generation do not subscribe to this illiberal future and are becoming increasingly impatient with both the monarchy and the military's continued hold on power. Thai youths overwhelmingly voted for democratic change in the form of the Future Forward Party, who campaigned on a platform of ending military coups, in the March 2019 elections.[73] Following the dissolution of the party, for having received a US$6 million loan from Thanathorn Juangroongruangkit, which the court deemed a donation, and therefore illegal, they commenced a series of university-based demonstrations that were growing in size and demands for change when the coronavirus struck.[74] After the resumption of demonstrations in July 2020, the August 2020 public statements of lawyer Anon Nampha and student Panusaya "Rung" Sithijirawattanakul on monarchical reform broke the ceiling for public discussions of the monarchy. For a time calling for monarchical reform became commonplace among protestors, and the monarch's periodic residence in Germany and his significant wealth both attracted public protests. There is, at the time of writing, no consensus on whether this current generation of protestors will succeed in enacting real political reform, but a generational shift of the dimensions seen in Thailand in 2020 will likely mean a long struggle is ahead.

Therefore, there is ample reason for the military-monarchy relationship to strengthen, as cooperation against a shared threat is in their mutual interest. There is considerable evidence that this is indeed occurring. Security agencies such as the Internal Security Operations Command and the Royal Security Command are organizing a conservative backlash. They are mobilizing civil society groups such as former communists, and also conducting information operations via social media platforms such as Twitter.[75] The use of lèse-majesté, after a hiatus, is returning in order to silence activist student leaders.[76] The monarch's impromptu statement to a foreign journalist in November 2020, that "Thailand was the land of compromise," looks increasingly to have been crafted to soothe the fears of Western onlookers rather than indicate any willingness to contemplate reform.[77]

Keep Your Friends Close and Your Enemies Closer: New Expectations Make for Uncomfortable Times

Facing a common threat may drive cooperation but this does not mean that the relationship is comfortable. The military is, in a sense, cornered. Having imbibed current royalist ideology even more deeply during Vajiralongkorn's reign, it is powerless to resist the edicts of the monarchy. And Vajiralongkorn is now having a substantial effect. The Thai military has long resisted reform. The last real attempt was that of Prime Minister Chuan Leekpai. Dual-hatted as a civilian defense minister in the 1990s, he worked with Thai army commander General Surayud Chulanont to map a reform program. The vision was the replacement of Cold War–vintage equipment with more capable and modern arms to make a "small but powerful Royal Thai Armed Forces." This would be achieved through a reduction in troop levels by 72,000 over 12 years, thereby freeing up resources for modernization.[78] But numbers ultimately rose. Similarly, Chuan's plans to change the military's command and organizational structure were abandoned.[79]

Vajiralongkorn's demands for change are more difficult to resist. Initially, his influence was on parade drill and haircuts. At the cremation ceremony of Bhumibol, observers heard the *mahadlek* marching to a new refrain ("Yok ok eup"!) while sharply rotating their heads 45 degrees.[80] Apart from the new salute, the police now have extremely short haircuts reminiscent of the Ayutthaya period and a new police uniform color at the behest of the new king.[81] Vajiralongkorn has now moved to exert influence on operations, training, structure, and doctrine. In the wake of the 2018 cave rescue of the 12 boys and their football coach, Vajiralongkorn decreed that the skills and knowledge acquired during the rescue be incorporated into the training of the Thailand's special forces, including its navy SEAL teams.[82] In 2019, he imposed a new training program on the army. The 10-week program, aimed at improving the stamina, diet, and attitude, of army recruits, would be implemented by a team of one hundred soldiers already trained under the methods of the Royal Security Command.[83] Most recently, some Thai army personnel are wearing a distinctive red-collared T-shirt beneath their standard camouflage uniform. These are graduates of a special three-month course run by the *mahadlek* wing of the Royal Security Command. The course covers mind, body, and palace protection, and teaches the palace code of values introduced by Rama VI (*rachasawat*).[84]

Some changes are not directly attributable to Vajiralongkorn but, as they appear in line with his connection with Australia and interest in physical fitness, may nonetheless reflect his growing influence on the Thai military. Thai army chief General Apirat has started restructuring Thai army divisions into Australian-style joint combat brigades.[85] This would be a significant reform, bringing units with diverse missions and specializations (for example, tanks and infantry) into single organizational and operational structures, with the object of achieving greater operational flexibility (combining armor and infantry has become common practice for counter-insurgency missions of Western militaries in the Middle East). I have heard informally that the new monarch's interest in military reform may in the future encompass adopting Australia's military doctrine.[86] There has also been the introduction of the "Smart Man Smart Soldier" program, introduced by the former army chief, now privy councilor, General Chalermchai Sitthisart, which explicitly aims at providing "inspiration for the people."[87]

Vajiralongkorn's very high--some would say severe—expectations with regard to military discipline and public image are also affecting the Thai security forces. In 2018, Vajiralongkorn signed an order expelling a high-ranking police general, Lt. Gen. Itthisak Krinchai, from the Royal Security Command for failing to behave as a role model, and not demonstrating the required sacrifice and dedication.[88] Although there is no official confirmation, there is speculation that another high-ranking police general, Lt. Gen. Surachate "Big Joke" Hakparn, may also have suffered the consequences of incurring the king's displeasure. Surachate, who had been a highly prominent spokesman for the immigration police and tipped for further promotion, was suddenly stripped of his rank in April 2019.[89] The reasons remain unknown, but some sources indicate that his management of police postings to a traffic management office in Bangkok may have been perceived as unsatisfactory.[90] There are also reports that Dhaveevatthana Palace in Bangkok is used to punish military officials deemed to have failed in the performance of their duties, including through having to undertake extremely demanding physical training.[91] Dhaveevatthana, as well as housing segments of the Royal Security Command, also contains a prison, the building of which was authorized during the time of the Yingluck administration (2011–14).

Finally, Vajiralongkorn has made appointments and accelerated promotions of favorites in a way that almost certainly has raised eyebrows and in some cases may have spurred resentment. Members of the royal household have been promoted at extraordinary speed, in one case from lowly lieutenant to major general in four years, a journey that would take entire careers for ordinary officers.[92] Given the instances of rapid ascent that have taken place in the monarch's private force, the RSC, this might seem less surprising for Thais. But there is evidence that the monarch's direction may have also affected outcomes in the mainstream force. In October 2020, former defense attaché to Germany Airbull Suttiwan was appointed to the top Thai air force job, over the heads of the normal contenders (the deputies, assistant, and chief of staff). This likely stoked anger among those who will conclude that royal connections have facilitated the rapid rise.[93] There is other evidence that palace connections are circumventing normal promotion and posting processes, in the police at least (some police officers have also resisted transfers to the palace police unit Ratchawallop Police Retainers, King's Guard 904 in the RSC, and been punished via disciplinary courses).[94] It is therefore plausible that similar palace influence is permeating Thai military promotional processes. In considering all of this, we must note that issues of favoritism and unfairness are not without historic precedent and have had serious consequences for the military-monarchy relationship. Rama VI founded a separate and favored paramilitary force, the Sua Pa (Wild tiger) regiment. Rama VII preferred royal family members for top positions. Both times disaffection ensued, contributing to attempts to overthrow the monarchy: the first attempt in 1912, which failed, and the second in 1932, which succeeded.[95]

Distrust below the Surface

In 2019, when the 1st and 11th Regiments of the King's Guard Ratchawallop were transferred from the army's 1st Division King's Guard to the Royal Security Command, parliamentarian and Secretary-General of the Future Forward Party Piyabutr Saengkanokkul asked two reasonable questions: (1) What was the emergency endangering the monarchy? and (2) Why were the Thai army and Thai ministry of defense, already explicitly tasked with protecting the monarchy, unable to do so?[96] No answer was given, and the order received the assent of all parliamentarians, apart from the Future Forward Party. Nonetheless, in debating the order the Thai parliament was clearly raising a valid question: What is the threat to the monarchy?

A pliable military at least prima facie committed to royalist ideology would appear to make for a solid partnership, including against the democracy movement that has subsequently arisen. So why has Vajiralongkorn decided to build his own force separate from the Thai armed forces and to spend a considerable proportion of his time in Germany? It is difficult to avoid the conclusion that there is a trust deficit in the military-monarchy partnership. Claudio Sopranzetti in this book notes that, under Rama X, fear has replaced love as the primary means of monarchical rule. At the same time, history and logic tell us that the coercive power of a military means that should it at any point decide that it would prefer "the role of chief executive instead of acting as a mere guardian," it has the material potential to attain this desire.[97]

Therefore, Rama X might well be prepared to take steps to raise the costs of disloyalty, even as he instills fear. This is certainly one way to understand why Rama X bolstered the Royal Security Command and, in addition, reduced the presence of regular Thai army units in urban Bangkok. In September 2018, the army announced that the 1st Cavalry Reconnaissance Company, 4th Tank Battalion, and 1st Cavalry Regiment would move to bases outside Bangkok in Lopburi and Saraburi.[98] The Army Intelligence Unit would move to Samut Sakhon. The official explanation was that the army had decided to ease traffic congestion. Indeed, there had been calls from opposition politicians for the army to reduce its holdings of land in downtown Bangkok to make way for parks, schools, and hospitals.[99] But the implications of the new force disposition, for a country that has experienced repeated coups, are impossible to ignore. The unavoidable conclusion is that moving units under the control of the army commander outside the perimeter of the city makes the Royal Security Command the principal repository of military force. This makes a coup without Vajiralongkorn's explicit assent more difficult.

Consistent with the less trustful relationship is the way in which the new monarch has dispensed with intermediaries in working with the Thai armed forces. In the Bhumibol era, the monarchy's control of the military was exercised through trusted advisers, principally General Prem Tinsulanonda, then president of the Privy Council. Prem vetted the promotional lists each year to ensure officers of the right caliber and political persuasions were ascending to the top spots.[100] The new king is reported to be more direct in managing the affairs of the military.[101] Prayuth, despite his expressed aspiration to become a second Prem Tinsulanonda, is highly unlikely to fulfill the role of intermediary between the palace and the military in the way that Prem did.[102]

Instead, Vajiralongkorn has his own direct and trusted personal connections, derived from his extensive experience of working with both the Royal Thai Army and the Royal Thai Air Force. As prince, Vajiralongkorn became close to Air Chief Marshal Chaiplik Disiyasirin, the chief of the Royal Thai Air Force in 2019.[103] His highly trusted personal private secretary, Air Chief Marshal Satitpong Sukvimol, is also ex–Thai air force. Vajiralongkorn may well have greater confidence in those military colleagues that he does in civilians. For example, Vajiralongkorn has increased the proportion of military officers serving in the Privy Council. In 2011 under Bhumibol, 42 percent (8 of 19) were military. In 2019 under Vajiralongkorn, this increased to 53 percent (8 of 15).[104] Of the current 11-member board of the Crown Property Bureau, eight, including the chairman, are military or police.[105] When he sent his privy councilors to discuss drought relief with the ministry of the interior, it was mostly his military appointees who attended the meeting.[106] At the same time, he is vetting the appointments process to ensure that control of the mainstream military remains in the hands of officers loyal to him.

Vajiralongkorn's balancing of military factions also suggests distrust. Vajiravudh has worked to stem the preponderance of senior army leaders from the army's Queen's Guard Division.[107] Prayuth himself is a former Queen's Guard, as are his deputy prime minister and confidante Prawit Wongsuwan and his interior minister, Anupong Paochinda. In the appointment of Apirat as army commander, this pattern was broken, and some have seen this as Vajiralongkorn acting to reassert the power of the King's Guard, to which he is closer.[108]

In sum, it is quite plausible that Vajiralongkorn may fear a backlash from the military itself. This could be from factions of the military, perhaps dissatisfied with the promotions process for the reasons set out earlier. They might even be conceivably dissatisfied with the political direction of the country. Currently, there are no signs of any division within the military, but there are historical precedents. During the 1950s the Thai military split, with the army and air force supporting Field Marshal Phibul Songkhram while more liberal factions within the navy supported former revolutionary and leftist lawyer Pridi Banomyong. Battles on the streets of Bangkok were the consequence. But a military move on the monarchy could also conceivably come from conservatives seeking a monarch more pliant and less hands-on with respect to the military, such as Bhumibol. One thing is certain: interfering with the military promotions process, such that there is frustration over lack of military promotion prospects, always carries risk. The 1932 revolution has already been mentioned. In more recent times we can add the 1991 and 2006 coups. The Thai coup of 1991 was in part the consequence of long running intra-army friction between various Chulachomklao Royal Military Academy (CRMA) class groups finally culminating in a major rift between the military and the government.[109] While there was not interference in promotions per se, there was dissatisfaction among class 5 CRMA graduates, that another CRMA group, class 7, had acquired higher military and political positions. In 2006 Prime Minister Thaksin Shinawatra was pushing the promotions of his classmates (class 10) from the Armed Forces Preparatory School at the expense of the choices of royal confidant General Prem.[110] This was one factor among several that contributed to the coup.

Conclusion

Every 3 February, the Thai military observes Veteran's Day (*wan thahan phan suek*). Leaders place wreaths at Victory Monument to commemorate fallen soldiers. In 2019, neither King Vajiralongkorn nor Prime Minister Prayuth attended. Instead, each sent a deputy. For Vajiralongkorn, General Surayud Chulanont attended, and for Prayuth, Deputy Prime Minister General Prawit

Wongsuwan. It was an eloquent statement of the way in which the government and the monarchy have come to represent separate poles of power in matters of defense and Thailand's armed forces. Increasingly, Vajiralongkorn is building a separate military, directly under his own command. With each day that passes, Vajiralongkorn's identity as a military king becomes more prominent. His four years at the Duntroon military college in Australia appear to have been formative. The legacy is a strong preference for physical fitness and correctness in matters of dress and presentation, especially for the military but also for his own staff and even for the broader Thai population. As a career military officer, albeit of unique status, Vajiralongkorn has his own network of military contacts and an intimate understanding of the business of organizing a military. He is influencing the promotions process in ways that could be fostering unease.

In the twilight years of Bhumibol's reign, Vajiralongkorn began the process of building a new military force under his personal command, the RSC. Since ascending the throne, the RSC has increased in size, legislative independence, and political and military importance as it has assumed the role of the major repository of military force within the capital. Largely unchallenged and unquestioned until recently, the precise need for this personal force has not been made fully transparent. The best guess is that the enlarged personal guard reflects both deep insecurity and a wish to return the profile of the monarchy to an even more absolutist character, when monarchs such as Vajiravudh and Prajadhipok exercised actual and not just ceremonial command and control over military forces.

The emergence of a vigorous democracy movement extolling monarchical reform may have justified, in Vajiralongkorn's estimation, the prudence of these military reforms. It may have also renewed the strength of the military-monarchy partnership sufficiently to conceal the distrust and irritation that abides within this profoundly important relationship.

Notes

1 Raymond, *Thai Military Power*, 69–73.

2 Jittraporn, "Kanchatratchakarnthaharn nai ratcha samai phrabatsomdet phrapokklaochaoyuhua pho so songphansiroihoksippaet," 61–69.

3 Jittraporn, "Kanchatratchakarnthaharn nai ratcha samai phrabatsomdet phrapokklaochaoyuhua pho so songphansiroihoksippaet," 85.

4 Hewison and Kengkij, "'Thai-Style Democracy.'"

5 Chong and Jenne, "Asian Military Evolutions."

6 Saichon, "Historical Legacy and the Emergence of Judicialization in the Thai State," 188.

7 "Prem: Bad Leaders Doomed to Failure," *The Nation*.

8 Handley, *The King Never Smiles*, 188–89.

9 Chinpha, Somdet phraboromma-orosathirat chaofa mahawachiralongkon sayam makut rachakuman, 75.

10 Handley, *The King Never Smiles*, 189.

11 "Education of the Crown Prince of Thailand in Australia," *Current Notes on International Affairs*.

12 "In-Brief," *Canberra Times*.

13 Australian Army, Report on the Royal Military College of Australia, 1974, 45.

14 Royal Military College of Australia, *Royal Military College Handbook, 1975*, 21.

15 Royal Military College of Australia, *Royal Military College Handbook, 1975*, 115–27.

16 Royal Military College of Australia, *Royal Military College Handbook, 1975*, 29.

17 "Royals at Duntroon," *Canberra Times*.

18 Conversation with staff at Bridges Memorial Library, Duntroon Royal Military College, 21 August 2019.

19 "Prince Graduates at RMC Duntroon," 22.

20 Royal Military College of Australia, *Royal Military College Handbook, 1975*, 128.

21 ANZAC stands for "Australian and New Zealand Army Corps," the combined force that landed at Gallipoli.

22 Chinpha, "Somdet phraboromma-orosathirat chaofa mahawachiralongkon sayam makut rachakuman," 109.

23 Chinpha, "Somdet phraboromma-orosathirat chaofa mahawachiralongkon sayam makut rachakuman," 129.

24 Phinit, *Banthuek prawatsat na mai ratchakanthi sip haeng borommaratchakriwong somdet phrachaoyuhua maha Vajiralongkorn bodinthara thepphaya warangkun*, 110.

25 Committee of Inquiry into the Royal Military College, Report of the Committee of Inquiry into the Royal Military College, 19.

26 Committee of Inquiry into the Royal Military College, Report of the Committee of Inquiry into the Royal Military College, 18.

27 Evans, "Hazing in the ADF," 116.

28 "Prince Graduates at RMC Duntroon," *Canberra Times*, 22.

29 ทรงพระเจริญ *Song phra charoen*, 24.

30 Commonwealth of Australia, Inspector-General of the Australian Defence Force Afghanistan Inquiry Report.

31 By 1975, the CPT controlled 412 villages, and another 6,000 villages were under CPT influence (Chai-Anan, Kusuma, and Suchit, *From Armed Suppression to Political Offensive*, 122).

32 Handley, *The King Never Smiles*, 264.

33 Marks, "The Meo Hill Tribe Problem in North Thailand."

34 Central Intelligence Agency, Intelligence Memorandum, "Insurgency in Thailand."

35 Author's visit to the Chinese Martyr's Museum, Doi Mae Salong, Chiang Rai, February 2018.

36 "Guerillas Attack Prince," *Canberra Times*.

37 "Phrapricha ro sip phu song klahan pok pong pracha jak phai khukkham," *Thai Rath Online*.

38 Apirat, "Phaen din khong rao nai moommong dan khwammankhong doi bigdaeng pol ek aphirat khongsomphong."

39 Ministry of Culture, *Nueng nai okat phra ratcha phithi maha mongkon chaleom phrachonphansa ha rop yisippaet karakadakhom songphanharoihasipha asirawad somdet phraboroma orosathirat chao fa mahawachiralongkon sayammaku-tratchakuman*, 22.

40 *Song phra charoen*, 78.

41 "Crown Prince Returns to Visit Some Old Friends," *Canberra Times*.

42 Prime Minister's Department, Untitled Media Release.

43 *Hasip phansa maha wachiralongkon*, 63

44 *Hasip phansa maha wachiralongkon*, 24.

45 Phinit, *Banthuek prawatsat*, 201–2.

46 Reed, "Thais Question King's Spending as Economy Takes a Hit from Covid-19," *Financial Times*.

47 Phinit, *Banthuek prawatsat*, 119.

48 *Government Gazette*, "Phraratchabanyat chatrabiap ratchakan krasuang kalahom."

49 Wassana, "Elite Royal Guards Go on Defense Ministry Payroll."

50 Wassana, "Elite Royal Guards Go on Defense Ministry Payroll."

51 *Government Gazette*, "Phraratchabanyat kanthawai khwam plot phai po so songphanharoihoksip lem roisamsipsi tonthi roiyisiphok ko ratchak-itchanubeksa siphok thanwakhom songphanharoihoksip."

52 "Mahad lek ying ongkarak sut-ngarm sa-nga," *YouTube*.

53 Thai Lawyer Blog, "All Royal Agencies Will Now Be Overseen by the King."

54 In this usage, the "904" refers to Vajiralongkorn, as the police previously had a code-name system for designating each royal family member as follows: 901 = Rama 9, 902 = Queen Sirikit, 903 = Ubolratana, 904 = Vajiralongkorn, etc. Plianchue bo ko to pho po pen bo ko tamruaj mahadlek ratchawallop raksa phra-ong hai pol tamruaj torsak phubangkhapkarn, *Manager Online*.

55 Thai Rath, "Nuai raksapra-ong kongthapthai."

56 Government Gazette, "Lem roisamsiphok ton phiset roi ngo ratchakitchanubeksa yisipsam mesayon songphanharoihoksipsong prakatsanaknaikratmontri rueang phraratchathan phrarachanuyat plian plaeng nuaithahanraksapraong lae nuaithahan nai phraong."

57 Government Gazette, "Lem roisamsiphok ton phiset roi ngo ratchakitchanubeksa yisipsam mesayon songphanharoihoksipsong prakatsanaknaikratmontri rueang phraratchathan phrarachanuyat plian plaeng nuaithahanraksapraong lae nuaithahan nai phraong."

58 Piyabutr, "Maihenduai woroko oonyaikamlang phon lae ngop khong piyabut saengoknokkun."

59 "Thai King's Yellow and Blue Volunteers Boost His Support, Visibility," *Reuters*.

60 Handley, *The King Never Smiles*, 222

61 Handley, *The King Never Smiles*, 236.

62 Handley, *The King Never Smiles*, 224.

63 Siam Commercial Bank, "SCB Executives and Staff Pledge Loyalty and Commitment to Royal Volunteer Spirit Program (904 Vor Por Ror)."

64 Pravit, "New Lecture at Thammasat University Extols Chakri Dynasty."

65 "King Doesn't Want Lavish Coronation," *Bangkok Post*.

66 "King Doesn't Want Lavish Coronation," *Bangkok Post*.

67 Mérieau, "Seeking More Power."

68 Mongkol, "Ombudsman Refers Oath Blunder to Constitutional Court."

69 Raymond, "Mnemonic Hegemony, Spatial Hierarchy and Thailand's Official Commemoration of the Second World War."

70 Pravit, "Monument Marking Defeat of Royalist Rebels Removed in Dead of Night." The Boworadet Rebellion was named after Prince Boworadet, a cousin of King Prajadhipok who led an armed counter-revolt against the People's Party a year after the 1932 revolution, attacking from outside Bangkok.

71 Panu and Panarat, "Thai Army Holds Ceremony Countering Pro-Democracy Protesters View of History."

72 Facebook post of Somsak Jeamteerasakul, dated 25 January. https://www.facebook.com/somsakjeam/posts/2653860824667180, accessed 9 December 2020.

73 "Is Thailand's Political Future with the Future Forward Party or the Military?," *Thai Enquirer*.

74 "Students Vow to Ramp Up Protests in Coming Weeks," *Bangkok Post*.

75 Presentation by Puangthong Pawakapan, Special Thai Update webinar, Southeast Asia Institute, Australian National University, 1 December 2020; with regards to information operations, on 30 November Twitter suspended an account @ji-tarsa_school created in September 2020 and responsible for tens of thousands of pro-royalist tweets. "Twitter Suspends Thai Royalist Account Linked to Influence Campaign," *Reuters*.

76 Beech and Suhartono, "A Feared Law to Protect the Monarchy Returns amid Thailand's Protests."

77 "King Declares Love for All Says Thailand 'Land of Compromise,'" *Bangkok Post*.

78 Matthews, "Civil-Military Relations in Thailand," 51.

79 Raymond, *Thai Military Power*, 131.

80 T-News, "Sinsongsai poet thima khamsang yok ok uep tha thamkhwamkhaorop mai khong thahannaiphraratphithi sa-nga ngot-ngam lae khem khaeng!!!."

81 Teeranai, "Model Soldiers to Implement HM King's Training Course."

82 Chayanit, "King Orders Military Training in Cave Rescue."

83 Teeranai, "Model Soldiers to Implement HM King's Training Course."

84 Wassana 'Nanuam, "Who Are the Red-Collared Soldiers?"

85 Pratya, "Monitor 'bigdaeng' chak phaen patirup kongthap lasut su The Great Hack lae buempuanmueang."

86 Private conversation with Thai military officer, August 2019. Doctrine is the basic principles of warfighting that guide training, procurement, and operational planning for military organizations. Doctrine has been a problematic area for the Thai military since it adopted military doctrine from the United States in the 1950s largely without adaptation. United States military doctrine is designed for a much larger organization with more extensive resources. Moreover, because each of the Thai services adopted the military doctrine of its counterpart in the United States, the armed forces as a whole have limited capacity to operate as a joint force. For a relatively small military such as the Thai military, a joint approach is a more efficient use of resources.

87 Smart Man Smart Soldier, "Tonkamlangphon thang thahan nai sangkat kongthapbok."

88 Teeranai, "King Expels Cop from Royal Guard for Lack of Dedication."

89 Teeranai, "Gov't Moves 'Big Joke' to Obscure Civilian Post."

90 Personal communication with Thai academic in 2019.

91 Pavin, "Dhaveevatthana Prison."

92 "Senthangkiarttiyot chaokhun phra sininat philatkalayani," BBC News.

93 Tappanai, "Dark Horse: Rise Of New Air Force Chief Raises Eyebrows."

94 "Gov't Seeks to Slap MP with Royal Insult Charge for Debate Expose," *Khaosod English*.

95 Kullada, *The Rise and Decline of Thai Absolutism*, 130; Directorate of Education and Research, *Prawat kongthapthai nai rop songroipi*, 255.

96 Piyabutr noted that the order referenced Article 172 of the 2017 Constitution of Thailand, which states that: "For the purpose of maintaining national or public safety or national economic security, or averting public calamity, the King may issue an Emergency Decree which shall have force as an Act. The issuance of an Emergency Decree under paragraph one shall be made only when the Council of Ministers is of the opinion that it is an emergency of necessity and urgency which is unavoidable" ("Maihenduai pho ro ko oonyaikamlangphon lae ngop khong piyabut saengkanokkun").

97 Chong and Jenne, "Asian Military Evolutions."

98 "Army Bases to Leave Capital to Ease Traffic," *Bangkok Post*.

99 "Thai Liberal Party Vows to Reform Thai Army," *Prachatai*.

100 Handley, "The King Never Smiles," 422.

101 Macan-markar, "All the King's Men."

102 Wassana, *Bigtu Nayok hoad man ha*, 66.

103 Chambers, "A Rebuke against a Sister and the Personalizing of Monarchical Control."

104 Lawyer's Council of Thailand under Royal Patronage, *Phrabatsomdet phrachao yuhua kap khana ongkhamontri*.

105 Crown Property Bureau Board, 2019.

106 Prachachat, "Kao ongkhamontri mahatthai nomnam phraratkrasae rapsang ro sip kae phailaeng."

107 The Queen's Guard denotes the 21st Infantry Regiment and is part of the 2nd Infantry Division, located east of Bangkok in the province of Prachinburi. Soldiers from the Queen's Guard were consistently promoted to the army commander position between 2007 and 2015, and many of the current government ministers within the Prayuth government were from this lineage.

108 Macan-markar, "All the King's Men."

109 Ukrist, "A Different Coup d'État," 125.

110 Ockey, "Broken Power: The Thai Military in the Aftermath of the 2006 Coup."

References

Apirat Kongsompong. "Phaen din khong rao nai moommong dan khwammankhong doi bigdaeng pol ek aphirat khongsomphong แผ่นดิน-ของเราในมุมมองด้านความมั่นคง โดย บิ๊กแดง พล.อ.อภิรัชต์ คงสมพงษ์" [Our homeland from the point of view of security]. *YouTube*, 11 October

2019. https://www.youtube.com/watch?v=L4nkevF1P8g, accessed 28 October 2019.

"Army Bases to Leave Capital to Ease Traffic." *Bangkok Post*, 4 September 2018. https://www.bangkokpost.com/thailand/general/1533362/army-bases-to-leave-capital-to-ease-traffic, accessed 23 September 2019.

Australian Army. Report on the Royal Military College of Australia, 1974. Canberra: Australian Government Publishing Service, 1975.

Battye, Noel Alfred. "The Military, Government and Society in Siam, 1868–1910: Politics and Military Reform during the Reign of King Chulalongkorn." PhD diss., Cornell University, 1974.

Beech, Hannah, and Muktita Suhartono. "A Feared Law to Protect the Monarchy Returns amid Thailand's Protests." *New York Times*, 25 November 2020. https://www.nytimes.com/2020/11/25/world/asia/thailand-protest-lese-majeste-monarchy.html, accessed 18 June 2021.

Chai-Anan Samudavanija, Kusuma Snitwongse, and Suchit Bunbongkarn. *From Armed Suppression to Political Offensive: Attitudinal Transformation of Thai Military Officers since 1976*. Bangkok: Institute of Security and International Studies, Chulalongkorn University, 1990.

Chambers, Paul. "A Rebuke against a Sister and the Personalizing of Monarchical Control." *New Mandala*, 9 February 2019. https://www.newmandala.org/a-rebuke-against-a-sister-and-the-personalising-of-monarchical-control/, accessed 23 September 2019.

Chayanit Itthipongmaetee. "King Orders Military Training in Cave Rescue." *Khaosod English*, 4 July 2018. http://www.khaosodenglish.com/featured/2018/07/04/king-orders-military-training-in-cave-rescue/, accessed 5 July 2018.

Central Intelligence Agency. Intelligence Memorandum, "Insurgency in Thailand," 30 October 1972, no. 2080/72. Approved for release 20 October 2009.

Chinpha Onrueang. "Somdet phraboromma-orosathirat chaofa mahawachira-longkon sayam makut rachakuman สมเด็จพระบรมโอรสาธิราชเจ้าฟ้ามหาวชิ-ราลงกรณสยามมกุฎราชกุมาร" [His Royal Highness Prince Vajiralongkorn]. Bangkok: Lions Club Dusit, 1973.

Chong, Alan, and Nicole Jenne. "Asian Military Evolutions: Entrenching Varieties of Civil-Military Fusion and Its Security Initiatives in Asia." In *Asian Military Evolutions: Civil-Military Relations in Asia*, ed. Alan Chong and Nicole Jenne, 1–29. Bristol: Bristol University Press, 2023.

Committee of Inquiry into the Royal Military College. Report of the Committee of Inquiry into the Royal Military College, 24 April 1970. Bridges Memorial Library, Royal Military College, Duntroon, Canberra.

Commonwealth of Australia. Inspector-General of the Australian Defence Force Afghanistan Inquiry Report. 2009. https://www.defence.gov.au/about/reviews-inquiries/afghanistan-inquiry, accessed 30 August 2023

"Crown Prince Returns to Visit Some Old Friends." *Canberra Times*, 5 December 1981, 2.

Crown Property Bureau Board. 2019. https://www.crownproperty.or.th/คณะกรรมการทรัพย์สินพระมหากษัตริย์, accessed 16 October 2019.

Directorate of Education and Research. *Prawat kongthapthai nai rop songroipi* ประวัติกองทัพไทยในรอบ ๒๐๐ ปี พ.ศ.๒๓๒๕–๒๕๒๕ [Royal Thai Armed Forces: History of the Thai armed forces over 200 years, B.E. 2325–2525 (AD 1782–1982)]. Bangkok: Supreme Command Headquarters, 1982.

"Education of the Crown Prince of Thailand in Australia." *Current Notes on International Affairs* 41.8 (August 1970):437.

Evans, R. "Hazing in the ADF: A Culture of Denial?" *Australian Army Journal*, Culture Edition, 10.3 (2013):113–27.

Government Gazette. "Lem roisamsiphok ton phiset roi ngo ratchakitchanubeksa yisipsam mesayon songphanharoihoksipsong prakat samnaknayokrattha-montri rueang phraratchathan phrarachanuyat plian plaeng nuaithahanrak-sapra-ong lae nuaithahan nai phraong เล่ม ๑๓๖ ตอนพิเศษ ๑๐๗ ง ราชกิจจานุเบกษา ๒๓ เมษายน ๒๕๖๒, ประกาศสำนักนายกรัฐมนตรี เรื่อง พระราชทานพระราชานุญาตเปลี่ยนแปลงหน่วยทหารรักษาพระองค์และ-หน่วยทหารในพระองค์" [Prime ministerial announcement regarding changes to Royal Security Units 136/100, 23 April 2019].

———. "Lem roisamsiphok tonthi roisam ko ratchakitchanubeksa samsip kanyayon songphanharoihoksipsong phra ratcha kamnot one atra kalang-phon lae ngoppramanbangsuan khongkongthapbok kongthapthai krasuang kalahom paipenkhong nuaibanchaka tawai khwamplotphairaksapraong sueng pensuanratchakan nai phraong pho so songphanharoihoksipsong เล่ม ๑๓๖ ตอนที่ ๑๐๓ ก ราชกิจจานุเบกษา ๓๐ กันยายน ๒๕๖๒, พระ-ราชกำหนด โอนอัตรากำลังพลและงบประมาณบางส่วน ของกองทัพบก กองทัพไทย กระทรวงกลาโหม ไปเป็นของหน่วยบัญชาการถวายความปลอด-ภัยรักษาพระองค์ซึ่งเป็นส่วนราชการในพระองค์ พ.ศ. ๒๕๖๒" [Royal order transferring personnel and budget from the army and ministry of defense to the Royal Security Command 136/103, 30 September 2019].

———. "Phraratchabanyat chatrabiap ratchakan krasuang kalahom (chabap thi song) pho so songphanharoihasiphok roisamsip thon thi roikao ko ratchak-itchanubeksa yisip phritchikayaon songphanharoihasiphok พระราชบัญญัติ-จัดระเบียบราชการกระทรวงกลาโหม (ฉบับที่ ๒) พ.ศ. ๒๕๕๖ ๑๓๐ ตอนที่ ๑๐๘ ก ราชกิจจานุเบกษา ๒๐ พฤศจิกายน ๒๕๕๖" [Regulation of the Ministry of Defense 120/109, 20 November 2013].

———. "Phraratchabanyat kanthawai khwam plot phai po so songphanharoi-hoksip lem roisamsipsi tonthi roiyisiphok ko ratchakitchanubeksa siphok thanwakhom songphanharoihoksip พระราชบัญญัติการถวายความปลอดภัย พ.ศ. ๒๕๖๐, เล่ม ๑๓๔ ตอนที่ ๑๒๖ ก ราชกิจจานุเบกษา ๑๖ ธันวาคม ๒๕๖๐" [Provision of Security Act 134/136, 16 December 2017].

———. "Phraratchakritsadika chat-rabiapratchakan lae kan borihan ngan bukkon khong ratchakan nai phra-ong pho so songphanharoihoksip lem roisamsipsi tonthi hasip-et ko ratchakitchanubeksa sip phruetsaphakhom songphan-haroihoksip พระราชกฤษฎีกาจัดระเบียบราชการและการบริหารงานบุค-คลของราชการในพระองค์ พ.ศ. ๒๕๖๐ เล่ม ๑๓๔ ตอนที่ ๕๑ ก ราชกิจ-จานุเบกษา ๑๐ พฤษภาคม ๒๕๖๐" [Regulation regarding administration of servants in the royal household, 10 May 2017, 134/51].

"Gov't Seeks to Slap MP with Royal Insult Charge for Debate Expose." *Khaosod English*, 20 February 2021. https://www.khaosodenglish.com/politics/2021/02/20/govt-seeks-to-slap-mp-with-royal-insult-charge-for-debate-expose/, accessed 30 August 2023.

"Guerillas Attack Prince." *Canberra Times*, 15 February 1977, 5.

Handley, Paul M. *The King Never Smiles: A Biography of Thailand's Bhumibol Adulyadej*. New Haven, CT: Yale University Press, 2006.

Hasip phansa mahawachiralongkon ๕๐ พรรษา มหาวชิราลงกรณ์ [Fiftieth birthday of Prince Vajiralongkorn]. Ayutthaya: Ratchapat Institute, 2002.

Hewison, Kevin, and Kengkij Kitirianglarp. "'Thai-Style Democracy': The Royalist Struggle for Thailand's Politics." In *Saying the Unsayable: Monarchy and Democracy in Thailand*, ed. Soren Ivarsson and Lotte Isager, 179–202. Copenhagen: NIAS Press, 2010.

"In-Brief," *Canberra Times*, 7 September 1970, 3.

"Is Thailand's Political Future with the Future Forward Party or the Military?." *Thai Enquirer*, 20 February 2020. https://www.thaienquirer.com/8143/opinion-is-thailands-political-future-with-the-future-forward-party-or-the-military/, accessed 27 March 2021.

Jittraporn Chaikanta. "การจัดราชการทหารในรัชสมัยพระบาทสมเด็จพระปกเกล้าเจ้าอยู่หัว (พ.ศ.๒๔๖๘—๒๔๗๗) Kanchatratchakarnthaharn nai ratcha samai phra-batsomdet phrapokklaochaoyuhua pho so songphansiroihoksippaet—Songphansiroichetsipchet" [The organization of the Royal Thai Armed Forces in the reign of King Rama VII, 1925–1935]. MA thesis, Chulalongkorn University, 1978.

"King Declares Love for All Says Thailand 'Land of Compromise.'" *Bangkok Post*, 2 November 2020, https://www.bangkokpost.com/thailand/politics/2012131/king-declares-love-for-all-calls-thailand-land-of-compromise, accessed 3 February 2021.

"King Doesn't Want Lavish Coronation." *Bangkok Post*, 23 June 2018. https://www.bangkokpost.com/news/general/1490554/king-doesnt-want-lavish-coronation, accessed 23 June 2018.

Kullada Kesboonchoo Mead. *The Rise and Decline of Thai Absolutism*. London: Routledge, 2004.

Lawyer's Council of Thailand under Royal Patronage. *Phrabatsomdet phrachao yuhua kap khana ongkhamontri* พระบาทสมเด็จพระเจ้าอยู่หัวกับคณะองค-มนตรี [The king and the Privy Council]. Bangkok: Amarin, 2013.

Macan-markar, Marwaan. "All the King's Men: Thai Military Power Shifts away from Prayuth." *Nikkei Asian Review*, 2 July 2019. https://asia.nikkei.com/Spotlight/Asia-Insight/All-the-king-s-men-Thai-military-power-shifts-away-from-Prayuth, accessed 19 September 2019.

"Mahad lek ying ongkarak sdt-ngarm sa-nga มหาดเล็กหญิงองค์รักษ์สุดงามสง่า" [The beautiful female *mahadlek*]. *YouTube*, 25 September 2017. https://www.youtube.com/watch?v=URliTdSA5_Q, accessed 19 September 2019.

Marks, Thomas. "The Meo Hill Tribe Problem in North Thailand." *Asian Survey* 13.10 (1973):929–44.

Matthews, Warren E. "Civil-Military Relations in Thailand: Military Autonomy or Civilian Control?" Master's thesis, Naval Postgraduate School, Monterey, California, 2005.

Mérieau, Eugénie. "Seeking More Power, Thailand's New King Is Moving the Country away from Being a Constitutional Monarchy." *The Conversation*, 3 February 2017. https://theconversation.com/seeking-more-power-thailands-new-king-is-moving-the-country-away-from-being-a-constitutional-monarchy-71637, accessed 24 October 2019.

Ministry of Culture. *เนื่องในโอกาสพระราชพิธีมหามงคลเฉลิมพระชนมพรรษา ๕ รอบ ๒๘ กรกฎาคม ๒๕๕๘ อาศิรวาท สมเด็จพระบรมโอรสาธิราช เจ้าฟ้ามหาวชิราลงกรณ์ สยามมกุฎราชกุมาร Nueng nai okat phra ratcha phithi maha mongkon chaleom phrachonphansa ha rop yisippaet karakadakhom songphanharoihasipha asirawad somdet phraboroma orosathirat chao fa mahawachiralongkon sayammakutratchakuman* [On the occasion of the sixtieth birthday of Prince Vajiralongkorn]. Bangkok: Rungsinkanphim, 2015.

Mongkol Bangprapa. "Ombudsman Refers Oath Blunder to Constitutional Court." *Bangkok Post*, 27 August 2019. https://www.bangkokpost.com/thailand/politics/1737663, accessed 30 August 2023.

Ockey, J. "Broken Power: The Thai Military in the Aftermath of the 2006 Coup" in Pavin, '*Good Coup' Gone Bad*, 49–78.

Panu Wongcha-um and Panarat Thepgumpanat. "Thai Army Holds Ceremony Countering Pro-Democracy Protesters View of History." *Reuters*, 25 June 2020.

https://www.reuters.com/article/us-thailand-protests-idCAKBN23W1FU, accessed 14 February 2021.

Pavin Chachavalpongpun. "Dhaveevatthana Prison: Hell on Earth in Thailand." *Japan Times*, 2 June 2017. https://www.japantimes.co.jp/opinion/2017/06/02/commentary/world-commentary/dhaveevatthana-prison-hell-earth-thailand/#.XY7YWUb7Suk, accessed 28 September 2019.

———, ed. *'Good Coup' Gone Bad: Thailand's Political Development since Thaksin's Downfall*. Singapore: Institute of Southeast Asian Studies, 2014.

Phinit Chanthon. *บันทึกประวัติศาสตร์หน้าใหม่ รัชกาลที่ ๑๐ แห่งบรมราชจักรีวงศ์ สมเด็จพระเจ้าอยู่หัวมหาวชิราลงกรณ์ บดินทรเทพยวรางกูร Banthuek prawatsat na mai ratchakanthi sip haeng borommaratchakriwong somdet phrachaoyuhua maha Vajiralongkorn bodinthara thepphaya warangkun* [Recording a new page in history: King Vajiralongkorn Rama X]. Bangkok: Panyachon Distributor, 2017.

"Phrapricha ro sip phu song klahan pok pong pracha jak phai khukkham พระปรีชา ร.10 ผู้ทรงกล้าหาญ ปกป้องประชาจากภัยคุกคาม" [The intuition of the royal hero Ror 10, protected the people from threats]. *Thai Rath Online*, 2 December 2016. https://www.thairath.co.th/content/796941, accessed 6 August 2019.

Piyabutr Saengkanokkul. "Maihenduai pho ro ko oonyaikamlangphon lae ngop khong piyabut saengkanokkun ไม่เห็นด้วย พ.ร.ก.โอนย้ายกำลังพลและงบ ของปิยบุตร แสงกนกกุล" [Disagree with the Act Transferring Personnel and Budget]. *Future Forward Party*, 17 October 2019. https://futureforward-party.org/8852, accessed 20 October 2019. See also "Piyabut aphiprai maihenduai pho ro ko oonyaikamlangphon lae ngop thahan ปิยบุตร" อภิปราย "ไม่เห็นด้วย" พ.ร.ก.โอนย้ายกำลังพลและงบทหารฯ 17 ตุลาคม 2562" [Piyabutr disagrees with the Act Transferring Personnel and Budget] *YouTube*, 17 October 2019. https://youtu.be/s4BSezj5WEs?si=jV2WWRX 3pUntwRe, accessed 30 August 2023.

"Plianchue bo ko to pho po pen bo ko tamruaj mahadlek ratchawallop raksa phra-ong hai pol tamruaj torsak phubangkhapkarn เปลี่ยนชื่อ บก.ถปฬพ.เป็น บก.ตำรวจมหาดเล็กราชวัลลภรักษาพระองค์ 904 ให้ พล.ต.ต.ต่อศักดิ์ ผู้บังคับการ" [Change of name: Mahadlek Ratchawallop 904 for Commander Major General Torsak]. *Manager Online*, 28 January 2019. https://mgronline.com/crime/detail/9620000009522, accessed 19 September.

Prachachat. "9 องคมนตรี-มหาดไทย น้อมนำพระราชกระแสรับสั่ง ร. 10 แก้ภัยแล้ง Kao ongkhamontri mahatthai nomnam phraratchakrasae rapsang ro sip kae phailaeng" [Nine privy councilors meet interior ministry to convey royal orders on solving drought]. *Prachachat*, 20 August 2019. https://www.prachachat.net/general/news-362495, accessed 16 October 2019.

Pratya Nongnut. "Monitor 'bigdaeng' chak phaen patiroop kongthap lasut su The Great Hack lae buempuanmueang มอนิเตอร์ 'บิกแดง' จากแผนปฏิรูป-กองทัพล่าสุด ส่ 'The Great Hack' และ 'บึ้มป่วนเมือง'" [Monitoring "big daeng" from the latest military reform plan to the Great Hack and country chaos]. *Matichon Weekly*, 9–15 August 2019. https://www.matichonweekly.com/column/article_220018, accessed 18 October 2019.

Pravit Rojanaphruk. "Monument Marking Defeat of Royalist Rebels Removed in Dead of Night." *Khaosod English*, 28 December 2018. http://www.khaosodenglish.com/politics/2018/12/28/monument-marking-defeat-of-royalist-rebels-removed-in-dead-of-night/, accessed 29 December 2018.

———. "New Lecture at Thammasat University Extols Chakri Dynasty." *Khaosod English*, 28 August 2018. http://www.khaosodenglish.com/news/2018/08/28/new-lecture-at-thammasat-university-extols-chakri-dynasty/, accessed 29 August 2018.

"Prayut Orders Armed Forces to Study Possibility of Voluntary Military Conscription." *The Nation*, 21 September 2019. https://www.nationthailand.com/news/30376519, accessed 21 September 2019.

"Prem: Bad Leaders Doomed to Failure." *The Nation*, 1 September, 2006, 9.

"Prince Graduates at RMC Duntroon, Rules Bent for Queen of Thailand." *Canberra Times*, 10 December 1975, 22.

Prime Minister's Department. Untitled Media Release. Canberra, 6 April 1987.

Raymond, Gregory Vincent. *Thai Military Power: A Culture of Strategic Accommodation*. Copenhagen: NIAS Press, 2018.

———. Mnemonic Hegemony, Spatial Hierarchy and Thailand's Official Commemoration of the Second World War." *South East Asia Research*, 26.2 (2018):176–93. https://doi.org/10.1177/0967828X18773607.

Reed, John. "Thais Question King's Spending as Economy Takes a Hit from Covid-19." *Financial Times*, 17 September 2020. https://www.ft.com/content/5982ddoc-5312-4918-847e-f206b1a0b192, accessed 30 August 2023.

Royal Military College of Australia. *Royal Military College Handbook, 1975*. Duntroon, Australian Capital Territory, 1975.

"Royals at Duntroon." *Canberra Times*, 3 December 1971, 7.

"Ruchak sip-ha ongkhamontri nai phrabatsomdet phrachao yu hua ratchakan thi sip รู้จัก 15 องคมนตรี ใน พระบาทสมเด็จพระเจ้าอยู่หัว รัชกาลที่ 10" [Know the 15 privy councilors of Rama X]. *Mthai*, 8 May 2019. https://news.mthai.com/webmaster-talk/728556.html, accessed 1 October 2019.

Saichon Sattayanurak. "Historical Legacy and the Emergence of Judicialization in the Thai State." In *Thai Politics in Translation: Monarchy, Democracy and the Supra-constitution*, ed. Michael K. Connors and Ukrist Pathmanand, 187–216. Copenhagen: NIAS Press, 2021.

"Senthangkiarttiyot chaokhun phra sininat philatkalayani เส้นทางเกียรติยศ เจ้าคุณพระสินีนาฏ พิลาสกัลยาณี" [Sineenat's promotional path]. BBC News, 29 July 2019. https://www.bbc.com/thai/thailand-49148671, accessed 10 August 2019.

Siam Commercial Bank. "SCB Executives and Staff Pledge Loyalty and Commitment to Royal Volunteer Spirit Program (904 VorPorRor)." 2019. https://www.scb.co.th/en/about-us/news/jul-2019/csr-nws-royalvolunteer-2562.html, accessed 18 October 2019.

Smart Man Smart Soldier. "Tonkamlangphon thang thahan nai sangkat kongthapbok ตอน กำลังพลทางทหารในสังกัดกองทัพบก" [Personnel in the army]. *YouTube*, 8 November 2018. https://www.youtube.com/watch?v=J34SAvDbGz0, accessed 14 October 2019.

Song phra charoen ทรงพระเจริญ [Long live the king]. Bangkok: DK Publishing, 2017.

Storey, Ian. "Thailand's Perennial Kra Canal Project: Pros, Cons and Potential Game Changers." *Perspective* [ISEAS, Yusof Ishak Institute] 76 (24 September 2019).

"Students Vow to Ramp Up Protests in Coming Weeks." *Bangkok Post*, 1 March 2020. https://www.bangkokpost.com/thailand/politics/1868569/students-vow-to-ramp-up-protests-in-coming-weeks, accessed 16 February 2021.

Tappanai. "Dark Horse: Rise Of New Air Force Chief Raises Eyebrows." *Khaosod English*, 6 October 2020. https://www.khaosodenglish.com/politics/2020/10/06/dark-horse-rise-of-new-air-force-chief-raises-eyebrows/, accessed 20 February 2021.

Teeranai Charuvastra. "King Expels Cop from Royal Guard for Lack of Dedication." *Khaosod English*, 2 November 2018. http://www.khaosodenglish.com/news/crimecourtscalamity/2018/11/02/king-expels-cop-from-royal-guard-for-lack-of-dedication/, accessed 3 November 2018.

———. "Gov't Moves 'Big Joke' to Obscure Civilian Post." *Khaosod English*, 9 April 2019. http://www.khaosodenglish.com/news/crimecourtscalamity/2019/04/09/govt-deflects-questions-on-big-joke-downfall/, accessed 28 September 2019.

———. "Model Soldiers to Implement HM King's Training Course." *Khaosod English*, 22 August 2019. http://www.khaosodenglish.com/politics/2019/08/22/model-soldiers-to-implement-hm-kings-training-course/, accessed 23 August 2019.

———. "Special Police Unit Rebranded as King's Guard." *Khaosod English*, 29 January 2019. www.khaosodenglish.com/politics/2019/01/29/special-police-unit-rebranded-as-kings-guard/. accessed 19 September 2019.

"Thai King's Yellow and Blue Volunteers Boost His Support, Visibility." *Reuters*, 4 September 2018. https://www.reuters.com/article/us-thailand-king-volunteers/thai-kings-yellow-and-blue-volunteers-boost-his-support-visibility-idUSKCN1LK036, accessed 5 September 2018.

Thai Lawyer Blog. "All Royal Agencies Will Now Be Overseen by the King." 4 May 2017. http://www.thailawforum.com/blog/all-royal-agencies-will-now-be-overseen-by-the-king, accessed 24 May 2019.

"Thai Liberal Party Vows to Reform Thai Army." *Prachatai*, 5 April 2018. https://prachatai.com/english/node/7707, accessed 20 July 2018.

Thai Rath. "Nuai raksapra-ong kongthapthai หน่วยรักษาพระองค์กองทัพไทย" [The King's Guard]. *YouTube*, 2 December 2014. https://www.youtube.com/watch?v=hnu6FyL2lkI, accessed 30 April 2020.

"Thailand's Rising Political Star Thanathorn under Fire as Election Nears." *The Straits Times*, 26 February 2019. https://www.straitstimes.com/asia/se-asia/thailands-rising-political-star-thanathorn-under-fire-as-election-nears, accessed 22 October 2019.

Thongchai Winichikul. "Thailand's Royal Democracy in Crisis." In *After the Coup: The National Council for Peace and Order and the Future of Thailand*, ed. Michael J. Montesano, Terence Chong, and Mark Heng, 282–307. Singapore: ISEAS, Yusof-Ishak Institute, 2019.

T-News. "Sinsongsai poet thima khamsang yok ok uep tha tham khwamkhaorop mai khongthaharn naiphraratchaphithi sa-nga ngot-ngam lae khem khaeng สิ้นสงสัย!!! เปิดทีมาคำสั่ง 'ยกอก … อึ๊บ' ท่าทำความเคารพใหม่ของทหาร-ในพระราชพิธีฯ สง่า งดงาม และเข้มแข็ง!" [End any doubt! The background of the order to "ok eup" posture that creates new respect for soldiers in royal ceremonies ornate, beautiful, and strong], 30 October 2017. https://bit.ly/2Bzraa1, accessed 26 September 2019.

"Twitter Suspends Thai Royalist Account Linked to Influence Campaign." *Reuters*, 30 November 2020. https://www.reuters.com/article/thailand-protests-royalists-idUSKBN28910J, accessed 3 December 2020.

Ukrist Pathmanand. "A Different Coup d'État." *Journal of Contemporary Asia* 38.1 (2008):124–42.

"Walking the Line." *Sydney Morning Herald*, 21–22 September 2019, 27 and 32–33.

Wassana Nanuam. "Elite Royal Guards Go on Defence Ministry Payroll." *Bangkok Post*, 13 February 2014. https://www.bangkokpost.com/opinion/opinion/394760/elite-royal-guards-go-on-defence-ministry-payroll%200n%2024%20February%202019, accessed 24 February 2019.

———. "Thahan Khodaeng Khue Khrai ทหาร คอแดง" คือ ใคร?" [Who are the red-collared soldiers?]. *LapLuangPrangChannel*.com, 8 September 2019. https://www.facebook.com/LLP.Exclusive/posts/2625801937451581/? locale=th_TH, accessed 30 August 2023.

———. *Bigtu Nayok hoad man ha บิ๊กตู่ นายกฯ โหดมันฮา* [Big Du Prime Minister]. Bangkok: Matichon, 2015.

"WikiLeaks Cables: Thai Leaders Doubt Suitability of Prince to Become King." *The Guardian*, 16 December 2010. https://www.theguardian.com/world/ 2010/dec/15/wikileaks-thailand-royal-succession-prince, accessed 21 October 2019.

5

What's Yours Is Mine: Transformation at the Crown Property Bureau

MICHAEL RUFFLES

THE SIAM KEMPINSKI HOTEL in Bangkok stands in a part of the city where the Skytrain intersects with giant malls, Thailand's oldest university, and cultural landmarks including a palace. It is largely royal land and all high-value real estate. For more than a decade, Thailand's Crown Property Bureau (CPB) owned an 80 percent stake not only in the hotel but the entire Kempinski brand worldwide, a luxury chain founded in Berlin in 1897 that by the end of 2020 boasted 76 five-star properties in 31 countries. That changed with the new reign. As King Bhumibol Adulyadej was lying comatose in Siriraj Hospital and his successor worked to consolidate his position, an equity transfer was arranged with the minority shareholder: companies controlled by Bahrain's royal family. The Thais cashed out, selling a 60 percent stake. The rulers of the Middle East kingdom increased their shareholding from an estimated 20 percent to 80 percent in a deal media reports indicate was worth one billion euro, or nearly 35 billion baht based on the exchange rate of the day. The deal was struck shortly before Bhumibol's death, and was finalized on 15 and 16 February 2017, just weeks after King Maha Vajiralongkorn presided over the funeral rite marking one hundred days of mourning.[1]

This was only the first example of Vajiralongkorn taking a strikingly different approach to crown property than his predecessors in the Chakri dynasty, and one that has ushered in the most radical change to the way royal finances are managed since the 1932 revolution. Where his father enabled if not cultivated an air of ambiguity over ownership of crown property, with possession held in some nebulous zone between the person and the state few dared to question, Vajiralongkorn has made it explicitly his own. He has taken direct control of the CPB, made its holdings part of his personal wealth rather than that of the state, and transferred significant shareholdings into his name. The changes in personnel at the organization are also telling, with loyal military men and hard-line royalists ousting technocrats in key board positions. More visibly from the outside, he has altered the capital city by reclaiming and expanding royal land, with institutions including parliament, the 80-year-old Dusit Zoo, and a 102-year-old turf club forced to relocate. Control of Sanam Luang, a public square adjacent to the Grand Palace and the Temple of the Emerald Buddha, has returned to the crown from the Bangkok Metropolitan Administration. In early 2020, the renovation of Ratchadamnoen Avenue also provoked concern that the CPB was trying to erase history.[2]

What was once secret and secretive is becoming harder to deny, as questions about royal wealth are being asked in parliament and street protests alike. The most glaring example came on 25 November 2020 when thousands of protesters gathered outside the headquarters of the Siam Commercial Bank in Chatuchak District.[3] The king's status as the bank's largest shareholder was the focus of attention, even ire, although the reality that he owns a sizeable stake was nothing new. Taken together, these developments indicate Vajiralongkorn is much more overtly interventionist than any other king since the end of absolute monarchy, solidifying both his financial clout and political power in the process. However, it is also a more precarious position to hold. In taking such steps, he has made himself more vulnerable to criticism.

The full picture of crown property and Vajiralongkorn's wealth remains elusive outside the palace, but the Kempinski deal was one piece of the puzzle. In mid-2018, guests who stayed two consecutive nights at the Bangkok hotel were offered a free, limited-edition game of Monopoly where a miniature tuk-tuk and hotel logo took the place of the famous thimble and boot. The most expensive property, Mayfair, was replaced with the Grand Palace.[4] Outside, the new king was playing monopoly for real.

Community Chest

When Bhumibol died in 2016, Vajiralongkorn stood to inherit control of an organization that had been radically transformed from a small bureaucratic anomaly into a giant corporate conglomerate. By the time he placed the crown on his head in an elaborate ceremony two and a half years later, the CPB had been transformed again. Remade by Rama X, it has come under more direct control with trusted military men in charge. It has also become much more controversial, with student demonstrators in 2020 taking aim at the king's wealth and demanding transparency and making the king's assets the subject of protests. Debate has even been held in parliament, where opposition figures have questioned increases to taxpayer spending on the monarchy at a time when the COVID-19 pandemic flattened the tourism-dependent economy.

Even those with excellent sources describe the CPB as opaque. The organization has also shown itself to be less inclined toward transparency under the new reign, abandoning the production of annual reports. In the final years of the Bhumibol era, these had been slickly compiled without divulging any meaningful financial data.[5] Requests for more recent data have gone unanswered. The most reliable sources suggest the bureau is among Thailand's largest conglomerates. It had US$6.7 billion in corporate investments as of 2010, with significant landholdings including large sections of Bangkok. Estimates of its total wealth vary between US$30 billion and US$60 billion.[6] Historically, Thailand's crown wealth has relied most heavily on land, banking, and cement: these have come to be known as the three pillars. The leading academic authority on the matter, Porphant Ouyyanont, found in 2005 that the "CPB's worth was equivalent to 15.8 percent of Thailand's GDP and 93.6 percent of the Thai government budget."[7] Porphant, a contributor to *King Bhumibol Adulyadej: A Life's Work*, based his estimate of the CPB's wealth on his landmark 2005 study and updated it both for the 2010 biography and in 2014. His later survey found the bureau's shareholdings in the Siam Commercial Bank (SCB) and Siam Cement Group (SCG), land worth 8,835 rai in the capital, and the various shareholdings of CPB Equity were worth US$43.8 billion.[8] The king's 23.4 percent stake in the bank was worth US$1.7 billion in late 2020, and 33.6 percent of Siam Cement Group was valued at US$4.5 billion.[9] Both stocks had a difficult year.

There are limitations to these educated guesses, otherwise they would not vary so wildly, and Porphant's calculations of the land value have been called into question.[10] They also typically neglect to include any mention of privately held property. In 2008, *Forbes Asia* explained the difficulty this way: "Aside from the bureau's holdings, the king [Bhumibol] also has extensive personal investments and landholdings. Porphant did not look at these assets, and no outside analysis could ever do more than guess at their value."[11] For example, the *Wall Street Journal* reported in 2016 that Bhumibol owned a 2.2 percent stake in the Minor International hotel and retail group.[12] As of early 2020, no one in the royal family was personally listed as a shareholder. There has been wide speculation about Vajiralongkorn's properties, and his business dealings in nightclubs and the like. There is no public database to keep track on any of these movements, and how donations flow into the palace and are disbursed for charity is a mystery. However, even taking a conservative approach to the estimates, Vajiralongkorn is often regarded as the richest individual monarch on earth. The combined wealth of other royal families, such as the Saudis, may outstrip the Thais, but his place at the top of royal rich lists seems secure. When *Forbes* placed Bhumibol above the Sultan of Brunei in 2011, the palace was at pains to point out the wealth was not the king's personally. Because of the changes of the past few years, that excuse is no longer valid.

The most quoted estimates usually mention little of the institution's income or expenses, which are thought to be exorbitant. The CPB also generates considerable money from rent, particularly its high-value commercial real estate in Bangkok, but none of this is reported publicly. There is a risk that inquiry into this subject could devolve into making semieducated mathematical guesses in the dark, especially after months of protests and as the long-term financial and political consequences of the coronavirus crisis are still uncertain, but there is much to explore and analyze about the way one of the world's richest monarchies has centralized wealth and used it to consolidate power.

The crown does rely on the public purse, with taxpayers funding security for the king and the budget for the 2020 financial year setting aside 29.7 billion baht both directly and indirectly for the institution across several ministries.[13] Most of this, nearly 20 billion baht, is directly supporting the monarchy's activities. The government put aside 7.685 billion baht for the Office of the Privy Council, Bureau of the Royal Household, and Royal

Security Command. A further 6.528 billion baht was slated for royal travel and receptions for heads of state, and, in *Prachatai*'s translation, the "maximum convenience and safety for flights of the royal family upon request." Under the commerce ministry's budget, 13 million baht was set aside for the exhibition of Sirivannavari brand products internationally, helping to prop up the fashion career of Vajiralongkorn's youngest daughter. Protesters have not taken kindly to using taxpayer money to this end, and during the 2020 demonstrations even staged a mocking fashion show on Silom Road as the princess held an event nearby. In total, the expenditure amounted to 0.93 percent of the annual budget. By way of comparison, more was allocated to royalty than the 26 billion baht for justice, 9 billion for foreign affairs, and 7.5 billion for commerce. It is a significant amount of money and supports an equally significant security operation.

The Move Forward Party investigated royal spending as part of its work on a parliamentary committee examining the budget. Even doing this much came as a shock to political figures and observers who felt the king should be above scrutiny, and who had routinely passed increases in the budget without so much as a murmur of opposition. *Financial Times* correspondent John Reed explained that the budget for the Royal Office alone had doubled between 2018 and 2020, while Move Forward questioned royal spending paid by other government departments. "The party also queried the Royal Office's use of aircraft, and were given by (Prime Minister) Prayuth (Chan-ocha)'s office an inventory of 38 planes and helicopters reserved for royal use," Reed reported. Move Forward's Thanathorn Juangroongruangkit was also reported to be critical of the transfer of royal assets to the king, pointing to his stakes in SCG and SCB. "The king is now a player in the market," he says. "It's just wrong. It's undemocratic."[14]

The protest movement that swept Thailand in 2020 has also put the issue in the spotlight. While the movement is fluid, key leaders have made demands for crown property to be returned to the state. The 10-point declaration at Thammasast University on 10 August 2020, which has become famous for shattering the ceiling of scrutiny on the monarchy, explicitly called for Vajiralongkorn's recent law changes to be revoked. They wanted to "make a clear division between the assets of the king under the control of the Ministry of Finance and his personal assets" and "reduce the amount of the national budget allocated to the king to be in line with the economic conditions of the country." Donations to and from royal charity funds should cease "in order for all of the assets of the monarchy to be auditable."[15] The CPB's headquarters were set to be the scene of a large rally, but it was switched to the SCB after dozens of shipping containers were placed on the street to block them. Protesters have also closed SCB accounts in a display of defiance against the bank's largest shareholder.

In the Beginning

The origins of the CPB can be traced to 1890, when under the reign of King Chulalongkorn an old department that managed the royal family's personal and discretionary spending became a more formal office within the government. In the era of absolute monarchy, having the bureau under the aegis of the government was more a distinction than a difference. By 1899 it had been moved under the Royal Secretariat and therefore became part of the palace administration, where it stayed until the 1932 revolution. But originally, the Privy Purse Bureau was established within the Finance Ministry and allocated 15 percent of government revenue, along with staff to manage it.

Revenue growth left the bureau with a surplus that in turn was invested in land, banking, and cement.[16] For all the economic turbulence and political upheaval that have followed in the more than 120 years since, these three pillars remain central to crown wealth. The first of these, investment in land, dovetailed with King Chulalongkorn's political needs. By controlling the physical space, he not only consolidated his hold on power but helped stave off or at least limit the influence of foreign investment at a time when colonial powers were circling across Asia, with British-controlled Burma to the west and French Indochina to the east only the closest examples.

The effect of the royal family's investment in row houses between 1885 and 1910 can still be seen in Bangkok today, as much of the development was in what is now considered the old royal center on Rattanakosin Island, areas on the eastern bank of the Chao Phraya River from Sampheng to Sathorn, and to the island's north. These row houses would typically be rented out cheaply to Chinese laborers. In 1902, the PPB held 4,805 rai or 22.5 percent of the land in Bangkok. This only grew in the decades that followed. "Prior to the Second World War, the PPB was estimated to own one third of the land in the capital." The primary motive, according to Porphant, was urban development, providing accommodation, and boosting business, rather than maximizing rental revenue.[17] There have been reports of a rise in rents under the new reign, although coming off a low base; with about 40,000 lease contracts across the country including 17,000 in Bangkok, any guesses about the income would be just that.

The crown's involvement in banking dates from 1904, when the Minister of Finance, Prince Mahisara Rajaharudaya, also referred to as Prince Mahit, sought an alternative to foreign institutions he saw as having "squeezed the blood from our traders"[18] and hindered the economy. His proposal for a bank has quaint beginnings: it was a semicovert operation known as the Book Club. A royal proclamation in 1906 conferred legitimacy, and it was soon after renamed the Siam Commercial Bank. The Privy Purse Bureau was a significant minority shareholder from day one.

> Of the 3,000 shares issued in 1906, 1,300 shares were taken up by Prince Mahit and his Book Club partners (who were mainly Sino-Thai merchants), and 300 shares were directly owned by the Privy Purse Bureau (PPB). A further 540 shares were taken up by German and Danish banking interests. Of the management board of seven, one was a PPB appointee and three others were Prince Mahit's Book Club associates.[19]

For the sake of comparison, Vajiralongkorn's personal stake in SCB is more than double that investment—23.38 percent as of 2020 (to be discussed subsequently in the chapter). The crown was likewise involved in cement from the beginning, putting up half the one million baht in total capital for the country's first cement plant in 1913. It also financed a loan to a prince who invested a further quarter. Siam Cement prospered quickly, as it was a monopoly in a time of urban expansion, and its ties to royal finances were strong from the outset. Today, the king owns a 33.64 percent stake. *A Life's Work* quotes Japanese historian Akira Suehiro as follows: "[The PPB was] a kind of proto-investment bank which exclusively served as the core organization to undertake private business on behalf of the king."[20]

House Rules

The way crown property has been managed has changed with each reign, but it would be simplistic to say that it reflects the monarch of the day. Political and economic circumstances have often shaped the crown's fortunes, as the crown's fortunes have in turn shaped politics and the economy. The

CPB as Vajiralongkorn controls it today exists partly by dint of his demand for it to be structured a certain way, partly thanks to a compliant military government acquiescing to those changes, and in large part because of the forces of history.

The two kings who followed Chulalongkorn are not viewed as kindly by history, although they faced a world war and global depression respectively. King Vajiravudh, Rama VI, has been described as a spendthrift and dilettante who was uninterested in business. Yet during his reign, several significant investments were made.[21] His successor King Prajadhipok's mishandling of the economy, even outlawing the teaching of economics, was among the factors contributing to the revolution that ended absolute monarchy in 1932.[22] The revolution and its aftermath—with a purge of princes, a coup, and a suppressed counter-revolution—nearly ended the crown, to say nothing of the threat to crown property. As constitutional monarchy was ushered in, allowances paid to royal family members were abolished. Budget figures show the allocation to the PPB was slashed to 440,000 baht a year, or 5 percent of the amount flowing a few years earlier. There was a further reduction of the PPB's expenditure after the 1935 abdication of King Prajadhipok. It was enough to maintain palaces, temples, and other properties, along with funding a few ceremonies, but it was a shadow of its former self.[23] The three years between the revolution and the abdication were spent not only in a struggle for political and constitutional control, but also in a battle of wills over property.[24] While overseas, Rama VII refused to sign a bill he believed would hand the Privy Purse to the government and subject the king to inheritance tax. His reported threat to sell off assets including palaces and the Emerald Buddha, perhaps apocryphal, was invoked in November 2020 by student leader Parit Chiwarak, although this was something of a distraction from the main point of the protests.[25] After Prajadhipok's abdication in 1935, with his ten-year-old nephew Prince Ananda Mahidol chosen as a successor but living in Switzerland, the People's Party rewrote the laws governing crown property.

The 1935 act split crown property in two ways. In the first category were the king's personal belongings, which would be subject to taxation, and in the other those assets that belonged to the crown as a state institution and would remain tax-free. A commission was set up to oversee the division. Importantly, control of crown property was brought under the auspices of the Ministry of Finance. In 1936, a more complex law was introduced, and, although it was amended in 1948, it served as the basis for how crown property was governed for decades until the law was overhauled again in 2017 and 2018. The Crown Property Act of 1936 divided the property in three ways.[26]

1. The king's private property: "property that belonged to the king before ascending to the throne; property conferred on the king by the state; or property acquired by the king by any means and at any time other than property acquired on account of kingship including any fruit accrued there from." This was liable to taxation.
2. Public property: defined as "property of the king which is used exclusively for the benefit of the state, e.g. palaces."
3. Remaining property that fell outside those two categories: in reality, this meant land and corporate investments that had formerly belonged to the PPB, and this is what has come to be known conventionally in Thailand as crown property.

The act sets out that, after administrative expenses were deducted, the income was for the king to spend "in his capacity as head of state." A board was created, to be headed by the minister of finance and therefore reliant on the government of the day, and including four other directors who were appointed by the king. Under Vajiralongkorn's reign, this number has expanded, and he has done away with the requirement for the finance minister to be on the board. Amendments to the Crown Property Act in 1948 laid the groundwork for the behemoth Vajiralongkorn would later inherit. These restructured the bureau as a juristic person and confirmed its tax-exempt status. It is a unique legal entity in a category of its own, and exactly how the CPB is defined under Thai law has eluded even those who should know. Porphant, drawing from a 2006 study by Thammasat University historian Somsak Jeamteerasakul, was at a loss in 2015:

> In the course of subsequent legal processes, the Council of State had to give rulings on the nature of the CPB on four occasions. Not one of the rulings was unanimous, and the four rulings conflicted. The Council agreed that the CPB was not a private company, government department, or state enterprise, and ultimately in 2001 ruled it was a "unit of the state," whatever that meant.[27]

Importantly, the 1948 law changed the management structure and gave the king more sway over day-to-day operations. Vajiralongkorn later went much further. But early in Bhumibol's reign, one of the royally appointed board members was named the director general of the CPB and granted full executive power. This role provided the board with more independence from government, leading to more active management in the decades that followed, although the director general was still answerable to the board. In Bhumibol's time, board members were typically bureaucrats with economic backgrounds or had political experience in the cabinet; those making a mark in the private sector might be tapped to join the CPB in other capacities, but they were not chosen for these positions.

The way revenue could be used was also overhauled. Instead of requiring it to be spent in the king's role as head of state, the money "may be dispersed only by the king, according to his disposition, in any way at all." In a different translation in 2015, Porphant, again relying on Somsak, wrote that the use of the CPB's resources and income "depends totally on the royal inclination"[28] and that the 1948 act stipulated the bureau's landed assets could not be seized or transferred. Precisely where the money went will never be known, but the changes did usher in a more profitable phase for the crown. This phase coincided with the national economy growing at an average of 7 percent a year, "from an agrarian backwater"[29] to a more complex, partly industrialized economy.

Roll the Dice

Under King Bhumibol, both the CPB and the monarchy went from strength to strength. In 1946, when the young man was named king, the bureau was bereft. Yet by the end of his reign, it was a powerhouse. It also evolved into a conglomerate that, while recognizing the value of contributing to the social good and being seen to do so, grew steadily more corporate and business-savvy as time went on. One factor that likely contributed to its success was stability. Over the course of 70 years under Bhumibol, only three men served as director general of the CPB. In each case, the king also appointed him as lord chamberlain in the Royal Household Bureau, or to the deputy position of grand chamberlain. In that way, the person tasked with overseeing and growing the crown's assets and income had intimate knowledge of the royal family's day-to-day expenses. As Porphant put it in *A Life's Work*, "This combination of roles undoubtedly ensured smooth administration."[30]

Vajiralongkorn has continued with this combination during his reign, installing a trusted adviser who had already been looking after his personal affairs for more than a decade and had been privy to the palace's inner workings.

The first to be appointed director general under Bhumibol's reign was Mom Thawiwong Thawansak. His tenure is of little relevance to this chapter other than to note that one of the bureau's first decisions was to go into business with Chanut Piyaoui, owner of the Princess Hotel. The result was the Dusit Thani, among Bangkok's first high-rise buildings and a landmark opposite Lumpini Park, which would expand into an international chain. The crown has since divested its stake in the Dusit Thani, although the CPB partnered with the hotel chain to create Siam Sindhorn and to purchase the Kempinski hotel business. To quote Porphant again: "The CPB went on to make similar ventures with several other hotels. The CPB applied the same model to joint ventures with shopping centres and commercial buildings."[31] In 1970, Poonperm Krairiksh was appointed after rising through palace ranks. By that time, the CPB had shares in 30 companies, including Siam City and Thai Danu banks. During Poonperm's tenure, SCG and SCB each blossomed to become conglomerates in their own rights. SCG bought up building and material companies, while SCB expanded into other financial products. In the late 1970s, the bureau had a 44 percent stake in SCG and a 50 percent stake in the bank. This is a higher proportion than today in both cases. Of the property portfolio, hotels were again prominent. In 1980, the CPB took out a stake in the Oriental and the Royal Orchid.

After Chirayu Isarangkun na Ayuthaya was parachuted out of the administration of General Prem Tinsulanonda (1980–88), he landed in a position where he would have a significant effect on Thailand's social and economic development for the next 30 years. Chirayu was appointed CPB director general on 28 July 1987. His term was notable for its longevity, its remarkable growth, and its handling of the Asian Financial Crisis of 1997 and the royal succession in 2016. An economist with degrees from England and Australia, Chirayu is a leading public proponent of the sufficiency economic theory who nevertheless oversaw the CPB as its assets and revenues skyrocketed. Under Chirayu, the CPB took a more commercial approach to property rents and land development, and the office became more open to joint ventures with multinationals. In a 2005 interview with Porphant, Chirayu said, "The fact that the CPB is the investment arm for the monarchy, with a long-term and continuous reputation for reliability, induces Thai and foreign investors to seek joint ventures. Hence the CPB is invited to take a minority stake as a passive partner."[32] This provided multiple opportunities for revenue and growth while managing the risk, albeit not mitigating it entirely.

By the mid-1990s, the bureau had sizeable investments in two conglomerates and had become one in its own right. Before the Asian Financial Crisis of 1997, its income had jumped from 563 million baht in 1987 to almost 2 billion baht in 1992 and 3 billion baht by 1997. The SCG had expanded and, by the mid-90s, had about 120 subsidiaries and affiliates. The bank had also enjoyed the boom and, by the eve of the 1997 financial crisis, had 77 subsidiaries ranging from financial asset management and real estate to sugar, entertainment, and beyond. The CPB's proportion of each was diluted, but in 1997 the CPB retained about 26 percent of the shares in SCB and 35 percent of SCG. Financial data from 1996 put the value of SCG assets at 180 billion baht and profits at 6.8 billion baht. Both these had roughly doubled from three years earlier. In the case of SCB, profits averaged 6.4 billion baht between 1992 and 1996, peaking at more than 9 billion baht in 1996. The CPB reaped the benefit of dividends. Between them, these two giants contributed 60 percent of the bureau's income at that time. Land added another 300–600 million baht a year, with the various shareholdings adding 870 million baht.[33]

Just as the CPB rode the boom, it was crushed in the bust that began in Thailand and spread through much of Southeast and East Asia. After the baht was floated in July 1997, it lost half its value against the US dollar in a matter of months. The stock exchange dropped 75 percent, layoffs were massive in many sectors, and the gross domestic product did not return to 1996 levels, in dollar terms, until 2006.[34] As the baht had long been pegged at 25 to the US dollar, many businesses had borrowed without hedging. Banks and financial institutions were among the biggest offenders and most exposed. Banks were especially hit as they borrowed in unhedged dollars and lent in baht, and this contributed to about 20 percent of the Siam Commercial Bank's liabilities. Real estate loans were also problematic. Of the SCB's total loans for 1998, 34 percent were non-performing. Over the next five years the average was 25 percent.[35] Also exposed was SCG, which had US$4.2 billion in unhedged foreign debts resulting in a $1.2 billion write-down in 1997.[36]

Dividends disappeared, and thereby about three-quarters of the CPB's income vanished. The SCB paid no dividend between 1998 and 2003, while SCG shareholders went without between 1998 and 2001. The bank itself was US$6.6 billion in debt, and the bureau had to pay to fulfill its obligation as a shareholder. The bureau borrowed "perhaps as much as US$222 million, to cover royal household expenses,"[37] although some experts doubt it actually took out a loan. A convoluted deal with the government meant that the finance ministry bought a large stake until it was repaid with about 78 hectares of land west of Victory Monument.[38] Chirayu told Porphant that there was "no panic" within the bureau,[39] but the response to the crisis shows there was a significant degree of concern. Both the SCB and SCG were overhauled with a renewed focus on their core businesses, about 400 companies and joint ventures were divested, changes were made to management, and new talent was introduced. Chirayu was also appointed as chair of both the bank and the cement giant, a move that could be interpreted as an attempt to restore confidence but equally could be read as a sign of how desperate the times were.

Inside the bureau, too, a high-powered group of Thai and foreign experts in finance and real estate were hired. Among them were Vichit Surapongchai, a former president of Bangkok Bank and then chairman of Siam Commercial Bank's executive committee, and Michael Selby, onetime adviser to Brunei's Prince Jefri.[40] In 1999, the bureau set about raising rents for its more commercial tenants. The bureau also created two companies as part of managing the fallout. CPB Property, established in 2000, took over management of land and property, while CPB Equity, established a year later, oversaw share portfolios and holdings in non-core companies. The two other giants recovered well once the crisis passed. SCG looked to exports, rising from 5 percent of the company's sales before the crisis to 40 percent by the early 2000s. By 2004, SCG's profits were higher than pre-crisis levels. A year later, the CPB's income had risen to 9.3 billion baht, roughly three times its pre-crisis level. Between 2008 and 2010, total incomes fluctuated between 9 and 11 billion baht.

The recovery appears impressive, although some have cautioned against accepting Porphant's analysis without some skepticism. Scholar Kevin Hewison warned Porphant had been too credulous in accepting Chirayu's account of the crisis, calling it "wholly uncritical."[41] However, the figures are likely reliable and have never been contradicted. They reveal the organization had long been becoming more professional and business-like in its focus on growth. There might have been concern at Bhumibol's appearance at the top of the *Forbes* list of richest royals, but he did not get there by accident. Vajiralongkorn would be even more deliberate about staying there.

Do Not Pass Go

The first major change to the CPB's operation under the reign of Rama X was set in motion months earlier, as King Bhumibol lay dying. It was essentially a billion-euro deal with the Bahraini royal family under which the Thai monarchy relinquished majority control of the Kempinski hotel chain and its various subsidiaries, retaining about one-fifth.[42] The arrangement formally transpired on 16 February 2017,[43] but it had been agreed to months before and pored over by lawyers at length. It was also worked out as Vajiralongkorn was consolidating his power behind the scenes and taking a deeper interest in the bureau's operations.[44] It is quite possible that if not for the arrest of a refugee soccer player from Melbourne the deal would have gone virtually unnoticed.

On the world stage, Kempinski was the CPB's most significant investment. The chain has five-star hotels and residences in more than 30 countries. The company has been in private hands since its inception, although ownership has shifted since it left the original family in the 1950s. The CPB has informed German authorities that it owns less than 25 percent of the holding company Kempinski AG, which owns the operating company Kempinski Hotels SA outright along with other subsidiaries. That stake is a fraction of what it once was.[45] Unlike the bureau itself, Kempinski does have obligations under German law to disclose certain financial matters including the results of audits, board changes, and major share adjustments. Between these and other statements on the public record, there is enough to illustrate a quarter of a century of Thai involvement in the hotel giant. In 1994, the Dusit Thani group and the SCB partnered to form Siam Sindhorn and purchase 83 percent of the Kempinski chain. In this way, on paper at least, the CPB's initial investment and involvement was circuitous. At the time, it held about a quarter of the shares in the bank, which in turn had a 50 percent stake in Siam Sindhorn. An interest in an international luxury hotel chain, however, did align neatly with other investments the CPB made during Bhumibol's reign. It was a time of expansion and optimism, but the partnership proved short-lived as the Asian Financial Crisis struck.

Four years later, it was reported Dusit Thani had sold its share to the bank. Kempinski's spokeswoman told trade publications it was likely the bank would also try to sell out of the hotel company. "She speculated that Dusit Thani was not prepared to fund Kempinski's expansion," *Travel Weekly* reported.[46] Not foreshadowed at the time was that one of the bank's shareholders would be an interested party. Six years later, in 2004, the bank opted out of Kempinski and the Crown Property Bureau bought in. Siam Sindhorn has since become a fully owned subsidiary of the CPB. Kempinksi's website says plainly that Thailand and Bahrain were the "two existing shareholders" between 2004 and 2017. It announced the equity swap between Bahrain and Thailand, with few specific details:

> Effective today, the two existing shareholders of Kempinski AG formalize previous plans for an equity transfer between them. The majority shares of Kempinski AG shall be held by the existing Bahraini shareholder, while the shareholder from Thailand will now own a minority. Both shareholders remain committed to Kempinski and its long-term success.[47]

Under the equity swap arrangement, the Thai companies that owned the majority of the shares sold roughly a 60 percent stake, reducing the various holdings from somewhere in the order of 80 percent to 20 percent. For the Bahraini companies involved, the proportions went in reverse: from 20 percent to 80 percent. The swap reportedly cost the Bahraini royal family one billion euro. The numbers, as reported in trade publications at the time and subsequently in mainstream media, are traced to inside sources as the terms of the deal include an agreement not to disclose the purchase price. International law firm Baker McKenzie advised the CPB on the sale and, in promoting its professional services, was not shy about saying it navigated several difficulties with the transaction. "The numerous cross-border elements of the transaction were a particular challenge for the negotiations with the buy-side," Primyadar Duangrat, the lead partner at Baker McKenzie Bangkok, said in a statement. Her German equivalent, Heiko Gotsche from Baker McKenzie Dusseldorf, said, "We had to consider a significant number of corporate, anti-trust and tax issues in Germany and various other jurisdictions."[48] German records reveal some of the nuance behind the deal.

On 24 February 2017, Kempinski informed the authorities that Acresfield Holding Limited, CPB International Holdings Limited, and CPB Equity Co. Ltd were no longer majority shareholders and held less than a quarter of the shares in the company. In the same announcement, KAY Investments Holding GmbH & Co.KG, Blitz F16-95 GmbH, and K Investments Inc. were named as the new majority shareholders. These companies are based in Bahrain.

Kempinski grew enormously in the years when Thai investment was at its greatest. When Reto Wittwer stepped down as president and CEO in 2014, he had overseen a chain that had expanded from 21 hotels in 1995 to 73, and a further 35 were in development or under construction at the time. As of the end of 2020, as the novel coronavirus pandemic caused chaos in the travel and tourism industry, the total stood at 76.

Internally, Kempinski's leadership changed significantly as the ownership shifted. Previously, executive officers included MR Disnadda Diskul and Michael Selby. MR Disnadda was private secretary to King Bhumibol's mother for 28 years and is a long-serving chairman of the charitable Mae Fah Luang Foundation.[49] Selby, a pivotal figure after the Asian Financial Crisis, held several positions within the CPB's various companies and was also on the Kempin Siam board. Selby left on 24 February 2016. Yos Euarchukiati, a top figure in the SCG and connected with several CPB subsidiaries and the Siam Piwat retail giant linked to Princess Sirindhorn, also left shortly thereafter. In the statement announcing the equity swap, Kempinski detailed the composition of the new supervisory board. Abdulla H. Saif, a trusted economic adviser to the Bahrain royal family and head of the Islamic Bank of Asia since 2007, was named chairman. Chumpol Na Lamlieng, who is involved in several CPB assets and assisted in overseeing the post-crisis restructure of the SCB and SCG, was named vice-chairman. His tenure ended on 23 November 2017.[50] Thai representation continues, albeit at a reduced level.

Precisely why the Thai companies were selling is not made clear in freely available documents. There was speculation from political sources in Bangkok that Kempinski was in some financial difficulty, but there is little evidence.[51] The balance sheets of Kempinski AG improved in the first years after the deal was struck. While they will no doubt suffer because of the pandemic, there is no indication the Bahrainis were sold a lemon. Being long-time shareholders, they would have known what they were buying.

Whether the crown was in some sort of financial strife, or whether the royal family was simply in need of cash, is another matter. The location of the Siam Kempinski Hotel itself in central Bangkok offers an alternative possibility. This is land closely associated with Princess Sirindhorn, sister of Vajiralongkorn, and adjacent not only to her palace but to major Siam Piwat developments to which she is tied. It may not be entirely coincidental that Siam Piwat joint venture IconSiam, one of the largest malls in Asia, was being built at that time on a prominent stretch of the Chao Phraya River. No doubt as the end of Bhumibol's reign was nearing, all senior members of the royal family were getting their financial affairs in order. The other point worth making is Vajiralongkorn once made extensive use of a Kempinski hotel in Munich, before taking up residence at the Grand Hotel Sonnenbichl for years on end. Who stood to benefit from the Kempinski sale and to what degree may never be known.

From the outside, the change to Kempinski has so far been subtle, which is unsurprising given multimillion-dollar projects take years to plan and develop. There are suspicions the reduced Thai involvement led to the chain abandoning a five-star heritage hotel on the Strand in Myanmar's Yangon, with Rosewood picking up the reins.[52] But the project had long been controversial and other explanations are possible. In Bangkok itself, the Kempinski brand is arguably more prominent now the CPB's development at Langsuan has come to fruition. However, it is Kempinski in name only. The Residences at Sindhorn Kempinski Hotel Bangkok in the Lumpini precinct has been developed independent of the German parent company. Siam Sindhorn licensed the name from Kempinski Hotels SA. The project's website states: "The role of the Kempinski group is limited to supervising the management of the residential facility."[53] Siam Sindhorn was not the only royally aligned company involved. Naturally, the country's largest industrial conglomerate, Siam Cement, played a part in the construction of the 33-story, 231-unit complex. Looking at the bigger picture and based on the announcements of the past few years, it is reasonable to conclude that since the change in ownership, Kempinski's greatest focus for growth has been in the Middle East and the Gulf.

The Bahrain connection is likely the only reason the equity swap came to light. While Kempinski did put out a statement and had kept German authorities informed per its legal obligations, the deal went almost unnoticed except in the esoteric world of travel trade websites. It was only after Bahraini refugee football player Hakeem al-Araibi was arrested at Suvarnabhumi Airport on 27 November 2018 that journalists and other interested observers began wondering about links between the Gulf and Southeast Asian kingdoms. Araibi, who had been granted asylum and Australian travel documents, was detained upon landing after taking a flight from Melbourne. [54] It was to have been his honeymoon, but Thai immigration police were waiting when he landed. His 77-day ordeal became an international incident, a three-way diplomatic standoff compounded by his status as a former Bahrain national football player who had been outspoken on human rights issues and corruption. Journalists and advocates alike were curious as to whether the Gulf kingdom held any unusual sway over Thailand. In the billion-euro Kempinski deal, Australian media reported that there was certainly speculation in Bangkok that Bahrain was calling in a favor. [55] After the international media storm and diplomatic pressure reached its zenith with the sight of the twenty-seven-year-old in shackles for a routine court appearance, Bahrain dropped its extradition demand and Araibi was returned to Melbourne. The two kingdoms continue to do business together.

Making a Move

If the changes at Kempinski meant ceding control, King Vajiralongkorn's moves at the CPB itself were all about seizing it. And he wasted no time. The day after Bhumibol's death, along with taking on more duties customarily performed by the monarch, he was "familiarizing himself with the workings of the CPB, one of the country's most important landowners and the holding vehicle for much of the monarchy's wealth." [56] A few weeks later, it was claimed Vajiralongkorn had made use of the bureau's assets in the past. The media reported, "At times, some Thais have questioned how the bureau's income should be used. In late 2014, for instance, the finance ministry said the bureau made a 200 million baht, or US$5.64 million, divorce payment, to 64-year-old Prince Vajiralongkorn's most recent spouse." [57] Whether this money came from the bureau or whether it was even paid is a matter of dispute. That former wife, now known as Srirasmi Suwadee, was stripped of her titles and royally bestowed surname, and several of her relatives were arrested on charges of profiting from their connection to the then crown prince. [58] The man who signed the order revoking the surname was Vajiralongkorn's private secretary,

Air Chief Marshal Satitpong Sukvimol.[59] Satitpong, a former top Royal Thai Air Force officer, had long been part of the crown prince's staff by the time of the succession. Since 2012, he had served as a grand chamberlain in the Royal Household Bureau. In January 2017, he was named in the *Royal Gazette* as the new king's caretaker and "manager of his personal assets and interests."[60] From there, his status only grew and now he is arguably the most powerful of all the king's men. In a financial sense, certainly, his clout is unmatched.

The first change to be widely reported came in July 2017, when the military government passed laws giving the monarch direct control over the CPB.[61] This was a major change, but the shift to total control did not happen in one fell swoop. English-language and international media reports, as detailed later, typically referred to each incremental development in isolation. But taken together, this series of announcements, proclamations, and law changes reveals a more sustained and concerted takeover period. On 2 May 2017, five agencies were transferred from various ministries to sit under Vajiralongkorn's control, namely the Royal Household Bureau, the Office of His Majesty's Principal Private Secretary, the Royal Thai Aide-De-Camp Department, the Office of Royal Court Security Police, and the Royal Security Command.[62] Four were reverting to crown control for the first time since the end of absolute monarchy in 1932, while the fifth, the police branch, was a newer addition. The new law also said that while the five agencies would continue to be funded by the public, any revenue they generated would not be returned to treasury. The money flowed in one direction. It is for others to analyze the changes to security arrangements (see Gregory V. Raymond's chapter herein), but it is worth noting the office that spends the money moved under the king's control within months of the bureau that makes the money. The next month, June 2017, brought a reshuffle of the king's staff. Satitpong won a promotion to lord chamberlain while Chirayu Isarangkun na Ayuthaya, who had been doing the job since the weeks before Bhumibol's death, returned to the rank of grand chamberlain.

It was on 16 July 2017, a Sunday, when the lawmakers handpicked by the military junta convened to change the Crown Property Act for the first time in 69 years.[63] The changes gave the monarch more power over royal wealth than at any stage since the revolution. Pavin Chachavalpongpun summarized the changes this way:

> There are two key characteristics of the legislation. First, the king is entitled to appoint the board members, as well as to remove them, at his

discretion. Second, the law prohibits the taking away of royal assets without the king's approval. This is the first time since 1948 that laws governing crown property have been amended. Under King Bhumibol, the board of directors for the royal assets answered to the finance minister. Now it is independent of the government. As a result, the independent status of the Crown Property Bureau augments Vajiralongkorn's power in making decisions about the future of the royal wealth."[64]

International media reports also noted the removal of the finance minister, whose presence had been "meant to ensure some semblance of government oversight. That requirement has now been removed, allowing Vajiralongkorn free rein to appoint who he likes to head the committee."[65] No time was wasted. On 17 July, as the announcement of the previous day's changes were being circulated, Satitpong was named chairman of the board. Four other military men were appointed; Chirayu, the director general, and two other incumbent board members stayed on.

The takeover was not complete. On 2 October, a 3.33 percent stake in the SCB was transferred from the CPB to the king in his own name. *Nikkei Asian Review* published the move a few days later,[66] citing a Securities and Exchange Commission report noting the CPB stake in the bank had reduced from 21.47 percent to 18.14 percent. "In a separate report filed with the SEC by the CPB, it was stated that the 3.33 percent holding had been transferred to King Vajiralongkorn, but there was no indication as to whether there was any payment for the stake," *Nikkei Asian Review* wrote. Based on the closing price of the day, the shares were worth 16.919 billion baht (US$507 million), and the king became the seventh-largest shareholder in Thailand's third-largest bank overnight. Reuters also reported the same details and had little success when it sought comment from the bureau:

> The Crown Property Bureau confirmed the transaction but declined comment on how the transfer fitted with changes to the way palace finances are run since the king took the throne late last year after the death of his revered father. "It is his majesty's private affair so I cannot comment further," said an official of the Crown Property Bureau who declined to be named because of the sensitivity of anything to do with Thailand's palace.[67]

In hindsight, this share transfer could be viewed as a test run. By the following year, all the bureau's shares in both the bank and Siam Cement would be held under the king's name. Making the shareholdings his own came as the king took personal possession of the rest of the CPB's assets.

Again, this did not appear to have been done by whim. Nor was it done with much in the way of stealth. On 12 March 2018, Satitpong was named director general of the CPB.[68] Chirayu, having held the position for 30 years, was made a privy councilor. By the year's end, only one board member would remain from the Bhumibol era, and the board would be stacked with army men.[69] Having trained as a soldier and spent time close to the armed forces, Vajiralongkorn installed people he could trust. In the weeks that followed, Satitpong took over other duties from Chirayu. The former air force official was installed as a director at Siam Cement Group on 28 March and chairman of the board. On 13 June, he was appointed a director at SCB. In addition to being chairman of the royal family's Deves Insurance, he is listed as the chair of Banbung Vejchakij Co., Ltd, Sriphath Co., Ltd, Sridharani Co., Ltd, Siam Sindhorn Co., Ltd, CPB Equity Co., Ltd, Siam Bioscience Co., Ltd, Apexcela Co., Ltd, and Doi Kham Co., Ltd.[70] The bank records that neither Satitpong nor any member of his family hold any personal shares in the SCB. His function is to act on behalf of the king. A member of Vajiralongkorn's staff for decades, Satitpong has long been entrusted with significant personal and official responsibilities. These appointments make him not only arguably the most powerful mandarin in the palace, but a significant player in Thailand's wider business community.

On 16 June 2018, the CPB announced on its website that its assets had been transferred to Vajiralongkorn's personal possession. At the time, there was a promise to pay tax. "This is in line with the king's wishes," according to one translation of the announcement.[71] However, a proclamation in July 2019 absolved the monarch of the requirement to pay taxes on properties used for state functions.[72] On 18 June 2019, Vajiralongkorn became the top shareholder of SCB and SCG.[73] In November 2019, the Crown Property Act was amended for the second time in 70 years to redefine the king's possessions to include what the monarchy had "accumulated under ancient royal traditions." Under Article 5 of the act, "any disputes over what assets are considered crown property under the ancient royal traditions are to be decided by the king himself."[74] The division between personal wealth and that belonging to the state, established in 1936 even if vaguely defined for much of the ninth reign, effectively vanished. It all belonged to Vajiralongkorn. All these changes occurred before the coronation on 4 May 2019.

As with so many takeovers in Thailand, men in uniform were central to proceedings. Along with Satitpong and the other military figures appointed to the CPB board, Vajiralongkorn installed in October 2018 newly minted Army Chief General Apirat Kongsompong, the son of the general who had led the 1991 coup against the Chatichai Choonhavan government (1988–91). On retiring from the army, Apirat was given a job in the palace and has since been made deputy director of the CPB. Privy councilor Ampon Kittiampon, who has a background in the public service and served as cabinet secretary to three governments, was also appointed. As of 2019, the CPB board contained 11 men mostly of military and police backgrounds, with one remaining from the previous reign. The urge to install trusted allies and advisers is natural, and, after spending a long time as crown prince, Vajiralongkorn appears to have arrived in power with a firm idea of how he wanted to establish control. However, strikingly absent from the new appointees is anyone with strong financial or business backgrounds. Ampon spent part of his career with the National Social and Development Board, but Apirat rose through the King's Guard. Another example is General Jakrapob Bhuridej, who is Vajiralongkorn's security chief. In bringing in new personnel Vajiralongkorn not only sent the message that the CPB was under new management, but also that the era of the technocrats was over.

Outside the boardroom, other changes were afoot. On 4 April 2018, the CPB ended its lease arrangement with the Royal Turf Club. After 102 years as a gathering ground for the business and military elite, and no small amount of politics, the club to the south of Chitralada Palace was shuttered by September.[75] Dusit Zoo, a popular attraction to the west of the palace, was similarly reclaimed with its final day of operation being 30 September. The old parliament buildings and Sanam Luang were also brought under the CPB, and the Ananta Samakhom Throne Hall was added to the list.[76] The historic Vimanmek Palace was closed to tourists in mid-2016 and is getting an 81 million baht renovation, including a large fishpond. The structure would be rebuilt from the foundations up and not reopen to the public.[77] There is also the demolition of Si Sao Thewes Mansion, the long-time home of Prem, who died in 2019 at aged ninety-eight. The property was meant to be the home of the army chief, until Prem simply continued to live there long past his retirement. After 40 years, any thought that it would return to the army was overridden. The property had finally been "returned" to the Royal Household Bureau.[78] Once the residence of Field Marshal Sarit Thanarat and located around the corner from the CPB's headquarters, it was a prominent part of the Dusit precinct Vajiralongkorn appears determined to reshape. The house was demolished in September 2020.

In the Bank

The acquisitions just discussed add to the difficulty of coming up with a total figure for Vajiralongkorn's wealth. The value of the land under the IconSiam luxury mega mall can be roughly estimated, but the value of a large square of land such as Sanam Luang would be a relatively meaningless figure. As a national asset, it would be nearly impossible to liquidate. Palaces might be priceless, but if a paying public is kept away or they serve few state functions they may end up being a drag on the balance sheet. Updating Porphant's informed calculations is easy enough: assuming 8,835 rai in Bangkok have appreciated, conservatively, another five percent in the years since, it would be worth about 1.1 trillion baht. Combined with the SCG and SCB shares, this works out to be about US$44 billion. It is a flawed figure, and likely to be a significant underestimate, but reveals that even a crown that appears to burn through its income continues to be rich in assets.

Vajiralongkorn, unlike his father, has no qualms about being seen to be rich. Where Bhumibol had benefited from having a degree of distance between his public persona and crown property, promoting an image of a beneficent father figure not wholly connected to the fortune being accumulated, Vajiralongkorn tied himself explicitly to the wealth. The series of announcements before the coronation puts this beyond doubt, but there are other indications. The CPB under Bhumibol also used philanthropy or CSR (corporate social responsibility) to show the money was being used for the good of the people, and as a way of enhancing the monarchy's image. CSR formed a substantial part of the bureau's final annual report in 2016. However, under Vajiralongkorn, CSR has vanished from the bureau's priorities. Former CPB employees, speaking anonymously, said that an entire office devoted to philanthropy was closed shortly after the succession.[79] Ending the annual reports not only shows less inclination toward transparency, but also provides one fewer way of showing crown wealth being used for a common good. The priority instead, according to one former insider, changed overnight to be purely profit.[80]

The simple explanation is that being wealthy is its own reward, but the moves in the boardroom and beyond suggest Vajiralongkorn has other motives in mind too. Rama X is only the latest king in the dynasty to use structures in Bangkok to consolidate and demonstrate power; indeed, this is true of Bangkok's very establishment in 1782. Writing in the twilight of the Bhumibol era, Serhat Ünaldi put it this way: "Urban space helped to protect and increase royal charisma in spite of the royal family's heavy involvement in mundane capitalist activities. At the same time, physical proximity to royal properties enabled people—whether mall operators or slum dwellers—to use that charisma for their own ends." Ünaldi concluded his book on the politics of space in Bangkok with a quote predicting: "The moment the Thai Crown Prince ascends to the throne, the future of tall buildings around Sa Pathum Palace will be totally different."[81] Vajiralongkorn has certainly transformed the city and the monarchy along with the Crown Property Bureau, and often in unexpected ways.

Vajiralongkorn's undoing of law changes enacted after the revolution can be viewed in concert with the replacement of a plaque commemorating the 1932 democratic movement for one with a Chakri dynasty motto, the disappearance of statues to revolutionary leaders on army bases, and the removal of references to Phaholyothin, a revolutionary leader and the second prime minister after the end of absolute monarchy.[82] In chapter 7 herein, Chatri Prakitnonthakan dissects the destruction and removal of buildings and monuments as a political tactic against the new People's Party movement and as part of a wider struggle over memory and history. Whether Vajiralongkorn envisages a complete return to absolute monarchy or is guarding against the possibility of a repeat of the revolution is up for debate. He is consolidating not only his family's assets, but also its power and place at the center of Thai life.

Vajiralongkorn has more direct control over a larger share of the country's wealth than any king since the revolution. It is also under unprecedented scrutiny, making it more precarious than ever. For now, he controls the board, but others are making moves to counter his monopoly. Without compromise, it could become a game where the winner takes it all.

Notes

1 Sanderson, "Stuck between Two Kings."

2 Pravit, "Scholar Fears Massive Renovation of Iconic Avenue May Erase History."

3 Thanthong-Knight, "Thai Protesters Target King's Wealth in Latest Bangkok Rally."

4 Francis, "Siam Kempinski Hotel Bangkok Debuts Its Very Own Monopoly Game."

5 Crown Property Bureau, http://www.crownproperty.or.th/.

6 Grossman and Faulder, *King Bhumibol Adulyadej*, 283–301.

7 Porphant, "Crown Property Bureau in Thailand and Its Role in Political Economy," 166–89.

8 Porphant, "Crown Property Bureau in Thailand and Its Role in Political Economy," 166–89.

9 Reed, "All the King's Money."

10 Hewison, Review of Porphant Ouyyanont, *Crown Property Bureau in Thailand*.

11 Cunningham, "The Crowning Fortune."

12 Hookway, "Thailand's Royal Fortune Looms over Crown Prince's Ascension to Throne."

13 "Government to Spend 29 Billion Baht on Monarchy," *Prachatai*.

14 Reed, *All the King's Money*.

15 "[Full statement] The Demonstration at Thammasat Proposes Monarchy Reform," *Prachatai*.

16 Grossman and Faulder, *King Bhumibol Adulyadej*, 285.

17 Grossman and Faulder, *King Bhumibol Adulyadej*.

18 Porphant, "The Crown Property Bureau in Thailand and the Crisis of 1997," 168.

19 Porphant, "The Crown Property Bureau in Thailand and the Crisis of 1997," 168.

20 Grossman and Faulder, *King Bhumibol Adulyadej*, 287.

21 Hewison, Review of Porphant Ouyyanont, *Crown Property Bureau in Thailand*, 539.

22 Baker and Pasuk, *A History of Thailand*, 117.

23 Grossman and Faulder, *King Bhumibol Adulyadej*, 287–88.

24 Baker and Pasuk, *A History of Thailand*, 119.

25 Cod, "Opinion: Making Outlandish Statements Hinders More than Helps the Student Movement."

26 Thai Laws, www.thailawforum.com/laws/Crown%20Property%20Act.pdf.

27 Porphant, "The Crown Property Bureau in Thailand and the Crisis of 1997," 171.

28 Porphant, "The Crown Property Bureau in Thailand and the Crisis of 1997," 171.

29 Grossman and Faulder, *King Bhumibol Adulyadej*, 289–90.

30 Grossman and Faulder, *King Bhumibol Adulyadej*, 289–90.

31 Grossman and Faulder, *King Bhumibol Adulyadej*, 289–90.

32 Porphant, "The Crown Property Bureau in Thailand and the Crisis of 1997," 171.

33 Grossman and Faulder, *King Bhumibol Adulyadej*, 293.

34 International Monetary Fund report on Thailand's GDP, https://www.imf.org/en/Countries/THA#countrydata.

35 Porphant, "The Crown Property Bureau in Thailand and the Crisis of 1997," 175.

36 "'Thailand's Royal Wealth' and 'Royal Wealth (Continued),'" *Asia Sentinel.*

37 Porphant, "The Crown Property Bureau in Thailand and the Crisis of 1997," 175–76.

38 Cunningham, "The Crowning Fortune."

39 Grossman and Faulder, *King Bhumibol Adulyadej*, 294.

40 Cunningham, "The Crowning Fortune."

41 Hewison, Review of Porphant Ouyyanont, *Crown Property Bureau in Thailand*, 539.

42 Sanderson, "Stuck between Two Kings."

43 Baker-McKenzie statement, 22 February 2017, https://www.legal-monitor.com/news/crown-property-bureau-sells-kempinski-hotels-group, accessed 12 April 2020.

44 Hookway, "Thailand's Royal Fortune Looms over Crown Prince's Ascension to Throne."

45 German public records accessed by the author (www.bundesanzeiger.de).

46 Spritzer, "Dusit Thani Sells Its Share of Kempinski."

47 Kempinski Hotels, https://www.kempinski.com/en/hotels/about-us/history/, accessed 14 June 2023; Kempinski AG Statement, 16 February 2017 (from library records).

48 Baker McKenzie statement, 22 February 2017.

49 Established in 1969 by King Bhumibol's mother to aid ethnic minorities, the Mae Fah Luang Foundation has become a large philanthropic organization with environmental and social projects.

50 Annual financial statements for the financial year from 1 January to 31 December 2017 and consolidated financial statements for the financial year from 1 January to 31 December 2018, among other documents, https://www.bundesanzeiger.de/ebanzwww/wexsservlet.

51 Confidential interview with source in Bangkok, March 2019.

52 "Rosewood Takes over Kempinski Heritage Hotel Plans," *Myanmore.*

53 The Residences at Sindhorn Kempinsi, https://theresidencesatsindhornkempin-ski.com/.

54 Massola, "I Was Crying Inside."

55 Truu, "Questions Raised over Thailand and Bahrain's Close Ties."

56 Hookway, "Crown Prince Has Hard Act to Follow."

57 Hookway, "Thailand's Royal Fortune Looms over Crown Prince's Ascension to Throne."

58 *Royal Gazette*; also in multiple Thai news reports.

59 "Akkharaphongpricha Name Withdrawn, Kedampang Used Instead," *Bangkok Post*.

60 "King Appoints Sathitpong," *Bangkok Post*.

61 Sopranzetti, "The Tightening Authoritarian Grip on Thailand," 230–32.

62 Teeranai, "King Granted Direct Control over Palace Agencies."

63 Teeranai, "New Law Places Crown Property under HM King."

64 Pavin, "A Very Wealthy Monarch Grows Wealthier."

65 "Thailand's King Given Direct Control of Palace Wealth," *Agence France-Presse*.

66 Ono, "Thai King Becomes Major Shareholder of Siam Commercial Bank."

67 Tostevin, "Over $500 Million in Thai Bank Shares Transferred on Behalf of King: SEC."

68 Crown Property Bureau, https://www.crownproperty.or.th/.

69 Mérieau, "Thailand in 2018: Military Dictatorship under Royal Command," 327–40.

70 SCB, https://www.scb.co.th/en/about-us/board-of-director/satitpong-sukvimol.html.

71 Sawitta Lefevre, "Assets Registered to Thai Crown Property Bureau to be Held under King's Name."

72 "Thai King Exempted from Tax on Some Land Properties," *Reuters*.

73 Ono, "Thai King Becomes Top Shareholder of Siam Cement."

74 Mérieau, "Thailand in 2018," 332.

75 Wassana, "Royal Turf Club Runs Its Last Race."

76 Mérieau, "Thailand in 2018," 333.

77 Teeranai, "Khaosod English Visits Demolished Vimanmek Palace."

78 Wassana, "Army Returns Prem's Home."

79 Confidential interview with a source in Bangkok, November 2019.

80 Confidential interview with a source in Bangkok, November 2019.

81 Ünaldi, *Working towards the Monarchy*, 220–26.

82 Pravit, "No Explanation: Democratic Revolt Leaders Statues Gone Missing."

References

"Akkharaphongpricha Name Withdrawn, Kerdampang Used Instead." *Bangkok Post*, 30 November 2014. https://www.bangkokpost.com/thailand/general/446153/family-name-withdrawn, accessed 7 July 2022.

Baker, Chris, and Pasuk Phongpaichit. *A History of Thailand*, 3rd ed. Cambridge: Cambridge University Press, 2014.

Cod Satrusayang. "Opinion: Making Outlandish Statements Hinders More than Helps the Student Movement." *Thai Inquirer*, 30 November 2020. www.thaienquirer.com/21162/opinion-making-outlandish-statements-hinders-more-than-helps-the-student-movement/, accessed 7 July 2022.

Cunningham, Susan J. "The Crowning Fortune." *Forbes Asia*, 22 August 2008. https://www.forbes.com/global/2008/0901/032.html?sh=7b15848e1433, accessed 7 July 2022.

Francis, Samantha. "Siam Kempinski Hotel Bangkok Debuts Its Very Own Monopoly Game." *DestinAsian*, 14 August 2018. https://www.destinasian.com/blog/news-briefs/siam-kempinski-hotel-bangkok-debuts-its-very-own-monopoly-game, accessed 7 July 2022.

"[Full statement] The Demonstration at Thammasat Proposes Monarchy Reform." *Prachatai*. https://prachatai.com/english/node/8709, accessed 7 July 2022.

"Government to Spend 29 Billion Baht on Monarchy," *Prachatai*. https://prachatai.com/english/node/8431, accessed 7 July 2022.

Grossman, Nicholas, and Dominic Faulder, eds. *King Bhumibol Adulyadej: A Life's Work*. Singapore: Editions Didier Millet, 2011.

Handley, Paul M. *The King Never Smiles: A Biography of Thailand's King Bhumibol Adulyadej*. New Haven, CT: Yale University Press, 2006.

Hewison, Kevin. Review of Porphant Ouyyanont, *Crown Property Bureau in Thailand and Its Role in Political Economy. Journal of Contemporary Asia* 46.3 (2016):538–40.

Hookway, James. "Crown Prince Has Hard Act to Follow, Tough Job Ahead." *Wall Street Journal*, 14 October 2016. https://www.wsj.com/articles/after-thai-kings-death-crown-prince-has-a-hard-act-to-follow-1476386698, accessed 7 July 2022.

———. "Thailand's Royal Fortune Looms over Crown Prince's Ascension to Throne." *Wall Street Journal*, 17 November 2016. https://www.wsj.com/articles/thailands-royal-fortune-looms-over-crown-prince-s-ascension-to-throne-1479378606, accessed 7 July 2022.

"King Appoints Sathitpong." *Bangkok Post*, 29 January 2017. https://www.bangkok-post.com/thailand/general/1188573/king-appoints-sathitpong, accessed 7 July 2022.

Massola, James. "I Was Crying Inside: Hakeem Al-Araibi on the Bungle that Landed Him in a Thai Jail." *Good Weekend*, 13 April 2019. https://www.smh.com.au/world/asia/i-was-crying-inside-melbourne-soccer-player-hakeem-al-araibi-on-the-bungle-that-landed-him-in-a-thai-jail-20190409-p51cck.html, accessed 7 July 2022.

Mérieau, Eugénie. "Thailand in 2018: Military Dictatorship under Royal Command." In *Southeast Asian Affairs*, ed. Daljit Singh and Malcolm Cook, 327–40. Singapore: ISEAS-Yusof Ishak Institute, 2019.

Ono, Yukako. "Thai King Becomes Major Shareholder of Siam Commercial Bank." *Nikkei Asian Review*, 6 October 2017. https://asia.nikkei.com/Economy/Thai-King-becomes-major-shareholder-of-Siam-Commercial-Bank, accessed 7 July 2022.

Ono, Yukako. "Thai King Becomes Top Shareholder of Siam Cement." *Nikkei Asia*, 18 June 2018. https://asia.nikkei.com/Politics/Thai-king-becomes-top-shareholder-of-Siam-Cement-Siam-Commercial, accessed 30 August 2023.

Pavin Chachavalpongpun. "A Very Wealthy Monarch Grows Wealthier." *Japan Times*, 9 September 2017. https://www.japantimes.co.jp/opinion/2017/09/09/commentary/world-commentary/wealthy-monarch-grows-wealthier/, accessed 7 July 2022.

Porphant Ouyyanont. "The Crown Property Bureau in Thailand and the Crisis of 1997." *Journal of Contemporary Asia* 38.1 (2008):166–89.

———. *Crown Property Bureau in Thailand and Its Role in Political Economy.* Trends in Southeast Asia series. Singapore: ISEAS, No. 13, 2015.

Pravit, Rojanaphruk. "No Explanation: Democratic Revolt Leaders Statues Gone Missing." *Khaosod English*, 27 January 2020. https://www.khaosodenglish.com/politics/2020/01/27/no-explanation-democratic-revolt-leaders-statues-gone-missing/, accessed 7 July 2022.

———. "Scholar Fears Massive Renovation of Iconic Avenue May Erase History." *Khaosod English*, 23 January 2020. https://www.khaosodenglish.com/news/2020/01/23/scholar-fears-massive-renovation-of-iconic-avenue-may-erase-history/, accessed 7 July 2022.

Reed, John. "All the King's Money." *Financial Times*, 13 October 2022. https://www.afr.com/world/asia/all-the-king-s-money-thailand-divided-over-a-us40b-question-20201014-p564xr, accessed 7 July 2022.

"Rosewood Takes over Kempinski Heritage Hotel Plans." *Myanmore*, 20 June 2018. https://www.myanmore.com/2018/06/rosewood-takes-over-kempinski-heritage-hotel-plans, accessed 7 July 2020.

Sanderson, Paul. "Stuck between Two Kings: A Possible Explanation for Hakeem Al-Araibi's Detention." *Sydney Morning Herald*, 4 May 2019. https://www.smh.com.au/world/asia/two-kings-a-billion-euros-and-an-australian-trapped-in-thailand-20190314-p5146l.html, accessed 7 July 2022.

Sawitta Lefevre, Amy. "Assets Registered to Thai Crown Property Bureau to be Held under King's Name." *Reuters*, 16 June 2018. https://www.reuters.com/article/us-thailand-king-property-idUSKBN1JC0EK, accessed 7 July 2022.

Sopranzetti, Claudio. "The Tightening Authoritarian Grip on Thailand." *Current History* 116.791 (2017):230–34.

Spritzer, Dinah A. "Dusit Thani Sells Its Share of Kempinski." *Travel Weekly*, 11 March 1998. https://www.travelweekly.com/Travel-News/Hotel-News/Dusit-Thani-Sells-Its-Share-of-Kempinski, accessed 7 July 2022.

Teeranai Charuvastra. "King Granted Direct Control over Palace Agencies." *Khaosod English*, 2 May 2017. https://www.khaosodenglish.com/politics/2017/05/02/king-granted-direct-control-palace-agencies/, accessed 7 July 2022.

———. "Khaosod English Visits Demolished Vimanmek Palace." *Khaosod English*, 25 July 2019. https://www.khaosodenglish.com/news/2019/07/25/khaosod-english-visits-demolished-vimanmek-palace, accessed 7 July 2022.

———. "New Law Places Crown Property under HM King." *Khaosod English*, 17 July 2017. https://www.khaosodenglish.com/politics/2017/07/17/new-law-places-crown-property-hm-king/, accessed 7 July 2022.

"Thai King Exempted from Tax on Some Land Properties." *Reuters*, 28 July 2019. https://www.reuters.com/article/us-thailand-king-tax-idUSKCN1UN0IB, accessed 7 July 2022.

"Thailand's King Given Direct Control of Palace Wealth." *Agence France-Presse*, 17 July 2017. https://www.france24.com/en/20170717-thailand-king-monarchy-military-junta-palace-wealth, accessed 7 July 2022.

"'Thailand's Royal Wealth' and 'Royal Wealth (Continued).'" *Asia Sentinel*, 2 March 2007. https://www.asiasentinel.com/p/royal-wealth-continued, accessed 7 July 2022.

Thanthong-Knight, Randy. "Thai Protesters Target King's Wealth in Latest Bangkok Rally." *Bloomberg*, 25 November 2020. https://www.bloomberg.com/news/articles/2020-11-25/thai-protesters-to-target-king-s-wealth-in-latest-bangkok-rally, accessed 30 August 2023.

Tostevin, Matthew. "Over $500 Million in Thai Bank Shares Transferred on Behalf of King: SEC." *Reuters*, 6 October 2017. https://news.yahoo.com/over-500-million-thai-bank-shares-transferred-behalf-090825200-finance.html, accessed 7 July 2022.

Truu, Maani. "Questions Raised over Thailand and Bahrain's Close Ties as Hakeem Al-Araibi's Detention Continues." *SBS News*, 8 February 2019. https://www.sbs.com.au/news/article/questions-raised-over-thailand-and-bahrains-close-ties-as-hakeem-al-araibis-detention-continues/louxibm8r, accessed 7 July 2022.

Ünaldi, Serhat. *Working towards the Monarchy: The Politics of Space in Downtown Bangkok*. Honolulu: University of Hawai'i Press, 2016.

Wassana Nanuam. "Army Returns Prem's Home." *Bangkok Post*, 30 October 2019. https://www.bangkokpost.com/thailand/general/1782654/army-returns-prems-home, accessed 7 July 2022.

———. "Royal Turf Club Runs Its Last Race." *Bangkok Post*, 17 September 2018. https://www.bangkokpost.com/thailand/general/1541106/royal-turf-club-runs-its-last-race, accessed 7 July 2022.

6

From Love to Fear:
Affective Governance in Times of Succession

CLAUDIO SOPRANZETTI

ON 4 MAY 2019, Vajiralongkorn received the Thai crown, officially becoming Rama X, the latest heir of a dynasty that began in 1736 and has since ruled over Siam and Thailand, after the country changed its name in 1939. Although the coronation took place in 2019, Vajiralongkorn effectively took power right after the passing of his father, King Bhumibol Adulyadej, in October 2016. Many expected him to have little interest in ruling, due to his reputation as an erratic playboy more concerned with planes, parties, women, and living in his German mansion than with filling his father's shoes. His first years in power, however, painted a very different picture, one of a forceful ruler, determined to put his house in order, while exercising control over the palace, royal coffers, military forces, and Thai society at large.

The process of establishing his rule started close to home. Almost immediately after taking the throne in 2016, the new king imposed tighter control over the palace's inner circles and the powerful figures who ran it under his late father. In the following three years, Vajiralongkorn stripped more than 60 palace officials of their ranks,[1] with official accusations that went from behavior unfit for senior bureaucrats to abuses of power for personal profit, from engagement in politics jeopardizing national security and disclosing the late king's health record to adultery and having lost his trust. These sudden falls from the very top of the royal circles spread fear among prominent families, with multiple sources close to the palace stating that people were developing contingency plans, moving money abroad, and putting things in place in case the king turned against them.[2] The king's adoption of fear as a tool of governance did not stop there. Military officers were also brought in line through a new array of rules—including strict haircuts and punishments for anyone who dared to cross the new king. Finally, Vajiralongkorn's reign began with a landmark legal case against Jatupat Boonpattararaksa, a law student at Khon Kaen University, who was accused on 4 December 2016 of violating the infamous lèse-majesté law for sharing on his Facebook account a biography of the new king produced by the BBC Thai.[3] From student activists to soldiers, from politicians to aristocratic families, many in Thailand quickly learned that the new monarch was possibly even more hands-on than his father and much less interested in love and devotion than in ensuring blind loyalty, demanding submission, and instilling fear.[4]

While the magnitude of this shift went well beyond anyone's expectations, a radical change occurring between the two leaders was in no way unpredictable, given their different styles and personal histories. Vajiralongkorn came to the throne as a sixty-four-year-old military man, as described by Gregory Raymond in a previous chapter. He was largely disliked by the former king's inner circles,[5] portrayed by official Thai media as a loyal son,[6] but had acquired a diffused fame of a mercurial and vindictive character, prone to punishing insubordination and handsomely rewarding abnegation: a thug, many murmured behind closed doors. His father had become king as a quiet and inoffensive nineteen-year-old, orphan of his father, and raised mostly in Switzerland. King Bhumibol took the throne in 1946, after the mysterious death of his brother, who was found shot in his room. A quiet and bookish young man, Bhumibol was brought back to Thailand as an irrelevant figurehead controlled by military governments and secluded in his palace. In the following years, the young Bhumibol started to travel to rural provinces, support local monks and temples, and establish development projects. These popular enterprises laid the carefully crafted groundwork for the construction of his unprecedented popularity among Thais, which solidified, especially since the nationalist days of Cold War and anti-communist propaganda, around a discursive equation between "loving the country" (*rak chat*) and "loving the king" (*rak nailuang*). Love, however, was only one side of how the relationship between Bhumibol and his subjects was to be organized. The other was the lèse-majesté law—a law stating that "whoever defames, insults or threatens the King, the Queen, the Heir Apparent, or the Regent shall be punished with imprisonment of three to fifteen years." Also known as Article 112, its number in the penal code, the law was introduced in its present form punishing both defamation and insult to the monarchy in 1957, at the same time as Bhumibol's popularity started to flourish. Those two pillars—love and legal protection—provided the foundations to Bhumibol's reign.[7] Over the following decades, the king acquired more and more power, cultivating his image of a loving, fair, and charismatic father of the nation, while also accumulating wealth and fencing off any criticism with the help of a growing propaganda machine, military and para-military forces, and the lèse-majesté law. It was in 2006, during his golden jubilee, that the love story between Thailand and Bhumibol was sealed with the "we love the king" campaign, a slogan stamped on yellow stickers that proliferated like wildfire across the country, from cabs to restaurants, from billboards to magazines. Once again, as the message of love for Bhumibol was broadcast across the country, lèse-majesté cases skyrocketed.[8] Nonetheless, even with those repressive measures on the rise, his dedication to the Thai people remained until the very end, a largely celebrated feature of his reign,[9] one framed in the language of love—a language largely abandoned by the new king.

This chapter aims at analyzing the shift from love to fear as central tools of royal governance in contemporary Thailand and showing how the deployment of these affects shapes the royal succession, how each system imagines the relation between ruler and subjects, and what political actions are made possible or prevented by each of them. Naturally, like many shifts in dominant epistemes, this is not a binary transition, and the idiom of love continues to be mobilized under the reign of Vajiralongkorn, as much as fear played a role under Bhumibol. However, I argue that the relative weight that these affects play in royal governance are shifting and that a focus on this shift is central to understanding contemporary Thai politics. As Ann Stoller has shown, there is a global tendency in political analysis to think about affective components of power as epiphenomenal, "a smokescreen of rule ... a ruse masking the dispassionate calculations that preoccupy states."[10] This tendency is also present in Thai studies where material explanations have often dominated the scene, focusing on shifting alliances among the elite,[11] political-economic transformations,[12] or regional inequalities.[13] While I consider these works essential and do not dismiss the importance of their material analyses—on which I myself often focused my attention— here I follow the lead of Nidhi Eoseewong and his reminder that any analysis of contemporary Thai politics needs to pay attention to its ever-changing political culture: the "ways of life, ways of thinking, and values of the society come to accept that legitimate powers must be related together in a certain way."[14] In particular, I build on Thannapat Jarernpanit's observation that this attention means also exploring "the struggle for the meaning of moral values and politics, as shaped by different emotions."[15]

This centrality of affects and emotions, I argue, is particularly important when dealing with royalty. Marshall Sahlins and David Graeber have shown in their erudite study of kingship that "the ordinary balance of power between king and people is often maintained through intense emotional engagement,"[16] and Thailand has not been an exception. This chapter, therefore, focuses on changes in the form of emotional engagement between the reign of Bhumibol and Vajiralongkorn and explores the shift from love to fear as the main form of what I call "affective governance"—a ruling through affects—deployed by the two monarchs. Contrary to what it may seem, I do not see this shift as a degeneration from a positive form of governance to a negative one, nor, to paraphrase Machiavelli's famous motto, as an argument as to whether it is safer for a prince to be feared or loved. Love should not be considered, as intuitively we may do, as a positive emotion, and fear a negative one. On the contrary, both emotions have been and continue to be equally productive forces that generate different systems of "affective governance" and management of the relation between the king and his subjects, defined by specific forms of emotive participation, repressive mechanisms, and acts of dissent. I leave to normative political scientists the task of arguing over which form is preferable. My objective is not to express moral or pragmatic judgments but rather to analyze the features of each form and the systems of participation, refusal, and repression that they generate.

A Brief History of Love, Governance, and Bodhisattvas

The connection among love, family, and political authority has a long history in Theravada Buddhist thought and its conception of kingship, one that I can barely begin to scratch the surface of here.[17] The *Vessantara Jātaka*, one of the most popular *jātaka*—stories about the past lives of the Buddha—in Theravada tradition offers one of the earliest formulations of the importance of love, and specifically filial love, to the management of a Buddhist kingdom.[18] As Patrick Jory has shown,

> the *Maha Chat* [ritual recitation of the *Vessantara Jātaka*] was a discourse not only about kingship, moral and ascetic self-cultivation, and royal power but also about relations within the family. That these issues were played out at the level of the family made the story much more realistic and accessible to a popular audience. The *Vessantara Jātaka* addressed issues of authority generally, and authority started in the family. The principal relationships dealt with in the story are those between father and son, mother and child, husband and wife, family and state, and the individual and society.[19]

In this narrative, love between father and children becomes the model for the relationship between the rulers and his subjects, in which the latter gives complete deference and obedience, and the former reciprocates with the ties of paternal love, dedication, and care while maintaining that "this love is strictly subordinated to the father's self-interest."[20]

While this view, which Thongchai Winichakul has called "paternalistic governance,"[21] existed in Buddhist thought since its origin, it was among the palaces and temples of Sukhothai that this idea was more fully developed and condensed in a text that came to be seen as the first local formulation of Buddhist cosmology and polity: the *Three Worlds of Phra Ruang*. This text, known in Thai as *Traiphum Phra Ruang*, was redacted in 1345 by Phraya Li-Thai (r. 1347–68) and describes the conditions and characteristics of all beings who inhabit the various realms of the Buddhist universe. Relevant to us, the *Traiphum* solidified the link between Buddhism and kingship and put love at the very center of the kingdom, laying the foundations for legitimizing a type of monarchical rule that mobilizes love as a tool of governance. This is the type of affective governance that the most successful of the Chakri monarchs were able to implement, the one that King Mongkut (r. 1851–68) started to build, his son Chulalongkorn (r. 1868–1910) strengthened, and Bhumibol more fully realized.[22] In particular, three ideas that emerged in the *Traiphum* about the ideal Buddhist monarch became central to this model: first, the concept of the *mahasammata* (great elect), which portrays the king as chosen by his equals to save the reign from chaos due to his virtues, his embodiment of the dhamma, and his destiny to become a buddha (bodhisattva); second, the concept of the *chakravartin*, the wheel-turning monarch, who rules with dharma and not the sword, and by so doing maintains the order of the worlds and expands his reign as of "the many princes and lords, … not one of them could raise arms against the Universal King. They felt only the love towards him. … They made their obeisance to the king and vowed their loyalty to him"[23]; and finally, the concept of the *dhammaraja*, the king who is "righteous and just. Be steadfast in the Ten Principles of Kingship. Love thy lords, thy ministers, thy people. Love all equally."[24] What unites them all is a conceptualization of love as the affective bonding of the reign: love from the monarch toward his people and his subjects toward him. Such love, if reciprocal, was never among equals. As we saw, the archetype of this love was that between father and children, a hierarchical love made of complete devotion or immediate disowning.

While it would be easy to look back at those conceptions as the stuff of epic novels and cosmological stories, their ideas continued to run deep throughout modern Thai history, resurfaced, together with the Ramkhamhaeng inscription—a stone stele dating back to 1292 describing the Sukhothai Kingdom—during the reign of Mongkut, and acquired a new solidity during the reign of Chulalongkorn. It was then, in fact, that love as a form of governance acquired one of its eerier undertones, which would come to color its deployment under King Bhumibol. Writing to his brother in 1874, after a serious crisis between him and his uncle, the then viceroy rumored of trying to dethrone him, Chulalongkorn says, "I want to tell the 'Young Siam' [a group of his supporters] that what the viceroy has done [visiting a foreign ambassador] clearly showed that he should not be con-sidered a citizen of the Siamese nation because he has no love for the country and no love for the [royal] family."[25] This argument, destined to be repeated over and over again in conservative Thai discourse, took love as a tool of governance to a new level. Not only should the ideal relation between ruler and subject be modeled after that of filial love, but also a failure to love equals an expulsion from the national body.

According to this view, to be Thai is to love the king, and to love the king is to be Thai, therefore it is impossible for Thais to feel anything short of love for their ruler. As Bowornsak Uwanno, one of the most prominent royalist intellectuals, argued 134 years after the crisis:

> [such an idea] is unknown in those materially developed but spiritually deteriorating countries. It cannot be appreciated by those who have never lived in a country where warm ties exist between the ruler and the people as father and children. The leaders of these countries are politicians who have equal status as all other citizens. The ties between them and those who

elect them are political in nature so that once expired, such ties no longer matter, and the latter can make whatever criticisms of their political leaders, citing the freedom of expression. However, Thai people, who love and revere their Father, will never let anyone unfairly criticize their King. Such is the socio-cultural dimension of the Thai monarchy, which those who never feel it will find it hard to understand, like those who are orphaned from birth can, unfortunately, never feel, and thus cannot understand, the love and bond between children and parents![26]

Ignoring for a moment the essentializing and gross historical inaccuracy of this statement, this tautological and conceptual shortcut, reverberating through the hallway of Thai history, lost prominence after the death of King Chulalongkorn, almost disappeared over the course of the early twentieth century, in which the Thai monarchs were unable to rule by love, and often to rule at all, but reemerged to become the core of a new form of affective governance during the reign of King Bhumibol. Contrary to what Uwanno's ahistorical statement claims, however, this form of governance is coming to an end with the rise to the throne of King Vajiralongkorn. Before we move to that, however, let us explore how love resurfaced from the 1960s as a central tool of affective governance in Thailand, what system of rule it created, and what political actions it allowed and repressed during the reign of Bhumibol.

Love under Bhumibol

The traditional conception of filial love as the ideal relation between king and subjects reemerged, especially during the Cold War, as a way to conceptualize the relation between citizens and their leaders, amid a potential communist insurrection developing in the country. This renewed centrality of love as a tool of governance, begun during the years of Phibun's dictatorship (1947–57), was fully developed under Sarit's leadership (1957–63), and continued as a trademark of Bhumibol's reign until his passing in 2016. It is hard, in fact, to understand the postwar development of Thai national-ism (*chatniyom*) and the new relationship crafted over that period among national leaders, state bureaucracy, and citizens without acknowledging the role of love. During the Phibun regime, much of state propaganda revolved around the "age-old theme of filial piety and the danger of communism. The duties of a good citizen were to believe in the principle of respect for elders;

sons and daughters should listen to their parents, and the parents should love their children."[27]

Once Sarit came to power, this same filial love was conceptualized as diffusing across the nation connecting the leader and the citizens, through the bureaucracy. In the opening speech of the conference of governors and regional police chiefs in 1960, Sarit said: "I feel that you are my ears, eyes, and heart, which I have given to the people. The well-being of the people is my heartfelt concern. I ask you to represent my heart, which wants to give love and concern for the people. ... Always remember that you are my *khaluang tangchai*, representing my heart. My heart is honest and loves the people, and thus you must love and be honest towards the people."[28] On the one hand, Sarit saw love as given out by the ruler, through his officers. On the other hand, he stressed the importance of love also flowing in the other direction, reiterating Chulalongkorn's idea that to love your ruler was to love the nation and hence to be part of it. A subtle shift occurred. Previous discourse focused on the love given by the leader/father to his subjects/ children, a love that implied reciprocity but did not focus on it. During this period, love came increasingly to be stressed as a form of affective governance that went both ways, and that needed to be reciprocated by the subjects as a demonstration of their membership in the national community. In a 1961 speech, talking about the Muslim majority provinces in the south of Thailand, Sarit said, "I would like to urge and incite you to consider your love for the Thai nation. Our nationalism should flow thick in our blood, especially in the period of this revolutionary government. I want my Thai brothers from Isan, the north, and the south to pour to the south and to settle and work there. ... Bring down Thai blood and the love of the nation."[29]

Over this period, particularly in relation to the communist threat presented as un-Thai precisely for its refusal to love the nation and love its leaders, filial love and love for the nation (*rak chat*) were connected and became a central feature of the nationalist discourse, in which the monarchy increasingly played a prominent role. By the time Sarit died in 1963, in fact, the object of love started to shift away from him to King Bhumibol: love for the nation became love for the king, and vice versa. The state propaganda machine was deployed in full force to build this affective bond through public education, state radio, and TV stressing the continuous acts of love for the nation by the monarch, from development projects to donation ceremonies, all the way to campaigns that attempted to enter the most private aspects of citizens' everyday life: their bathrooms. In 1966 soap bars were distributed around the countryside. These soap bars, as they got used, revealed seven layers of slogans exhorting people to love the king, follow Buddhism, and fight communism.[30]

While the soaps may not have been the most successful piece of propaganda, over the following decades an idea started to take form, an idea most powerfully formulated in the work of Thannapat Jarernpanit, as quoted here:

> As a Thai, if you do not love the nation and the monarchy, then you are "bad," a sinner betraying your country and the king, and someone lacking gratitude towards the motherland (*pandin*). This discourse of gratitude to the motherland (*katanyu, rukun tor pandin*) is closely associated to royal-nationalist doctrine and the concept of goodness in Thai morality. Consequently, the feeling of love is combined with religious belief, goodness, and faith or loyalty to king and nation as promoted in royal-nationalist ideology. It is a feeling of love embedded in the cognition and consciousness of the Thai people.[31]

Three moments, in particular, were central to this process of embedding love for the monarchy in the collective consciousness and its emergence as a tool of governance over the reign of Bhumibol: the 1973 students uprising, the 1987 sixtieth birthday of Bhumibol, and the 2006 celebration of his sixtieth year on the throne.

On 14 October 1973, as students revolted against the government of Thanom Kittikachorn (1963–73), Bhumibol intervened, for the first time in his reign, in national politics and pushed Thanom out of power. This shift of the monarch from a passive to an active role had a deep influence on the king's popularity, lifting Bhumibol's status. Some members of the student movement, underlining their loyalty to the nation, praised the monarch by displaying the picture of the king during demonstrations. Yuk argued that the students were "motivated by love to the nation," and some Thai academics called this the birth of a new nationalism,[32] a nationalism from below which could legitimize and equate its love for the nation with its love for the monarchy.[33]

This nationalism that connected the love of the king with that of the nation was at the center of the celebration of the king's sixtieth birthday on 5 December 1987. For the occasion, the state propaganda machine organized a nationwide chanting for the king. "He rules the land with righteousness for the progress of the country, the people, and the religion," the chant recited. It continued:

> He never thinks about the obstacles, dangers, and troubles for him. He has a strong intention to perform the royal duty with perseverance and the strength of his endurance and benevolence. He loves the people like a father loves his children. When it is cold he gives warmth and when it is warm he gives water. When he goes to places with suffering, the suffering is gone because of his power, like the rain in the hot summer. He is firmly in dharma. He is the foremost Buddhist. Because of his power, kindness, and grace, the unity, happiness, peace, and progress happen to all the Thai people in every place in Thailand.[34]

This prayer reiterated all the elements of Buddhist kingship drafted centuries before in the *Three Worlds of Phra Ruang* and depicted the king as the holder of *barami*, a moral charisma that motivates the love of his subjects.[35] Prime Minister Prem Tinsulanonda (1980–88) stressed this aspect after the celebration: "You [King Bhumibol] closely share the suffering and the happiness with the people in order to extend your *barami* over them and to get rid of their suffering and create peace and happiness for the people. ... His [the king's] development projects result in progress of the countryside and prosperity of the land. ... This causes the real love and a sense of belonging towards their birthplace."[36]

These celebrations represented one more step toward the adoption of love for the monarch as a tool of governance and a defining characteristic of national identity. Yet it was only during the king's 2006 Diamond Jubilee that the Ministry of Culture enshrined this diffused feeling into the popular campaign "we love the king" (*rao rak nailuang*), which became, for the following decade until Bhumibol's death, "the convenient umbrella for organizing political sentiments around the monarchy, especially where military interventionism has the potential to raise troubling questions about elite motivations."[37] The "we love the king" campaign may have been the single most successful marketing campaign run by the Ministry of Culture under Bhumibol, with the slogan printed on T-shirts, bumper stickers, wristbands, coffee mugs, and any other imaginable piece of merchandise. Between 2006 and 2016, it became impossible to spend time anywhere in Thailand without being confronted with the seemingly handwritten message "*rao rak nailuang*" with a red heart encircling the word *rak* (love). This logo was originally penned in 2002 by secondary-school student Nop-abha "Yui"

Devakula as part of a nationwide competition to express the nation's love for the king. The winner was no ordinary girl, but the granddaughter of Lord Chamberlain Kaewkwan Vajarodaya, one of the most powerful figures in Bhumibol's palace, and one of those whom Vajiralongkorn would get rid of as soon as he took the throne. In an interview with the *Pattaya Mail* for Bhumibol's eighty-first birthday, the girl, then a university student, explained how she came up with the famous logo: "I drew characters with a computer mouse, not a pen. ... It does have a child-like quality which I thought appropriate to dedicate to the father of our country and of all the Thai people."[38]

The logo and its style perfectly condensed a central aspect of love as affective governance. On the one hand, as Yui showed, it confirmed a specific relation between the ruler and his subject: while the first is elevated as the father of the nation, the second is infantilized and reduced to the role of a child. On the other hand, the inclusion of the word *rao* (we) suggests a collectivity that is defined and bathed in that love. In other words, the slogan does not refer to personal love, but a communal one. Framed as "we love the king" and not "I love the king," it interpolates a national collective into this affect and creates a direct connection and almost mutual exclusion between love for the king and Thainess. To be Thai, the slogan implied, is to love the king and, therefore, not loving the king means forfeiting Thainess. "If you don't love the king, never come back to Thailand!" and "Get a new nationality!" are common responses to critics of the monarchy.[39] This sentiment was by definition collective and required complete devotion from each of the royal subjects.[40]

Since 2006, love became a centerpiece to the ideology of hyper-royalism explored by Thongchai Winichakul, yet a feature largely ignored by him.[41] This centrality, however, made love for the king a highly contested and policed field. As an article in the *Financial Times Magazine* after the passing of Bhumibol stated, "It is impossible to generalise about how—and to what degree—devotion, affection, and fear bind Thai citizens to their kings. As one Thai journalist has put it, if it's compulsory to love the monarchy, you end up with two kinds of people: those who love the monarchy and those who lie about their love for the monarchy."[42] Policing and silencing the second attitude, therefore, was a central aspect of love as affective governance, one that framed which political actions were possible or not under the rule of love. As Irene Stengs showed:

All views on political core issues such a redistribution of wealth, corruption, human rights, and democracy are sucked in the vortex of the persistent political antagonisms, to surface as elaboration of the slogan "we love the king" (*rao rak nailuang*). The ideology of the Thai people's unconditional love for their king is controlled and enforced through a strict lèse-majesté law that precludes even the most trivial criticism of the king or the monarchy in general. The combination of a pervasive royalism, in which every person and party seek to appear more royalist than any other, and a general internalized self-censorship are central to grasping the transformation of the worship of the monarchy in recent years.[43]

The Other Side of Love: The Paradox of Article 112

Possibly the most famous example of the use of love as a defining characteristic of Thainess under hyper-royalism took place in 2010, at the peak of the Red Shirt mobilization. In a ceremony to accept a best supporting actor award on 16 May 2010, in the middle of the military crackdown, a well-known Thai actor said, "if you hate the father, don't love him anymore, please leave, because this is the home of the father. This is the land of the father. I love the king, and I believe that every one of us here loves the king. We are the entire same color. My head is belonging to the king." This speech was followed immediately by an Internet attack against another actor—for walking out in the middle of the speech. Also at the ceremony, the actor's daughter had been captured on TV not singing a song with lyrics composed by the king. She was also attacked. "Overnight both the father and the actor's daughter were bombarded with accusations and contract cancellations, and pressured into stating that they were loyal monarchists."[44] While this may be the most visible example of the need for complete submission to love, it was not the only one. As we saw, love as governance, since its discussion in the *Vessantara Jātaka*, demanded complete devotion. This characteristic was only reinforced during the Cold War and even more so under hyper-royalism after 2006. This was the dark side of love as governance: hate, anger, and violence toward anyone who did not profess undying love toward the monarch.

Love, especially when presented as both filial and collective love for the king and the nation, requires complete submission. To love someone is to do so unconditionally, constantly, and personally. Love demands a direct connection and spares no one. It requires everyone involved in the relationship to conform to this affective relation. As Jitlada Meesuk has argued, "the need for uniformity as imposed on citizens by the state has developed into hostility against differences and individuation."[45] This is the ultimate paradox of love as a tool of governance, its production of anger and hate toward anyone who refuses that emotional bonding. Not to love the father is to refuse to be part of the family, and this is not perceived simply as an attack on the father but on the whole social body. It is therefore not by chance that the launching of the "we love the king" campaign, followed by the 2006 coup, corresponded with an unprecedented surge in lèse-majesté cases. According to David Streckfuss, before 2006 the highest number of arrests in a single year was 36 in 1977, the year of the heightened royalist and anti-communist fever at the peak of Thailand's Cold War, and after that reduced to a few cases a year. Since 2006, however, the number skyrocketed. Between 2006 and 2008, the average number jumped to 60 cases a year, with a record of 126 cases in 2007.[46] From then to the death of Bhumibol, the cases stabilized with an average of 75 per year.[47]

Over this period, particularly telling was the case of Junya Yimprasert, founder of the Thai Labor Campaign. In 2010, she published in *Time-up Thailand* a controversial article titled "Why I Don't Love the King." In this long piece, Junya narrates the end of her love story with King Bhumibol, how she was raised to feel unquestioning love for him, how that love was central to the mainstream rejection of communism in the 1970s, and how the events of the 1992 pro-democracy protest, the 2006 military coup, and, most of all, the violent dispersal of the Red Shirts in 2010 brought her to question that love. "From the day I was born, the royal family had my love, but slowly they have been losing that love," she concludes. "If the palace makes me choose between loving the royal family and loving the Thai people I can only choose the latter."[48] This piece was a direct refusal to love and showed what space for political actions was open by this form of affective governance as well as how central it is for this system to enforce love, with any means necessary. Junya's declaration and her decoupling and opposition between loving the royal family and loving the nation, the opposite of what state propaganda had told her and everybody else for decades, attracted immediate public attention and soon came under the attack of the state's repressive machine. In 2010, Junya left Thailand, and in 2013 she was accused of lèse-majesté. "Three of my friends were interviewed by the Department of Special Investigation (DSI) and the Attorney-General," she declared, "who asked them questions about me. They were told that the interview was in relation to my article entitled 'Why I don't love the king.'"[49]

Junya was able to leave the country and live as a political refugee in Finland. Soon after her case, the deployment of lèse-majesté law to enforce Bhumibol's rule of love expanded. This time it was not only directed to political opponents and public figures but increasingly to "ordinary people, many of whom violated the law out of carelessness or ignorance to the proper conducts, such as sharing messages, clicking 'like' for some of those messages, writing a graffiti on the wall of a public toilet, and so on."[50] Love required complete submission by every member of the collective, no matter how ordinary, and its shadow extended over everyone. This repression of any refusal to love, moreover, was not carried out only by courts but also on social media by self-appointed defenders of the monarchy. A prominent example of this dynamic is provided by the Social Sanction Facebook page, created in February 2012 by royalist forces to target and shame people expressing anti-monarchy feelings. As reported in a 2011 Netizen report, "The main discourse used on the Social Sanction page to attack its opponents was centered around the notion of Thainess under the absolute monarchy, such as 'being Thai is being loyal to the monarch, the owner of the kingdom,' 'whoever questions, criticizes, or does not express love toward the monarch is considered alien, ungrateful, and evil.' The discourse frequently used expressions such as 'ungrateful,' 'dead wood,' 'traitor,' etc."[51]

The intimate relation between love and repression intensified with the passing of Bhumibol. On 13 October 2016, as the news of the king's death was communicated, Twitter exploded with declarations of love for the monarch. "The hashtag that got the highest retweet is #เรารักในหลวง (we love the king), followed by #ทรงพระเจริญ (long live the king), and #ขอเป็นข้ารองพระบาททุกชาติไป (May I be your humble servant in all my lives)." Once again, the Ministry of Culture reiterated the message and distributed at the king's funeral a souvenir book titled *What Can We Do to Confidently Say "We Love the King"?*[52] At the same time, attacks on anyone who showed less than complete submission to love skyrocketed both online and in person, with people not wearing black being dragged through the streets and forced to kneel in front of images of the king and an online campaign accusing anyone who was not professing love to be anti-monarchic and therefore an enemy of the nation.

While this dynamic colored the last decades of Bhumibol's reign, it suddenly changed just before Vajiralongkorn officially took the throne. In an unexpected development, in 2018 the number of new cases of lèse-majesté dropped to zero, something that had not happened in decades. In February 2018, the attorney general issued an instruction to the state's prosecutor that in cases of lèse-majesté, after the police investigations, all the materials from the police must be delivered to the attorney general's office, and the attorney general will be the only person to decide whether to charge. As Thongchai has shown, "The state's prosecutors at the lower levels should not make any decision, even comments, as they had done before. This action, as it is understood, is a measure to stem the abuses of LM."[53]

Some argued that this change may have been the result of international attention toward lèse-majesté. Yet, this seems unlikely given Vajiralongkorn's clear disdain of international opinion regarding other decisions (e.g., the taking of a formal concubine). This change, I argue, was rather the result of a new form of affective governance relying on fear rather than love, an attempt to rule by instilling terror that did not require complete submission, at least until the 2020 protests started to show publicly that fear was not enough to silence people's dissatisfaction with the new monarch. It was then that lèse-majesté law was reintroduced by Vajiralongkorn. Before I explore this process, however, let me once again look at conceptualizations of fear as governance in the Thai tradition.

A Brief History of Fear as Governance

"Few keywords in the field of politics have been so neglected as fear," argued John Keane.[54] Fear as a concept, he continued, "tends to be used as a 'face-value' term—as a concept that does not merit even a definition because it is presumed that everyone who has experienced fear in their lives, or has learned about it from others, knows what it is." This is true also for Thai political thought, in which fear has not received the same attention that love has. There is no ancient or contemporary text on which to rely to understand the role of fear in relation to governance.[55] However, we can still individuate two forms of fear that have played a central role in Thai politics.

First, it is an outward fear, an emotion directed toward a public enemy, presented as external to the body politics, that operates as the main object of aversion and helps define the nation in opposition to it. In early Siamese history, this enemy was the Burmese, during the Cold War the communists,[56] and more recently the "Thaksin system," the Red Shirts, and anti-monarchic forces at large.[57] While the object of fear changed, the deployment of this affect to unify the country's body politics remained a constant of modern Thai history. Nonetheless, next to this fear of enemies presented as attacking the country, a second use of this emotion existed: an inward fear, which has little to do with political leaders' defining a common object of apprehension, but rather is mobilized to obtain submission. Although this fear is also created, wielded, or manipulated by political leaders, its specific purpose is to guarantee their hold on power. Where the first mode of fear involves a fear of external dangers, separate from an imagined collectivity, this second mode of political fear is more intimate, less fabulist, and it arises from the vertical conflicts and cleavages endemic to society.[58] This is the type of fear waged by the new monarch, a fear that aims to silence dissent and quash any form of insubordination.[59]

Of this form of fear, we find reference in traditional Thai political thought, especially in relation to the idea of power as influence, or *itthipon*, a form of power associated with *chao pho* (godfathers) and *nak leng* (thugs).[60] In this conceptualization, *itthipon* is a kind of power that is used to gain personal profit and "can be rooted in socioeconomic force (money), physical force (ability to gain compliance by physical coercion), or psychological force (the threat of using one or both of the former)."[61] This form of power, in other words, relies on establishing control over the leader's entourage and, as Persons has shown, "*itthipon* leaders have two primary tactics for controlling the entourage. They woo them and fear them at the same time. ... Leaders' weapons for gaining compliance are twofold: they create indebtedness through generosity, and they reinforce fear of consequences should clients fail to comply."[62] *Itthipon* as a system of rewards and punishments describes quite appropriately royal governance under Vajiralongkorn.

Fear under Vajiralongkorn

Vajiralongkorn's adoption of fear as a way of controlling his subjects did not begin with his ascension to the throne. Rather, his life as the prince was defined by this strategy. As Pavin Chachavalpongpun has shown:

Even prior to the death of Bhumibol, Vajiralongkorn relied on fear for his own rearrangement of power. He allowed a faction under his control to purge another perceived to be disloyal to him. The cases of Suriyan Sucharitpolwong, or Moh Yong, Police Major Prakrom Warunprapha, and Major General Phisitsak Seniwongse na Ayutthaya—all of whom worked for Vajiralongkorn, most visibly in the "Bike for Mum" project—reiterated that death could become a reward for those who breached his trust. ... His former consort, Srirasmi, has been put under house arrest in a Rachaburi house, shaved and dressed as a nun. Her family members and relatives were imprisoned on dubious charges. Pongpat Chayaphan, a former Royal Thai Police officer who was the head of the country's Central Investigation Bureau, was convicted in 2015 for profiting from a gambling den, violating a forestry-related law, and money laundering. Srirasmi is his niece. Earlier in 2014, Police General Akrawut Limrat, a close aide to Pongpat, was also found dead following a mysterious fall from a building. Vajiralongkorn's estranged sons, Juthavachara, Vacharaesorn, Chakriwat, and Vatcharawee—who live in exile in the United States with their mother Sujarinee Vivacharawongse, née Yuvathida Polpraserth—have been banned from coming home. These extreme punitive measures reiterated the fact that fear once again functions as a controlling device over his subjects, even those with royal blood.[63]

Since taking the throne, Vajiralongkorn has erected fear to a system of affective governance, profoundly different from the one deployed by his father. The case of the Vajarodaya family is particularly telling. As we saw before, the handwriting behind the "we love the king" campaign belonged to Nop-abha Devakula, the granddaughter of Lord Chamberlain Kaewkwan Vajarodaya, the patriarch of one of the most influential clans in Bhumibol's palace and one of the families that have fallen dramatically victim of Vajiralongkorn's shift from love to fear. Kaewkwan was a childhood friend of King Bhumibol, and the former king appointed him as lord chamberlain of the Royal Household Bureau in 1987, a position he retained until Bhumibol died in 2016. This effectively put Kaewkwan in charge of a palace bureaucracy of several thousand officials that manage royal affairs. But since 2009, it was widely known that his sons Ratthanwut and Watcharakitti were the de facto chamberlains. Moreover, over the past two decades, Kaewkwan's nephew Distorn Vajarodaya became particularly close to Bhumibol. Distorn was chairman of the king's Rajanukhrao Foundation and a grand chamberlain in the Royal Household Bureau, a position just below that of his grandfather. Over the last years of Bhumibol's life, he was often seen accompanying the king. Soon after Vajiralongkorn ascended to the throne, however, his fate dramatically changed. In November 2017, the new king purged Distorn and four other members of his clan from the palace. The former king's confidant was stripped of his power in the palace, forced to re-enter military training at the age of fifty-three, and is now working as a housemaid who serves drinks to guests of the new king. While this is just one of the many cases of public punishment performed by Vajiralongkorn, it is significant in two ways. First, the same family that penned the "we love the king" slogan is now a scare story that Thai elites and members of the palace tell one another.[64] Second, their fate reveals the methods of punishment and expulsion from Vajiralongkorn's inner circle. As Hobbes showed centuries ago, the cultivation of fear as a political tool "depends upon clearly formulated laws and specified punishments."[65] Vajiralongkorn's treatment of fallen elites follows this rule. Each of these cases was in fact publicly announced in the *Royal Gazette*, transforming these personal conflicts into cautionary tales for other members of the elite.

A different strategy, however, has been deployed against political critics and opponents, a strategy more reliant on silent fear than public punishment. As Michael Taussig has argued, paranoia can also be constructed by the state through techniques of silencing and by the "strategic use of uncertainty and mystery."[66] Here the most infamous cases are those of Kasalong and Phu Chana, the two assistants of the also disappeared monarchy critic Surachai Danwattananusorn, who were killed in Laos, dismembered, and dumped in the Mekong River where they refloated at the end of January 2019. While there is no evidence directly linking the king to these murders, their occurrence contributed to generate the climate of widespread fear that has characterized the first years of Vajiralongkorn's reign. In this relation between publicity and secrecy is located the repressive nature of fear as a tool of governance, Vajiralongkorn's key weapon for keeping his opponents in line.

The departure from Bhumibol could not be starker, not just in terms of using fear but also ignoring royal acts that fostered love. Crowd-pleasing rituals of royal patronage, central to Bhumibol's reign and his creation of filial love, have lost centrality for Vajiralongkorn and were replaced by acts of punishment. Five weeks after his coronation, on 9 January 2018, the new king delivered university degrees to students of Chiang Mai Rajabhat University, a practice established by the late king. Vajiralongkorn kept the students waiting for more than four hours. This was only the first sign of his emerging style of leadership. The following day, Vijiralongkorn demanded changes to a constitutional draft voted on in a popular referendum in August 2016 under a military junta that prevented anti-charter activists and politicians from campaigning. The changes provided the king with complete control over the appointment of a regent in his absence, canceled the need for a parliamentary countersignature to royal orders, and re-established royal crisis powers that had been taken away from the palace in the 2016 draft, including the ability to impose executive and legislative vetoes and the right to dissolve the legislative assembly. Overall, with the new constitution, Vajiralongkorn wields more power over the parliament than his father ever did.

This new heightened control is performed also through the other side of *itthipon* leadership, the rewarding of his most loyal aides. General Jakrapob Bhuridej, Vajiralongkorn's chief of security, and his family are prime examples of this dynamic. Jakrapob has accumulated massive personal power and his brother Jirapob has been appointed to the Crime Suppression Bureau, a powerful branch of the police that now operates under the influence of the palace. Vajiralongkorn has also appointed Paiboon Kumchaya, a general-turned-minister of justice, as privy councilor, effectively giving the king direct control of any legal process against critics of the monarchy. And yet, between 2018 and 2020, no case of lèse-majesté was brought to court. This, I believe, was one of the effects of the shift from the rule of love to the rule of fear, valid as long as fear worked as a way of squashing opposition. Fear as a mode of "affective governance," in fact, does not need a direct connection. We can see something being done to someone else and develop a fear of the one who did it. The same does not happen with love. Love needs complete and total submission. It requires devotion and continuous practice. We do not fall in love because someone we barely know feels love for someone, at least not generally speaking. Fear instead needs less continuous checks. It hovers quietly about the relationships between the powerful and the powerless, subtly influencing everyday conduct without requiring much in the way of active intimidation.[67] In this sense, fear is much less pervasive than love was and it does not demand the creation of a collectivity policing its borders. Fear may be used as a cautionary tale or, as a Thai proverb goes, "by hitting the chicken to show the monkey." In this sense, Vajiralongkorn's system of fear does not require the average Thai person's devotion, but only submission by the people who represent potential threats—aristocrats, military, politicians, and well-known opponents. In other words, fear demands the persecution of disloyal members of the palace, the centralization of military and economic power in the king's hands, and the control over the new parliament and well-known opponents but does not require the application of lèse-majesté law against ordinary citizens, at least as long as those ordinary citizens remain fearful of the king. When this fear dissipates, however, the entire arsenal of punishment is once again brought into action, as it was after the 2020 protests.

The Limits of Fear under Vajiralongkorn

On 10 August 2020, Panusaya Sithijirawattanakul, a twenty-one-year-old student of Thammasat University, read in front of a crowd a document destined to make history. "There was fear lurking inside me, deep fear of the consequences," Panusaya told the BBC Thai, thinking back to the moments before going on stage. "I knew my life would never be the same again."[68] Panusaya read a series of unprecedented demands: to take away the monarch's legal immunity, to eliminate the lèse-majesté law, to cut the monarchy's funds, to make its investments transparent and taxable, to prohibit members of the royal family from expressing political opinions, to suspend all forms of monarchic propaganda, to investigate the disappearance in recent years of various critics of the monarchy, and to make it illegal for the monarch to support a coup d'état. The 10 demands, instead of alienating supporters from the movement, galvanized it and broadened its base far beyond students, attracting blue- and white-collar workers, people of various generations and social classes, including some former Red Shirt activists.

The enormity of this shift and the powerful refusal to submit to the rule of fear invoked by Panusaya has been expressed by Thak Chaloemtiarana in an online seminar titled "Uprising in Thailand," organized at the University of Wisconsin–Madison. "I never thought that in my lifetime I would have witnessed the bravery of young people who presented their 10 demands to modernize and democratize the Thai monarchy," the Thai scholar declared.

> I watched this unfold as when listening to Khun Rung reading the ten demands on August 10. I was shocked, proud, ashamed, and fearful. I was shocked that the demands were made publicly, calling attention to the fact that the monarchy is still a major factor in Thai politics and hindering democratization. A lot of us have thought about it but none of us dares say

it in public. I was proud of the bravery of the Thai students at this time. I
was ashamed that I had lacked the courage to say publicly my own thoughts
about the Thai monarchy. Even though I have written about it at the
beginning of my professional career, I and many others of my generation
have fallen prey to self-censorship that kept us from articulating what was
on our minds. I and my fellow colleagues of this generation failed to speak
truth to power. I am fearful that there may be violent reprisal because calls
for the reform of the monarchy affect the political legitimacy of the military.
Having decided to not let this fear paralyze them, a new generation of activists,
with the support of red shirts protesters, rallied against this system under
the slogan #ให้มันจบที่รุ่นเรา (let it end in our generation) ... protesters are
not simply "letting" it end at whatever time it wishes. The fearful wait-and-see
attitude toward the new reign that pervaded Thailand in the aftermath of
Bhumibol's death four years ago has been superseded by a decisive impa-
tience: we're sick of waiting; we've seen enough; let's get it over with now.[69]

If love called citizens into action, into massive parades and rituals of
adulation, into standing up before movies or cheering at passing royal cars,
fear was meant to paralyze them, to drive them to inaction. And yet it did
not work. When faced with fear, humans have a series of possible responses.
The hope of a ruler who deploys this affect as a tool of governance is that
the flight mechanism would kick in, pushing people into inaction. These
activists, however, went for the opposite reaction and started to fight. As a
result, lèse-majesté law was resuscitated by Vajiralongkorn, and 67 activists
have been charged between 2020 and 2022.[70] In June 2020, Prime Minister
General Prayuth Chan-ocha had stated that 112 prosecutions had stopped
"because the king was kind enough to instruct that it should not be used."[71]
These charges suggest that he changed his mind. However, ruling by fear is
a delicate business as, once defeated, fear can lose its grip. At least two of the
accused, in fact, responded to the news declaring that they are not afraid of
the consequences, [72] suggesting that Vajiralongkorn's rule of fear may be
starting to crack.

Conclusion

In this chapter, I have analyzed love and fear as tools of affective governance
deployed by Bhumibol and Vajiralongkorn as a way to explore how the
relationship between monarch and subjects has been imagined and performed by each monarch. It would be easy to see this shift from love to fear

as a move from monarchical power to despotism, following Montesquieu's discussion of ruling by fear.[73] However, I do not share this view. Rather, I attempted to show both love and fear as equally productive forces that generate specific systems of affective governance, each with its own forms of emotive participation and repressive mechanisms. To refuse to love or refuse to fear are both acts of defiance but the form they take, the political action they generate, and the type of pushbacks they encounter are different, if equally violent. In this sense, I disagree with readings that would see Bhumibol as less despotic than Vajiralongkorn and, based on their record in uses of lèse-majesté law, one could even argue the opposite. Rather, I think that for kings who are traditionally seen as gods, as in Thailand, acting like a god is central to be seen as one. Bhumibol interpreted this through an established model of a benevolent god, a superior fatherly figure to be loved unconditionally. Vajiralongkorn so far seems to interpret this according to another model of divinity, a god to be feared and obeyed, but less concerned with the opinions of ordinary people and less obsessed with small acts of defiance. Here, rather than the distinction between monarch and despot, dear to Montesquieu, maybe more relevant is the one proposed by David Graeber and Marshal Sahlins between divine monarchs, "who act like gods—that is with arbitrariness and impunity," and sacred kings, "who are actually considered to 'be' god."[74] In this sense, for Vajiralongkorn being seen as a god may be less important than being able to act like one. As a consequence, his rule may be crueler with public acts of defiance, but at the same time less concerned with what people say in the privacy of their homes. And this opens a space for opposition unknown under the rule of love. Acting like a god requires an audience willing to let one stage this performance and participate in it. Many in contemporary Thailand seem to be increasingly tired of this show, and an actor without an audience, very often, does not last long.

Notes

1 These numbers are based on reported news but there are suggestions they may in fact be higher.

2 Pavin, "Kingdom of Fear"; Sopranzetti, "From Love to Fear."

3 For a detailed analysis of the case, see Haberkorn, "Dictatorship, Monarchy, and Freedom of Expression in Thailand," 199.

4 Sopranzetti, "From Love to Fear"; Haberkorn, "Dictatorship, Monarchy, and Freedom of Expression in Thailand"; Pavin, "Kingdom of Fear"; Chambers, "Arch-Royalist Autocracy Unlimited."

5 Marshall, *Kingdom in Crisis.*

6 Jackson, *A Grateful Son, A Military King.*

7 Handley, *The King Never Smiles.*

8 Thongchai, "Thailand's Hyper-royalism."

9 De Rooij, "The King and His Cult"; Araya and Sukree, "An Analysis of Twitter in the Passing of His Majesty King Bhumibol"; Stengs, "United in Competitive Mourning."

10 Stoler, "Affective States," 6.

11 McCargo, "Network Monarchy"; Funston, *Divided over Thaksin*; Kasian, "Toppling Thaksin"; McCargo and Ukrist, *The Thaksinization of Thailand*; Chambers, "In the Shadow of the Soldier's Boot"; Chambers, "Arch-Royalist Autocracy Unlimited"; Naruemon, "Contending Political Networks"; Mérieau, "Thailand's Deep State."

12 Hewison and Veerayooth, *Military, Monarchy and Repression*; Puangchon, *Royal Capitalism*; Hewison, "Rebellion, Repression and the Red Shirts"; Apichat, Yukti, and Niti, *Re-examining the Political Landscape of Thailand.*

13 Saowanee, "Red Bangkok?"; Walker, "Royal Sufficiency and Elite Misrepresentation of Rural Livelihoods"; Walker, *Thailand's Political Peasants*; Keyes, "From Peasants to Cosmopolitan Villagers"; Porphant, *A Regional Economic History of Thailand*; Saowanee, "Sticky Rice in the Blood."

14 Nidhi, "The Thai Cultural Constitution."

15 Thannapat, "The Moral Disintegration and the Politics of Cultural Emotions," 718.

16 Graeber and Sahlins, *On Kings*, 11.

17 In order to make this analysis somewhat contained I focus particularly on love as *rak*. In so doing I do not do justice to the notion of *metta* as loving-kindness in the *Vessantara Jātaka*. This decision is motivated by the fact that the idiom of *rak* (not as *metta*) was mobilized by Bhumibol propaganda.

18 Supatra, "Ideas of Love in Thai Tradition-Reading Heritage."

19 Jory, *Thailand's Theory of Monarchy*, 54.

20 Jory, *Thailand's Theory of Monarchy*, 54.

21 Thongchai, "Thailand's Hyper-royalism," 15.

22 Sturm, *The King's Nation.*

23 Reynolds and Reynolds, *Three Worlds according to King Ruang*, 177.

24 Reynolds and Reynolds, *Three Worlds according to King Ruang*, 179.

25 As reported in Sturm, *The King's Nation*, 117.

26 Borwornsal, *Ten Principles of a Righteous King and the King of Thailand*, 24.

27 Thak, *Thailand: The Politics of Despotic Paternalism*, 65.

28 Cited in Thak, *Thailand: The Politics of Despotic Paternalism*, 105.

29 Cited in Thak, *Thailand: The Politics of Despotic Paternalism*, 132.

30 Handley, *The King Never Smiles*, 149.

31 Thannapat, "The Moral Disintegration and the Politics of Cultural Emotions," 22.

32 Junya, "Why I Don't Love the King."

33 Sturm, *The King's Nation*, 199.

34 Cited in Khanakammakan Amnuaikan Chat-ngan Chalermphrakiat, *Raingan Kantittam Lae Pramoenphon Kanchat-ngan Chaloemphrakiat Phrabatsomdet Phraparam Intaramahaphum Iphonadunyadetmaharat Nueangnai Warokatmahamongkon Chaloemphrachonmaphansa 5 Rop*, 7.

35 Sopranzetti, "Thai Ideas of Power."

36 Cited in Sturm, *The King's Nation*, 245.

37 Farrelly, "Why Democracy Struggles," 282.

38 Cummins, "The People's King."

39 Junya, "Why I Don't Love the King."

40 Saichon, "Kan Sang 'Khwam Pen Thai.'"

41 Thongchai defines hyper-royalism thus:

> First, it is the permeation of royalism in everyday life and the increased demand for expressed loyalty to the monarchy. Second, hyper-royalism indulges in exaggeration and exaltation. Members of the royal family are often touted by royalists and acolytes as being at the best in every aspect of social affairs. Hyperbole becomes normative; eulogies become truth. Third, the manufacture and encouragement of hyper-royalism have not been exclusive to the palace or state. Civil society actively involves itself in the production and circulation of hyper-royalism while participating in the suppression of critics of the monarchy. Finally, the control of public discourse on the monarchy protects hyper-royalism. When royalism is akin to religion, detractors become blasphemers. Article 112 has been the main instrument for this purpose.

See Thongchai, "Confessions to Lèse-majesté," 5.

42 Peel, "Thailand's Monarchy."

43 Stengs, "United in Competitive Mourning," x.

44 Araya and Sukree, "An Analysis of Twitter in the Passing of His Majesty King Bhumibol Adulyadej," 188.

45 Jitlada, *A Grieving Nation*, 66.

46 Streckfuss, "Freedom and Silencing under the Neo-absolutism Monarchy Regime in Thailand," 106–7.

47 Thongchai, "Confessions to L2èse-majesté."

48 Junya, "Why I Don't Love the King."

49 Newsdesk 2013, available at https://www.equaltimes.org/thailand-where-insulting-the-king-gets-you-locked-up?lang=en.

50 Thongchai, "Confessions to Lèse-majesté," 10.

51 Thaweeporn, "Thai Netizen Network Annual Report: Thai Freedom and Internet Culture, 2011."

52 Jitlada, *A Grieving Nation*, 39.

53 Thongchai, "Confessions to Lèse-majesté," 16.

54 Keane, "Fear and Democracy," 12–13.

55 This is not to say that fear as an emotion is not contemplated in canonical Buddhist texts—quite the contrary. But rather, fear is not associated with governance in the same way in which love is in those texts, or even in the same way in which it has been explored in European political thought by the likes of Machiavelli and Montesquieu. An apparent exception to this is Aung San Suu Kyi's *Freedom from Fear* (1991). In this text, as explored by Houtman, she advocates for "the Buddhist concept of 'righteousness' (*dhamma*) which permits 'absence of fear' (*abhaya*)" (*Mental Culture in Burmese Crisis Politics*, 95). Here, in line with a much longer Buddhist tradition evident in the *Mangala Sutta*, she engages with the theme of obtaining freedom from danger and fear, but not on the role of fear as a tool of governance.

56 Thak, *Thailand: The Politics of Despotic Paternalism*.

57 Thongchai, "Thongchai Winichakul on the 'Red Germs.'"

58 For a theoretical engagement with the role of fear in politics, see Robin, *Fear*.

59 This type of fear is discussed in classical Western political thought by Machiavelli and Montesquieu.

60 On this concept, see Sopranzetti, *Owners of the Map*, 250–53.

61 Persons, *The Way Thais Lead*, 137.

62 Persons, *The Way Thais Lead*, 137.

63 Pavin, "Kingdom of Fear (and Favour)"; Pavin, "Kingdom of Fear: Royal Governance under Thailand's King Vajiralongkorn."

64 Sopranzetti, "From Love to Fear."

65 Robin, *Fear*, 46.

66 Taussig, *The Nervous System*, 16–17.

67 Robin, *Fear*, 19.

68 "The Student Daring to Challenge Thailand's Monarchy," *BBC*.

69 In Peera, "The Law Ought to Be King."

70 "Table of Section 112 Cases in the Era of Student-Government Rally Since 2020," *ILaw Report.*

71 Beech and Sukartono, "A Feared Law to Protect the Monarchy Returns amid Thailand's Protests."

72 Patsaravalee Tanakitvibulpon, a twenty-five-year-old engineering student and prominent activist accused of defaming the monarchy, declared to Reuters: "I am not afraid. I understand that invoking this law is the government's plan to suppress us" (Chayut and Panarat, "Thai Protest Leaders Face Charges of Insulting Monarchy"). Similarly, Parit responded to his summon stating, "I am not scared. I am more worried about the country if they are still using this 112 in politics like this. This will cause the monarchy to deteriorate further" (Beech and Sukartono, "A Feared Law to Protect the Monarchy Returns amid Thailand's Protests").

73 Baron de Montesquieu and de Secondat Monstesquieu, *Persian Letters.*

74 Graeber and Sahlins, *On Kings,* 400.

References

Apichat Satitniramai, Yukti Mukdawijitra, and Niti Pawakapan. *Re-examining the Political Landscape of Thailand.* Bangkok: Thailand Universities Healthy Public Policy, Thai Health Promotion Foundation, 2013.

Araya Pudtal and Sukree Sinthupinyo. "An Analysis of Twitter in the Passing of His Majesty King Bhumibol Adulyadej." *International International Journal of Machine Learning and Computing* 7.6 (2017):187–93.

Aung San Suu Kyi. *Freedom from Fear: and Other Writings.* Penguin Books, 1991.

Baron de Montesquieu and Charles de Secondat Montesquieu. *Persian Letters.* Oxford: Oxford University Press, 2008.

Beech, Hannah, and Muktita Suhartono. "A Feared Law to Protect the Monarchy Returns amid Thailand's Protests." *New York Times,* 25 November 2020. https://www.nytimes.com/2020/11/25/world/asia/thailand-protest-lese-majeste-monarchy.html, accessed 8 July 2022.

Borwornsak Uwanno. *Ten Principles of a Righteous King and the King of Thailand.* Bangkok: King Prajadhipok's Institute, 2008.

Chambers, Paul. "Arch-Royalist Autocracy Unlimited: Civil-Military Relations in Contemporary Thailand." In *Rights and Security in India, Myanmar, and Thailand,* ed. Chosein Yamahata, Sueo Sudo, and Takashi Matsugi, 193–217. Singapore: Palgrave Macmillan, 2020.

———. "In the Land of Democratic Rollback: Military Authoritarianism and Monarchical Primacy in Thailand." *National Security, Statecentricity, and Governance in East Asia*. Cham: Springer, 2018.

———. "In the Shadow of the Soldier's Boot: Assessing Civil-Military Relations in Thailand." In *Legitimacy Crisis in Thailand*, ed. Mark Askew, 197–234. Chiang Mai: Silkworm Books, 2010.

Chayut Setboonsarng and Panarat Thepgumpanat. "Thai Protest Leaders Face Charges of Insulting Monarchy." *Reuters*, 30 November 2020. https://www.reuters.com/article/us-thailand-protests-idUSKBN28A0SC, accessed 8 July 2022.

Cummins, Peter. "The People's King—His Majesty King Bhumibol Adulyadej the Great Turns 81." *Pattaya Mail*, 2008. http://pattayamail.com/801/special.shtml, accessed 8 July 2022.

de Rooij, Laurens. "The King and His Cult: Thailand's Monarch and the Religious Culture." In *Religious Transformation in Modern Asia: A Transnational Movement*, Numen Book Series 148, ed. David Kim, 274–96. New York: Brill, 2015.

Farrelly, Nicholas. "Why Democracy Struggles: Thailand's Elite Coup Culture." *Australian Journal of International Affairs* 67.3 (2013):281–96.

Funston, John. *Divided over Thaksin: Thailand's Coup and Problematic Transition*. Chiang Mai: Silkworm Books, 2009.

Graeber, David, and Marshall David Sahlins. *On Kings*. Chicago: Hau Books, 2017.

Haberkorn, Tyrell. "Dictatorship, Monarchy, and Freedom of Expression in Thailand." *The Journal of Asian Studies* 77.4 (2018):935–43.

Handley, Paul M. *The King Never Smiles: A Biography of Thailand's Bhumibol Adulyadej*. New Haven, CT: Yale University Press, 2006.

Hewison, Kevin. "Rebellion, Repression and the Red Shirts." Paper read at East Asia Forum Quarterly, 2010.

——— and Veerayooth Kanchoochat. *Military, Monarchy and Repression: Assessing Thailand's Authoritarian Turn*. London: Routledge, 2018.

Houtman, G. *Mental Culture in Burmese Crisis Politics: Aung San Suu Kyi and the National League for Democracy*. Tokyo: Institute for the Study of Languages and Cultures of Asia and Africa, 1999.

Jackson, Peter A. *Grateful Son, A Military King: Thai Media Accounts of the Accession of Rama X to the Throne*. Singapore: ISEAS-Yusof Ishak Institute, 2017.

Jitlada Meesuk. *A Grieving Nation: Exploring Thainess in the Space of Emotion*. Lund: Lund University, 2017.

Jory, Patrick. *Thailand's Theory of Monarchy: The Vessantara Jataka and the Idea of the Perfect Man*. Albany, NY: SUNY Press, 2016.

Junya Yimprasert. "Why I Don't Love the King." Time-Up Thailand, 2010. https://www.academia.edu/3701626/Why_I_dont_Love_the_King, accessed 8 July 2022.

Kasian Tejapira. "Toppling Thaksin." *New Left Review* 29 (2006):5–37.

Keane, John. "Fear and Democracy." In *Violence and Politics: Globalization's Paradox*, ed. Kenton Worcester, Sally Avery Bermanzohn, and Mark Unger, 226–45. London: Routledge, 2002.

Keyes, Charles. "From Peasants to Cosmopolitan Villagers: The Transformation of 'Rural' Northeastern Thailand." Paper presented at the Association for Asian Studies annual meeting, Honolulu, 3 April 2011.

Khanakammakan Amnuaikan Chat-ngan Chalemphrakiat Phrabatsomdet Phrachaoyuhua [Organizing committee for the honoring of His Majesty the King]. *Raingan Kantittam Lae Pramoenphon Kanchat-ngan Chaloemphrakiat Phrabatsomdet Phraparam Intaramahaphum Iphonadunyadetmaharat Nueangnai Warokatmahamongkon Chaloemphrachonmaphansa 5 Rop* [Report on the evaluation of the organization of the ceremonies on the occasion of the 60th birthday of His Majesty King Bhumibol]. Bangkok: War Veteran Organization Press, 1989.

Marshall, Andrew MacGregor. *A Kingdom in Crisis: Thailand's Struggle for Democracy in the Twenty-First Century*. London: Zed Books, 2014.

McCargo, Duncan. "Network Monarchy and Legitimacy Crises in Thailand." *The Pacific Review* 18.4 (2005):499–519.

——— and Ukrist Patthamānan. *The Thaksinization of Thailand*. Copenhagen: NIAS Press, 2005.

Mérieau, Eugénie. "Thailand's Deep State, Royal Power and the Constitutional Court (1997–2015)." *Journal of Contemporary Asia* 26.3 (2016):1–22.

Naruemon Thabchumpon. "Contending Political Networks: A Study of the "Yellow Shirts" and "'Red Shirts' in Thailand's Politics." *Southeast Asian Studies* 5.1 (2016):93–113.

Nidhi Eoseewong. "The Thai Cultural Constitution." *Kyoto Review of Southeast Asia* 3 (March 2003). https://kyotoreview.org/issue-3-nations-and-stories/the-thai-cultural-constitution/, acccessed 8 July 2022.

Pavin Chachavapongpun. "Kingdom of Fear (and Favour)." *New Mandala*, 18 April 2017. https://www.newmandala.org/kingdom-fear-favour/, accessed 8 July 2022.

———. "Kingdom of Fear: Royal Governance under Thailand's King Vajiralongkorn." *Journal of Current Southeast Asian Affairs*, 3 July 2022.

https://journals.sagepub.com/doi/10.1177/18681034221111176, accessed 8 July 2022.

Peel, Michael. "Thailand's Monarchy: Where Does Love End and Dread Begin?." *Financial Times,* 12 October 2017. https://www.ft.com/content/149d82a4-ae17-11e7-beba-5521c713abf4, accessed 8 July 2022.

Peera Songkunnatham. "The Law Ought to Be King." *Boston Review of Books,* 1 October 2020. https://bostonreview.net/articles/peera-songkunnatham-the-law-ought-be-king/, accessed 8 July 2022.

Persons, Larry S. *The Way Thais Lead: Face as Social Capital.* Bangkok: Silkworm Books, 2016.

Porphant Ouyyanont. *A Regional Economic History of Thailand.* Singapore: ISEAS-Yusof Ishak Institute, 2017.

Puangchon Unchanam. *Royal Capitalism: Wealth, Class, and Monarchy in Thailand.* Madison: University of Wisconsin Press, 2020.

Reynolds, Frank E., and Mani B. Reynolds. *Three Worlds according to King Ruang: A Thai Buddhist Cosmology,* Berkeley Buddhist Studies Series 4. Berkeley: Group in Buddhist Studies, University of California, Berkeley, 1982.

Robin, Corey. *Fear: The History of a Political Idea.* Oxford: Oxford University Press, 2004.

Saichon Sattayanurak. "Kan Sang 'Khwam Pen Thai' Krasae Lak Lae 'Khwam Jing' Thi 'Khwam Pen Thai' Sang" [The construction of mainstream thought on "Thainess" and the "truth" constructed by "Thainess"]. *Fa Diao Kan* 3.4 (2005):40–67.

Saowanee T. Alexander. "Red Bangkok? Exploring Political Struggles in the Thai Capital." *Critical Asian Studies* 50.4 (2018):647–63.

———. "Sticky Rice in the Blood: Isan People's Involvement in Thailand's 2020 Anti-Government Protests." *Critical Asian Studies* 53.1 (2021):1–14.

Sopranzetti, Claudio. "From Love to Fear: The Rise of King Vajiralongkorn." *Al Jazeera,* 11 April 2017. https://www.aljazeera.com/opinions/2017/4/11/from-love-to-fear-the-rise-of-king-vajiralongkorn, accessed 8 July 2022.

———. *Owners of the Map: Motorcycle Taxi Drivers, Mobility, and Politics in Bangkok.* Berkeley: University of California Press, 2018.

———. "Thai Ideas of Power." In *Coup, King, Crisis: A Critical Interregnum in Thailand,* ed. Pavin Chachavalpongpun, 57–82. Yale Southeast Asia Studies Monograph 68. New Haven, CT: Yale Southeast Asia Studies, 2020.

Stengs, Irene. "United in Competitive Mourning: Commemorative Spectacle in Tribute to King Bhumibol Adulyadej of Thailand." In *The Secular Sacred,* ed. Markus Balkenhol, Ernst van den Hemel, and Irene Stengs, 263–84. Cham: Springer, 2020.

Stoler, Ann Laura. "Affective States." In *A Companion to the Anthropology of Politics*, ed. David Nugent and Joan Vincent, 4–20. London: Blackwell Publishing, 2004.

Streckfuss, David. "Freedom and Silencing under the Neo-absolutist Monarchy Regime in Thailand, 2006–2011." In *"Good Coup" Gone Bad: Thailand's Political Developments since Thaksin's Downfall*, ed. Pavin Chachavalpongpun, 109–38. Singapore: Institute of Southeast Asian Studies, 2014.

"The Student Daring to Challenge Thailand's Monarchy." *BBC*, 17 September 2020. https://www.bbc.com/news/world-asia-54182002, accessed 8 July 2022.

Sturm, Andreas. *The King's Nation: A Study of the Emergence and Development of Nation and Nationalism in Thailand*. London: London School of Economics and Political Science, 2006.

Supatra Boonpanyarote. "Ideas of Love in Thai Tradition-Reading Heritage." *Veridian E-Journal* [Silpakorn University (Humanities, Social Sciences and Arts)] 8.4 (2015):72–84.

Suthachai Yimprasert. "Latthi Chatniyom Kap Kan Totan Chakkraphatniyom Amerika Nai Samai 14 Tulakhom Poso 2516 Thueng 6 Tulakhom Poso 2519" [Nationalism and anti-American imperialism from 14 October 1973 to 6 October 1976]. In *Khamprakat Chatniyom Mai* [New nationalism], ed. Narong Petchprasert, 127–40. Bangkok: Amarin Book Center, 2000.

"Table of Section 112 Cases in the Era of Student-Government Rally Since 2020." *ILaw Report*, 2021. https://www.facebook.com/iLawClub/posts/10164889739020551/, accessed 8 July 2022.

Taussig, Michael. *The Nervous System*. New York: Routledge, 1992.

"Thailand: Where 'Insulting' the King Gets You Locked Up." *Equal Times*, 16 August 2013. https://www.equaltimes.org/thailand-where-insulting-the-king-gets-you-locked-up, accessed 8 July 2022.

Thak Chaloemtiarana. *Thailand: The Politics of Despotic Paternalism*. Ithaca, NY: Cornell University Press, 2007.

Thannapat Jarernpanit. "The Moral Disintegration and the Politics of Cultural Emotions within Thailand's Current, Deeply Divided Political Conflicts." *Humanities, Arts and Social Sciences Studies* (27 December 2018):717–36.

Thaweeporn Kummetha. "Thai Netizen Network Annual Report: Thai Freedom and Internet Culture, 2011." Thai Netizen Network.

Thongchai Winichakul. "Confessions to Lèse-majesté: A Lens into the Rule of Law in Thailand." In *The Legacies of the Past in the Modern Rule of Law in Thailand*. Japan External Trade Organization (JETRO), 2019. https://www.ide.go.jp/library/Japanese/Publish/Reports/InterimReport/2018/pdf/2018_2_40_026_ch01.pdf, accessed 8 July 2022.

———. "The Monarchy and Anti-Monarchy: Two Elephants in the Room of Thai Politics and the State of Denial," In *'Good Coup' Gone Bad: Thailand's Political Developments since Thaksin's Downfall*, ed. Pavin Chachavalpong-pun, 79–108. Singapore: Institute of Southeast Asian Studies, 2014.

———.*Thailand's Hyper-Royalism: Its Past Success and Present Predicament.* Trends in Southeast Asia 7. Singapore: ISEAS–Yusof Ishak Institute, 2016.

———. "Thongchai Winichakul on the 'Red Germs,'" *New Mandala,* 3 May 2010. http://asiapacific.anu.edu.au/newmandala/2010/05/03/thongchai-winichakul-on-the-red-germs/ (accessed 15 May 2010), now available at https://www.newmandala.org/thongchai-winichakul-on-the-red-germs/.

Walker, Andrew. "Royal Sufficiency and Elite Misrepresentation of Rural Livelihoods." *Saying the Unsayable: Monarchy and Democracy in Thailand,* ed. Lotte Isager and Søen Ivarsson, 241–65. Copenhagen: NIAS Press, 2010.

———. *Thailand's Political Peasants: Power in the Modern Rural Economy.* New Perspectives in Southeast Asian Studies. Madison: University of Wisconsin Press, 2012.

7

Destroying Monuments, Erasing Democracy: Coup, Monarchy, and the Politics of Memory in Thailand

CHATRI PRAKITNONTHAKAN

AFTER THE COUP D'ÉTAT of 2014 and especially after the ascension of King Maha Vajiralongkorn to the throne, one very interesting phenomenon occurred in the architectural world. This is the destruction of a significant number of buildings and monuments related to the memory of the People's Party—the group whose revolution in 1932 changed the form of government in Thailand from an absolute monarchy to a democracy and who had a leading role in Thai politics from 1932 to 1947.[1]

It is normal for constructions to be demolished if their condition deteriorates or if there would be a benefit from using a new form. But I believe that the destruction over the past few years of buildings and memorials related to the People's Party may not have conformed to any normal conditions for demolition. What is important is that many memorials that have been destroyed had been properly registered as historical monuments and according to the law should have been given special protection as national assets. A survey shows that, after the coup of 2014, at least 11 buildings, monuments, or political symbols memorializing the People's Party have been removed, destroyed, or renamed.[2] Nine of these 11 cases occurred during the reign of King Maha Vajiralongkorn. They consist of the People's Party plaque in Bangkok, the Constitution Defense Monument in Bangkok, the statue of Phraya Phahon Phonphayuhasena in Lopburi, the statue of Field Marshal Phibun Songkhram in Lopburi, the statue of Field Marshal Phibun Songkhram at the

National Defense Studies Institute in Bangkok, the Phibun Historical Studies Center in Chiang Rai, the General Phraya Phahon Phonphayuhasena Museum in Lopburi, Fort Phahonyothin in Lopburi, and Fort Phibun Songkhram.

Buildings and monuments are not only physical things constructed in response to the requirements of humans. Many serve as symbols that are loaded with historical memories of the people and society. Some are symbols of cities, some are symbols of the nation, some are symbols of principles, and some are sites of political expression. Therefore, their destruction is not merely the destruction of brick, stone, cement, and metal, but the destruction of memory, history, principles held by people through the symbolism of the monuments, freedom of political expression, and the identity of a great number of people who see themselves through these structures.[3] In some cases, this can be considered the first step in the destruction of humanity that may eventually lead to violence and genocide.[4]

Through constant monitoring of this phenomenon, I have formed a hypothesis that the destruction of these buildings and monuments is directly related to political struggle. It is an attempt to erase and destroy the historical memory of the People's Party, which is being revived by the young generation as a symbol of the struggle for real democracy. What is important is that this attempt is a phenomenon inseparable from the deterioration of the image of the monarchy in Thai society after the 2014 coup. To speak clearly, as the image of the monarchy has deteriorated, it appears that the destruction has increased to the same degree.

This chapter follows this hypothesis with the aim of studying and explaining this phenomenon of destruction by answering the basic questions of how this phenomenon arose, which agencies have had a role in the destruction, how this is related to the deteriorating image of the monarchy, and finally what possible direction the political response of the public to this destruction could take.

The Second Emergence of the People's Party after the 2006 Coup

To understand the phenomenon of the destruction of monuments, the first question that must be answered is how these structures, which are related to the memory of the People's Party, have become political symbols in Thailand over the past few years.

The political nature of Thailand that has existed for decades, throughout almost the entirety of the last reign, is characterized by the overlapping use of two forms of national executive power: a formal power and a non-formal power that exists beyond the law. The characteristics of this second form of power are especially interesting and have attracted the study of many scholars who have given different definitions such as *itthipon*[5] (influence), the Network Monarchy,[6] and the Deep State.[7] If we remove the differences in the details, we find a common central proposal arguing that Thai politics has an overlapping of a normal state structure, which is formal and regulated by universal democratic rules, and a secret structure of traditional elite groups, be they the military, the government bureaucracy, or monarchical networks, which are linked through a royalist ideology. The informal structure oversees and directs the normal state in a way that is outside democratic rule. This oversight takes many forms, from advice, conversations, and pressure to the extreme violence of a coup. Coups in Thai society have been made into something that is normal, that is not evil nor an instance of a rebellion overthrowing democracy. They are explained as one way of solving political problems, especially corruption among politicians, although in fact coups are a veneer to conceal the real objectives of the traditional elites in intervening in and controlling the normal state so as to prevent damage to the interests of these groups.[8]

However, the coup of 2006 failed to conceal the informal power that exercised control behind the scenes and irrevocably changed the political landscape. Kasian Tejapira suggests that in its true essence this coup was a coup for the throne,[9] and, whether intentionally or not, the monarchy stepped into an unprecedented more direct political role,[10] to the point where many sides see that the monarchy has become a political opponent. The unavoidable consequence has been a loss of image for the monarchy and the reduced strength of "royalist ideology," which was once the center that effortlessly held together all sectors in Thai society but which is beginning to be challenged and questioned. But it is regrettable that this ideological challenge, instead of leading to adaptation as a solution to the problem, has led to an intensification into "hyper-royalism,"[11] which creates more problems such that this ideology is no longer capable of gaining the unified acceptance of all sectors of society.

These features have effected a change in the struggle for democracy since the 2006 coup, prompting the young generation to launch more criticisms of the role of the monarchy. What is interesting, and which arose at the same time, is that the pro-democracy side has striven to use those symbols related to the People's Party, even though the People's Party had earlier been almost completely forgotten and whose narrative was discussed only in a narrow framework in academic circles, and even then from the perspective of almost complete erasure.[12] The group had never been elevated as a symbol in the struggle for democracy in any way. But this would suddenly change after the 2006 coup through the phenomenon of using monuments related to the People's Party in a wide number of locations as the venues for many rallies to oppose the coup.[13] The important ones are discussed next.

Figure 7.1 Jaran Ditapichai, one of the UDD leaders, lights red candles around the People's Party plaque on 24 June 2009 to commemorate the seventy-seventh anniversary of the 1932 revolution. (*Image*: Prachatai)

The People's Party plaque was a brass plaque, about 1 foot in diameter, embedded into the road in the vicinity of Dusit Palace in 1936 at the spot where it is believed that Phraya Phahon Phonphayuhasena (head of the People's Party) stood to read the proclamation of the change of government at dawn on 24 June 1932 (fig. 7.1). This plaque was never used as a symbol in political rallies, even when the People's Party lost power. The plaque faded from the memory of society until the coup of 2006, after which many groups of political activists used it more and more until it became one of the principal sites for anti-coup rallies. The People's Party plaque was also turned into a logo by several groups of demonstrators in a way that had never been seen before.

The Constitution Defense Monument was built as a memorial to the suppression of the Boworadet Rebellion in 1933 led by Prince Boworadet Kridakara to reinstate King Prajadhipok, Rama VII, to power. It was constructed in the Bang Khen area, which was the site of a large battle during the rebellion.[14] Once the People's Party lost political power, the importance of this monument was gradually reduced until almost no one recognized it. But after the large rallies of the Red Shirts in 2010, which were followed by the brutal dispersal of protestors and the deaths of almost one hundred people, the Constitution Defense Monument began to serve frequently as a political rally site among the Red Shirts and students. Soon, it became another important political venue.

Construction of the Democracy Monument was completed in 1940 to symbolize the change in the form of government. All the proportions and components of the length and breadth of the monument were designed with reference to the date of the change of government, 24 June 1932. This monument is considered the most important site proclaiming the political ideology of the People's Party. However, after the People's Party lost power, the implications and meaning of the monument faded, even though the monument became a site for significant political rallies in Thailand in the events of 14 October 1973, May 1992, and countless others. But at none of these times was any connection made to the ideology of the People's Party. After the 2006 coup, almost every political rally at the monument (with the exception of the rally of the People's Democratic Reform Committee, which supported the coup) has to a greater or lesser degree addressed or referred back to the memory of the People's Party era. It may be said that the meaning of this monument has returned to its original meaning.

Apart from the three examples just given, many other monuments in the provinces were constructed in the People's Party époque, which also had never been widely used as political symbols until after the 2006 coup. Important dates in the era of the People's Party have since been celebrated with political activities,[15] including the trend of reproducing pictures and speeches of People's Party members from the past as political symbols in a way that had never been seen before.

I have analyzed this phenomenon in detail in other articles so I will offer only a short summary here.[16] The revival of the memory of the People's Party and the use of various monuments constructed during the People's Party time as venues for political rallies has come about as a result of the history of the party, under different interpretations. The most important effect of the People's Party was the revolution to overthrow the absolute monarchy and to limit the power of the monarch within a constitution. But over time, there emerged a movement striving to increase the power of the monarchy, with an astounding surge in hyper-royalism. Since there is no historical period or symbol that would serve to oppose this ideology more forcefully than the People's Party, it was only logical that the opponents of the coup would be enchanted by the history and memories of this revolutionary era. The narrative and old images of the events at dawn on 24 June 1932 demonstrate the victory of the People's Party over the absolute monarchy, and many other events of that time have been the subject of inquiry, research, study, and even new interpretations.

This phenomenon grew considerably and replaced other symbols in the struggle for democracy that were previously powerful in Thai society, whether these symbols were related to the events of October 1976 or May 1992. These two events, even though they also represented struggles for democracy, were still viewed within the framework of royalist concepts and ideologies. The monarchy in both events was described as being above the conflict and on the same side as democracy. It was perceived to have played an important role in ending the violence that occurred.[17] But this description can no longer be justified. Hence, it should be no surprise why the events of October 1976 and May 1992 were powerless and have almost never been discussed among pro-democracy forces after the 2006 coup. For this reason, it would not be an exaggeration to say that many of the material objects, including monuments, related to the memory of the People's Party have become the most forceful political symbols to encourage and reaffirm the pro-democracy forces. These forces indicate that, in the current political struggle, the monarchy has become an opponent. But for them, there is hope, because in at least one historical period, the People's Party succeeded. From another perspective, it can be said that these memories have come to represent an ideal, which gives the pro-democracy forces the strength to fight "hyper-royalism." In the current context, it seems that there is a "re-emergence of the People's Party." This provides an answer as to why the narrative, the memory, and the monuments related to the People's Party have resumed an important political role in contemporary Thai politics.

Erasing the Memory of the People's Party after the 2014 Coup

The revival of the People's Party as a contemporary political symbol raised alarms and great concern among the government, military, and network monarchy, and a concrete response came very quickly after the 2014 coup.

Not long after this coup, the Royal Plaza, which had been a public space for the people and was the place where the People's Party plaque was embedded, was put off limits. It was forbidden to arrange any political activities in the area, which was reserved specifically for government and royal ceremonies only. At the Democracy Monument, flower gardens began to completely surround the base of the monument together with an iron fence to keep out anti-coup protesters. Meanwhile, at the Constitution Defense Monument and all People's Party monuments in the provinces, officials were very strict about using the rally venues and many were fenced off to prevent people from getting close to the monuments. Political and academic activities on important dates related to the People's Party, particularly 24 June, were especially targeted by security officials. Many activities had to be abandoned or postponed indefinitely.[18]

However, preventing the use of these monuments seems to have been only the first step. In fact, destruction was the real ultimate goal. The first case occurred just five months after the coup. Mueang Buriram Municipality carried out the removal of the Buriram Province Constitution Monument, which was built at the time of the People's Party as a symbol of the change in the form of government to democracy.[19] Despite public protest, the removal went ahead in November 2014 with the official reason of solving traffic problems. This was not destruction, but removal to a site in front of the old provincial hall.[20] However, in 2017, the relocated monument was permanently broken into pieces so that the space could be used to build a replica royal funeral pyre at the time of the cremation of King Bhumibol.[21]

The second case is the Supreme Court complex next to Sanam Luang, where construction commenced in 1939. The complex served as a memorial to the restoration of complete juridical sovereignty one year earlier. (Siam had lost this sovereignty under the Bowring Treaty, signed in 1855.) This was regarded as another important achievement of the People's Party.[22] The building was designed in an Art Deco architectural style, which integrated the democratic ideology of the People's Party. It was also demolished. Although the idea of demolishing these buildings had been around for many decades, it had never come to fruition because of voices opposing the unreasonableness of the project and the unnecessary waste of taxpayers' money. At the beginning of 2013 however, the Office of the Judiciary, as the project owner, embarked on the demolition with the objective of constructing in its place a new Supreme Court building in the style of "traditional Thai architecture" resembling a temple and former palace, which reflected "royalist ideology."[23] When news of the demolition broke out, a wave of opposition arose, particularly from academics in a wide circle. Because of the status of the building as a National Historic Site, the Department of Fine Arts filed a complaint with the police to prosecute those responsible for the demolition and to halt the project. Even though the complaint could not halt the demolition, the process was slowed by the widespread opposition from civil society. However, after the 2014 coup, the demolition continued quietly and smoothly.[24]

The third case is the Constitution Defense Monument. Although the demolition plan was initiated much earlier, it was similar to the case of the Supreme Court complex because it had never actually been implemented. But once a group of Red Shirt protesters first used the monument as the site of a political rally in 2010, efforts to demolish the monument restarted in earnest, apparently to pave the way for the construction of a Skytrain station. However, the Department of Fine Arts again intervened in the demolition and registered the monument as a National Historical Site in 2015.[25] Therefore, the demolition plan could not go ahead. The Mass Rapid Transit Authority of Thailand, in its capacity as project owner, could only move the monument at the beginning of November 2016 to a nearby site, which did not obstruct construction.[26] Even though this explanation demonstrates clear efforts at demolition after the 2014 coup, demolition did not come about easily. The media, civil society, and even agencies of the state itself such as the Department of Fine Arts expressed broad dissenting opinions, making it difficult, or even impossible in some cases, to carry out the demolition. But the situation changed completely after the death of King Bhumibol.

Erasing the Memory of the People's Party during the Reign of King Maha Vajiralongkorn

Since 2017 the method of demolishing monuments relating to the memory of the People's Party has changed. First, in almost all demolitions, no agency has shown itself to be responsible. This is different from previously, when a state agency was responsible for the demolition. Second, in the rare cases where the responsible agency is known, all the officials concerned are united in refusing to express any opinion at all. Third, almost all the demolitions follow no systematic plan that would be in line with rules and regulations. This prevents society from knowing the reason for the action. Again, it is different from the earlier period when the public was informed of the reason for the demolition (even if the reason was not convincing). And finally, the number and frequency of demolitions are significantly higher.

Figure 7.2 The People's Party plaque (left) was removed in April 2017, when a new brass plaque of the same size was embedded in its place (right). (*Image*: Wasawat Lukharang/BBC Thai)

The disappearance of the People's Party plaque in the middle of April 2017 has left no clues, has no agency claiming responsibility, and has no explanation from those involved (fig. 7.2). This was the first instance of the new form of demolition where initially there were attempts by many branches of the media to question various state agencies who were involved, but in the end the answer was "don't know" or, if not, "no comment."

Later, in December 2018, the Constitution Defense Monument disappeared without trace from its site in the same way, without anyone taking responsibility. This case is very interesting since it had been announced that the monument had already been registered as a National Historic Site by the Department of Fine Arts. It therefore had a special status requiring proper protection. The Department of Fine Arts had once forbidden efforts to demolish the monument after the 2014 coup. But the department chose to remain silent about its demolition in 2018 and gave almost no news to the media. Even today, some students and members of the public are demanding an explanation from the Department of Fine Arts. The responses from the department remain vague and fail to explain how a National Historic Site of such a large size could disappear.

This phenomenon intensified in early 2020, beginning with the removal of the statues of Phraya Phahon Phonphayuhasena and Field Marshal Phibun Songkhram, which stood in the Artillery Center (Fort Phahonyothin) in Lopburi Province, again without anyone knowing where they had been moved.[27] The statue of Phibun in front of the National Defense Studies Institute was removed at the end of January 2020 with no further details on the removal.[28] In February, there was a news report that the name of the Phibun Historical Studies Center in Chiang Rai Province had been changed to simply the "Historical Studies Center." Shortly afterward, the name of the General Phraya Phahon Phonphayuhasena Museum at the Artillery Center in Lopburi Province was changed to the "Artillery Museum." Fort Pha-holyothin in Lopburi Province was given the new name of "Fort Bhumibol," at the same time as Fort Phibun Songkhram in Lopburi Province was renamed "Fort Sirikit" on 20 March 2020.[29]

The most recent case erupted at the end of January when the website of the Crown Property Bureau revealed a photograph of a plan to renovate the facades on both sides of Ratchadamnoen Avenue, built in the Art Deco style and popular at the time of the People's Party. This was changed into a neoclassical architectural style, typical of that during the Chulalongkorn reign.[30] As with other cases, no clear information was given to the public regarding the project, its origin, rationale, budget, or period of implemen-tation.[31]

Another point of interest about the erasure of the memory of the People's Party during this period is the reintroduction of the concept of "nation, religions, and monarchy" and "hyper-royalism." For example, after the destruction of the People's Party plaque, a new brass plaque of the same size was embedded in its place with the inscription: "May Siam be blessed with prosperity forever. May the people be happy and cheerful and become the strength of the country. The respect for Phra Ratanattaya (the Three Jewels—Buddha, Dhamma, Sangha), one's state, one's family, and the faithfulness towards one's King will contribute to the prosperity of one's state."

This message is engraved on the new plaque, intentionally countering the message that was engraved on the old People's Party plaque, which read: "Here at dawn on 24 June 1932, the People's Party brought into being the constitution for the sake of the country's prosperity." The message on the People's Party plaque emphasized the beginning point of the prosperity of Thai society by linking it to the creation of a democratic form of government. But the message on the new plaque conveys that the real prosperity of Thailand is adherence to the concept of "nation, religions, and monarchy."[32]

In addition, only ten months after the demolition of the Constitution Defense Monument, the army set up new rooms in the Royal Thai Army Museum named "Boworadet Room" and "Si Sitthisongkhram Room"[33] to commemorate Prince Boworadet and Colonel Phraya Si Sitthisongkhram (Din Tharab), core leaders of the Boworadet Rebellion and loyalists to the monarchy who aimed to restore royal power to King Prajadhipok. This case again reflects endeavors to destroy democratic ideology through worshipping adversaries of the People's Party and devotees of royalism.

Even today, Thai society is perplexed as to why, since 2017, monuments related to the memory of the People's Party have been destroyed, because no agency has explained the real reason. But from the nature of the destruction, which is aimed directly at the memory of the People's Party, and the attempts to replace it with a new set of memories centered on the monarchy as already explained, there has emerged in parallel a diminution in the role and image of the monarchy in the eyes of the people. The fact is that the monarchy has become a subject of unprecedented criticisms and questions. The more the criticisms, the more the legacy of memories related to the People's Party is targeted for destruction.

The "Third" Emergence:
The Politics of the Memory of the People's Party

Despite the intensifying wave of demolitions, if the success in obliterating the memories and casting them into public oblivion is to be assessed, I believe the mission has failed completely, beginning with the removal of the People's Party plaque and replacing it with a new one. This has not only failed in creating a new meaning, but, in direct contrast, the People's Party plaque has reappeared in the political arena in cyberspace. Importantly, there has been a trend in manufacturing replicas in many forms, including commemorative coins, desk calendars, mugs, T-shirts, card games, and watches (fig. 7.3). It can be said that the purpose of its forced disappearance has motivated Thai society to revisit and remember the People's Party plaque to a greater and broader degree than before. The outcome is interesting because it is believed to have changed a single historical artefact into a political symbol of the masses, which has been imitated and reproduced in huge quantities through a variety of processes. This phenomenon has been explained by some as the equivalent of the third emergence of the People's Party.[34]

Figure 7.3 Various everyday objects inspired by the People's Party plaque, Democracy Monument, and Constitution Defense Monument. (*Image*: Chatri Prakitnonthakan)

I agree with this explanation and further argue that the third emergence does not only stem from a "spiritual" political perspective of memory and ideology in the same way as after the 2006 coup, but also from a "physical" re-emergence of a historical artefact. Even though the original physical objects have been destroyed, imitations in many forms have been created in their place and reproduced for wide distribution among the members of the public in new ways, which the state cannot control or eliminate. The political importance and power of historical artefacts is no longer derived from their inherent authenticity alone.

Imitation and mass reproduction have demonstrated an equally forceful role of political symbols. Certainly, the original plaque carries more value as a historical artefact. But in terms of political symbolism, the difference between the original and a replica is not greatly important. Physical copies offer flexibility in interpretation, can be freely extended to different modern forms, and can interact with people in broad circles without the need to experience the actual site or the originality of the artefact. Under this premise the reconstitution, preservation, and extension of the history and memory of the People's Party can be broadened.

The destruction of the Constitution Defense Monument achieved a similar result in that it led to a significantly greater interest in recovering and reconstructing the narrative about the suppression of the Boworadet Rebellion and the monument itself. The new narrative has proliferated online, together with widespread replicas of the Constitution Defense Monument

Figure 7.4 People hold a banner with the slogan "Khana Ratsadon has never died," seen at various anti-dictatorship demonstrations in 2020. (*Image*: Prachatai)

Figure 7.5 People hold a huge replica of the People's Party plaque during a rally marking the ninetieth anniversary of the 1932 revolution at Lan Khon Mueang Town Square on 24 June 2022. (*Image*: Maew Som Prachatai)

in various forms (although not as many as with the People's Party plaque) in both physical form and in virtual form in cyberspace. For example, images of the Constitution Defense Monument represented an inspiration for the design contest of election campaign posters, which was one part of a course at the Faculty of Architecture and Planning, Thammasat University,[35] and the making of small-scale display models of the Constitution Defense Monument for sale. Similarly, the removal of the statues of Phraya Phahon Phonphayuhasena and Phibun and the renaming of various government sites gave rise to recovery, reconstruction, and reproduction in many different fashions, including news reports,[36] documentaries,[37] and even artistic creations.[38] All this shifted the ideological struggle from the actual physical space in the real world, centered on the monuments and symbolic objects of the People's Party, to a similar site in cyberspace unbounded by the real symbolic objects or actual historic sites.

But the third emergence of the People's Party in the form of diverse physical replicas and new kinds of political spaces in cyberspace should not be overrated (at least during the period of writing this chapter), because I personally see that the current ideological political struggle is calling for a struggle in both places. If either is lacking, it is likely to complicate the conceptual and ideological movement. However, in the recent past we have begun to witness spatial progress, which owns an important meaning. In the nationwide protests in 2020, it was noticeable that the introduction of symbols relating to the People's Party, images of the People's Party leaders, past speeches of the People's Party leaders, and reproductions of the People's Party plaque became key components of the rallies (fig. 7.4 and 7.5). What was immensely vital was that at the large rally at Sanam Luang on 20 September 2020, a new version of the People's Party plaque was brought out and the protest leaders embedded it in the Sanam Luang ground.[39] This action implicitly communicated the idea that the memory of the People's Party had not died and that the new generation of demonstrators today has relived the commitment of the People's Party to bring real democracy to the country.

This situation showcases an increasingly vehement struggle over the history and memory of the People's Party while locating it along a current political fault line centered on the monarchy. It will be difficult, if not impossible, to predict the end point of the struggle over the memory of the People's Party. The enforced disappearance of objects related to the memory of the past may continue, and indeed may drive it completely out of the people's consciousness. Or indeed, it may further intensify the memory of the People's Party, remaking it into a strong political symbol capable of overcoming hyper-royalism.

Notes

This chapter adds new information and content to my chapter titled "Khana Ratsadon Lang Ratthaprahan 19 Kanya 49" [The People's Party after the coup d'état of 19 September 1947], in *Sinlapa Satthapatyakam Khana Ratsadon*, 311–63.

1 Charnvit, *Prawat Kanmueang Thai: 2475–2500*, 121–314.

2 "[Text+Pictures] Ruam List Moradok Khana Ratsadon Hai Pai," *Prachatai*.

3 For examples and discussion of these issues, see Mitchell, "Monuments, Memorials, and the Politics of Memory," 442–59; Nidhi, "Songkram Anusawari Kap Rat Thai"; Forty and Küchler, *The Art of Forgetting*; Kusno, *The Appearances of Memory*, 1–24; Reynolds, *Icons of Identity as Sites of Protest*; and Chatri, *Sinlapa Satthapatyakam Khana Ratsadon*.

4 Bevan, *The Destruction of Memory*.

5 Tamada, "Itthiphon and Amnat."

6 McCargo, "Network Monarchy and Legitimacy Crises in Thailand."

7 Mérieau, "Thailand's Deep State, Royal Power and the Constitutional Court (1997–2015)."

8 Farrelly, "Why Democracy Struggles."

9 Kasian, *Ratthaprahan Kap Prachathipatai Thai*, 22–26.

10 Examples are the emergence of "judicialization," which originated from an address by King Rama IX to the president of the Supreme Administrative Court and the president of the Supreme Court on 25 April 2006 and the attendance of HM the Queen at the funeral of a People's Alliance for Democracy protestor on 13 October 2008.

11 Thongchai, *Thailand's Hyper-royalism*.

12 Only Pridi Bhanomyong was remembered and spoken of in a positive way, but then not until the 1990s. He was thought of as a special case with a separate explanation. For further details, see Somsak, "24 Mithuna: Kan Tikhwam 4 Baep."

13 Thanavi, "A Dark Spot on a Royal Space."

14 Sarunyou, "Anusawari Prap Kabot Kap Kan Ramluek Wirachon Phu Phithak Kan Patiwat Pho. So. 2475."

15 Chatri, *Sinlapa Satthapatyakam Khana Ratsadon*, 312–40.

16 Chatri, *Sinlapa Satthapatyakam Khana Ratsadon*, 340–46.

17 In the case of the events of 14 October 1973, see Prajak, *Lae Laeo Khwam Khlueanwai Ko Prakot*, 464–559.

18 For examples, see Sarunyou, *Ratsadonthipatai*, 281.

19 The Buriram Province Constitution Monument was originally built at the time of the People's Party in a design that consisted merely of a round pillar topped by a tray containing a model of the constitution. Later, in the 1980s, the design underwent a major modification, but it still had a symbolic tray and constitution as the main component of the monument. It was eventually demolished in 2014.

20 "Wichan Sanan!," *MGR Online*.

21 Kridpuj, "Phan Rathathamanun Nai Wat Chaimonkhon, Cho Buriram."

22 Chatri, *Sinlapa Satthapatyakam Khana Ratsadon*, 276–79.

23 See Chatri, "Ultra-Thai Architecture after the 2006 Coup d'État," 120–39.

24 Chatri, *Sinlapa Satthapatyakam Khana* Ratsadon, 293–310.

25 "Prakat Krom Sinlapakon Rueang Rai Chue Boranasathan Nai Khet Krung Thep Mahanakhon," 12.

26 "Yai Laeo Ngiap Ngiap 'Anusawari Laksi' Sanyalak Prap Kabot Boworadet."

27 In fact, the original demolition plan was made at the end of December 2019 but when news of the demolition spread through various media, it was postponed until the middle of January 2020. See "Khana Ratsadon," *BBC Thai*.

28 "[Text+Pictures] Ruam List Moradok Khana Ratsadon Hai Pai," *Prachatai*.

29 The formal name of Fort Bhumibol is "His Majesty King Bhumibol Adulyadej the Great Fort" and of Fort Sirikit is "Her Majesty Queen Sirikit Fort." See "Prakat

Samnak Nayok Rathamontri Rueang Phraratchathan Plian Plaeng Nam Khai Thahan," *Royal Thai Government Gazette*, 2.

30 "Scholar Fears Massive Renovation of Iconic Avenue May Erase History," *Khaosod English*.

31 Just one day after the photograph appeared on the website of the Crown Property Bureau, it disappeared and to this day no one has come out to give detailed information.

32 The substitution with the new plaque was however not seen to be completely successful because it was not popular or discussed and did not become a site for conservatives to show their strength.

33 "Tho. Bo. Chai Chue 'Boworadet' Tang Pen Chue Hong," *Matichon Online*.

34 Thanapol, "The Third Emergence of the People's Party."

35 PAPSThammasat, "Remember When We Tried to Remember."

36 Anna, "Uprooting Democracy."

37 "Khana Ratsadon," *BBC Thai*.

38 "Khwam Songcham Haeng Chat Prawatsat Thi Thuk 'Khoefiw,'" *Matichon Online*.

39 "Mut Khana Ratsadon," *BBC Thai*.

References

Anna Lawattanatrakul. "Uprooting Democracy: The War of Memory and the Lost Legacy of the People's Party." *Prachatai English*, 19 December 2019. https://prachatai.com/english/node/8312, accessed 14 April 2021.

Bevan, Robert. *The Destruction of Memory: Architecture at War*. London: Reaktion Books, 2006.

Charnvit Kasetsiri. *Prawat Kanmueang Thai: 2475–2500* [Thai political history: 1947–1972]. Bangkok: Foundation for the Promotion of Social Sciences and Humanities Textbooks Project, 2001.

Chatri Prakitnonthakan. *Sinlapa Satthapatyakam Khana Ratsadon: Sanyalak Thang Kanmueang Nai Choeng Udomkan* [Art and architecture of the People's Party: Political symbols and ideologies]. Bangkok: Matichon, 2020.

———. "Ultra-Thai Architecture after the 2006 Coup d'état." *South East Asia Research* 28.2 (2020):120–39.

Farrelly, Nicholas. "Why Democracy Struggles: Thailand's Elite Coup Culture." *Australian Journal of International Affairs* 67.3 (2013):281–96.

Forty, Adrian, and Susanne Küchler, eds. *The Art of Forgetting*. Oxford: Berg Publishers, 2001.

Kasian Tejapira. *Rathaprahan Kap Prachathipatai Thai* [Coups and Thai democracy]. Bangkok: Foundation for the Promotion of Social Sciences and Humanities Textbooks Project, 2007.

"Khana Ratsadon: Sun Kan Thahan Puen Yai Lopburi Triam Buangsuang Anu-sawari Chomphon Po.—Phraya Phahon Kon Rue Thon" [People's Party: Artillery Center Lopburi prepares ceremony for statues of Field Marshal P-Phraya Phahon before Demolition]. *BBC Thai*, 27 December 2019. https://www.bbc.com/thai/thailand-50923944, accessed 24 March 2020.

"Khana Ratsadon: Yuean Lopburi Du Moradok Thi Luea Yu Khong Chomphon Po. Phibunsongkhram Lae Kan Aphiwat 2475" [People's Party: Visit to Lopburi to see what remains of Field Marshal P. Phibunsongkhram and the 1932 Revolution]. *BBC Thai*, 16 February 2020. https://www.bbc.com/thai/thailand-51519715, accessed 24 March 2020.

"Khwam Songcham Haeng Chat Prawatsat Thi Thuk 'Khoefiw' Lae Ik Rueang Lao Khong Anusawari" [National memory, history under 'curfew' and another narrative of monuments]. *Matichon Online*, 30 March 2020. https://www.matichon.co.th/prachachuen/news_2104182, accessed 31 March 2020.

Kridpuj Dhansandors. "Phan Rathathamanun Nai Wat Chaimonkhon, Cho Buriram: Khwam Songcham Khong Khana Ratsadon Nai Isan Thi Yang Khong Yu" [Constitution Tray in Wat Chai Mongkol, Buriram Province: The memory of the People's Party in the northeast still remains]. *The Isaan Record*, 27 January 2020. https://theisaanrecord.co/2020/01/27/constitution-in-a-temple/, accessed 25 November 2020.

Kusno, Abidin. *The Appearances of Memory: Mnemonic Practices of Architecture and Urban Form in Indonesia*. Durham, NC: Duke University Press, 2010.

McCargo, Duncan. "Network Monarchy and Legitimacy Crises in Thailand." *Pacific Review* 18.4 (December 2005):499–519.

Mérieau, Eugénie. "Thailand's Deep State, Royal Power and the Constitutional Court (1997–2015)." *Journal of Contemporary Asia* 46.3 (2016):445–66.

Mitchell, Katharyne. "Monuments, Memorials, and the Politics of Memory." *Urban Geography* 24 (2003):442–59.

"Mut Khana Ratsadon: Bueang Lang Phithi Fang Mut Khana Ratsadon 2563" [People's Party plaque: Behind the ceremony of embedding the 2020 People's Party plaque]. *BBC Thai*, 21 September 2020. https://www.bbc.com/thai/thailand-54232265, accessed 14 February 2021.

Nidhi Eoseewong. "Songkram Anusawari Kap Rat Thai" [The monuments, war, and the Thai state]. *Sinlapa Wathanatham* [Art and culture magazine] 11.3 (1990):80–102.

PAPSThammasat. "Remember When We Tried to Remember." *PAPSThammasat*, 15 October 2019. https://www.facebook.com/PAPSThammasat/posts/pfbidoEn3kbgfHJ8unrbDajWFWPiwP1CZyE4jF1xKzEcfCVsDc2qQd4zqh oWVsUMhip6JPl, accessed 24 March 2020.

Prajak Kongkirati. *Lae Laeo Khwam Khlueanwai Ko Prakot: Kan Mueang Lae Wathanatham Khong Naksueksa Lae Panyachon Kon 14 Tula* [And then came the movement: The politics and culture of students and intellectuals before 14 October]. Bangkok: Thammasat University Press, 2005.

"Prakat Krom Sinlapakon Rueang Rai Chue Boranasathan Nai Khet Krung Thep Mahanakhon" [Announcement of the Department of Fine Arts on the list of historic sites in the area of the Bangkok metropolis]. *Royal Thai Government Gazette*, vol. 135, special section 165 ngo, 30 September 2015. http://www.ratchakitcha.soc.go.th/DATA/PDF/2561/E/165/10.PDF, accessed 24 March 2020.

"Prakat Samnak Nayok Rathamontri Rueang Phraratchathan Plian Plaeng Nam Khai Thahan" [Announcement of the Prime Minister's Office on the change of name bestowed on military forts]. *Royal Thai Government Gazette*, vol. 137, special section 68 ngo, 20 March 2020. http://www.ratchakitcha.soc.go.th/DATA/PDF/2563/E/068/T_0002.PDF, accessed 26 March 2020.

Reynolds, Craig. *Icons of Identity as Sites of Protest: Burma and Thailand Compared*. Academia Sinica Prosea Research Paper No. 30 (March). Taipei: Academia Sinica, 2000.

Sarunyou Thepsongkraow. "Anusawari Prap Kabot Kap Kan Ramluek Wirachon Phu Phithak Kan Patiwat Pho. So. 2475" [The Rebellion Suppression Monument and the remembrance of the heroic protectors of the 1932 revolution]. *Sinlapa Wathanatham* [Art and culture magazine] 34.12 (2013): 112–29.

———. *Ratsadonthipatai: Kan Mueang Amnat Lae Songcham Khong (Khana) Ratsadon* [Citizens' rule: Politics, power, and the memory of the People's Party]. Bangkok: Matichon, 2019.

"Scholar Fears Massive Renovation of Iconic Avenue May Erase History." *Khaosod English*, 23 January 2020. https://www.khaosodenglish.com/news/2020/01/23/scholar-fears-massive-renovation-of-iconic-avenue-may-erase-history/, accessed 24 March 2020.

Somsak Jeamteerasakul. "24 Mithuna: Kan Tikhwan 4 Baep" [Twenty-four June: Four interpretations]. In *Somsak's Work*, 17 June 2006. http://somsakwork.blogspot.com/2006/06/causes-mutation-in-existing-structural.html, accessed 14 May 2020.

Tamada, Yoshifumi. "Itthiphon and Amnat: An Informal Aspect of Thai Politics." *Southeast Asian Studies* 28.4 (1991):455–66.

"[Text+Pictures] Ruam List Moradok Khana Ratsadon Hai Pai" [List of missing People's Party legacy]. *Prachatai*, 26 March 2020. https://prachatai.com/journal/2020/03/86941, accessed 24 April 2020.

Thanapol Eawsakul. "The Third Emergence of the People's Party." In *The 101. World*, trans. Tyrell Haberkorn, 25 June 2018. https://www.the101.world/the-third-emergence-of-the-peoples-party/, accessed 24 March 2020.

Thanavi Chotpradit. "A Dark Spot on a Royal Space: The Art of the People's Party and the Politics of Thai (Art) History." *Southeast of Now: Directions in Contemporary and Modern Art in Asia* 1.1 (March 2017):131–57.

"Tho. Bo. Chai Chue 'Boworadet' Tang Pen Chue Hong Thi Prap Prung Mai Nai Kong Banchakan Kong Thap Bok" [Army uses the name "Boworadet" to name newly renovated room at army headquarters]. *Matichon Online*, 9 October 2019. https://www.matichon.co.th/politics/news_1705178, accessed 24 March 2020.

Thongchai Winichakul. *Thailand's Hyper-royalism: Its Past Success and Present Predicament*. Trends in Southeast Asia 7. Singapore: ISEAS-Yusof Ishak Institute, 2016.

"Wichan Sanan! Thup Anusawari Prachathipatai Buriram, Ang Sang Fai Charachon Dichiton" [Howls of criticism! Buriram Democracy Monument dismantled, supposedly to put in digital traffic lights]. *MGR Online*, 7 November 2014. https://mgronline.com/local/detail/9570000128508, accessed 25 November 2020.

"Yai Laeo Ngiap Ngiap 'Anusawari Laksi' Sanyalak Prap Kabot Boworadet" [Laksi Monument silently moved, symbol of the suppression of the Boworadet Rebellion]. *Matichon Online*, 4 November 2016. https://www.matichon.co.th/politics/news_347403, accessed 25 November 2020.

8

Untamed and Unrestrained: On Vajiralongkorn's Life Overseas

PAVIN CHACHAVALPONGPUN

IT IS TOO SOON TO PREDICT what kind of international royal tours King Vajiralongkorn will undertake and what they will look like. Indeed, it remains unanswered whether any international royal tours will ever happen in his reign. His father, King Bhumibol Adulyadej, although crowned in 1946, waited for 13 years before embarking on the first in a series of international royal tours in 1959. But then, Bhumibol was only thirty-two years old. In 2019, the year that marked the official coronation of Vajiralongkorn, he was sixty-seven, and time is precious for an old king. He is already the oldest monarch to have ascended to the throne in Thai history. The discussion here on Vajiralongkorn's international royal tours is fundamental in asking if international recognition is still deemed imperative in the strengthening of the royal institution in Thailand. With this question in mind, I set out to examine Vajiralongkorn's life and activities abroad and their effects on his position and image at the international level. This is in turn useful in determining whether his activities are in some ways affected, or even constrained, by the quest for international recognition.

The chapter argues that, from childhood to adulthood, Vajiralongkorn had developed certain personality traits based on his experiences overseas that put him at odds with his father, Bhumibol. A spoiled prince then and an indulgent king now, Vajiralongkorn has broken the essence of Thai kingship molded by Bhumibol, and parts of this development came about during his visits or stays overseas. The change of international environment after the Cold War also plays its part in unlocking conditions and expectations of the world vis-à-vis the Thai monarchy. Vajiralongkorn, as a newly crowned monarch, is taking advantage of such change, by behaving with few international constraints. This explains why his habits and lifestyles during life overseas have remained erratic. For example, on the one hand, he has craved privacy, choosing seclusion in the German countryside to enjoy his cycling. On the other hand, he has called for public attention, such as when wearing a tiny crop top and sporting a fake Yakuza-style tattoo while roaming the streets of Munich. To properly understand Vajiralongkorn's outlook on life overseas is therefore difficult. What is easier to conclude is that the negative image has become a part of the king's trademark—a subject of ridicule among Thais, foreigners, and international media today.[1]

The chapter is divided into three parts. First, it explores Vajiralongkorn's socialization abroad, as a student in England and a cadet in Australia, which formed the foundation of his character later in life. Second, the chapter analyses the linkages between Vajiralongkorn's personal lifestyles, his responsibilities as a royal, and changing international conditions. A simple question in this discussion is whether the Thai monarch today continues to require international recognition of his reign. And third, the chapter delves into how international society, including international media, is perceiving Vajiralongkorn's behavior, both in the personal and public sense, and how the Thai palace has responded to such scrutiny, under what conditions and what legal machinations, for ultimately the protection of the royal image and prestige overseas.

Early Exposure to "Foreignness"

Vajiralongkorn was born in 1952. In 1956, he entered kindergarten at the Chitralada School inside the Dusit Palace, where he studied until he completed grade seven. Groomed to become Thailand's future king, Vajiralongkorn was sent to England in 1966 to begin his Western education. The choice of England was obvious. It has a monarchical system and has served as a desired traditional educational hub for members of the Siamese royal family. King Vajiravudh (Rama VI), Vajiralongkorn's great granduncle, for example, went to Sandhurst and Oxford University.[2] While the United States was fast becoming an emergent superpower in the post–World War II period, it was not selected as a place for Vajiralongkorn's education. Many decades earlier, Prince Rangsit Prayurasakdi said to the Mahidol family, "The United States is a republic and thus unsuitable for raising royalty."[3] By sending Vajiralongkorn to England, this by no means was meant to depreciate the importance of the United States as a key political ally of Thailand during the Cold War. In fact, the Massachusetts Institute of Technology was a choice of Princess Ubolratana Rajakanya, the eldest daughter of Bhumibol and elder sister of Vajiralongkorn, for her higher education in 1969.

Details of Vajiralongkorn's early schooling in England are largely unknown to the Thai public. He was sent to be educated at some private educational institutions, first enrolling at a prep school, King's Mead, in Seaford, Sussex, and then at Millfield School in Somerset. He eventually completed his secondary education in July 1970. Millfield is a boarding school notoriously known as the most expensive educational establishment in Britain, a mecca for children of plutocrats who could not pass legitimately into Eton or Roedean. Vajiralongkorn spent his adolescent years at Millfield, where some of his personal characteristics undoubtedly developed. Despite being a home for the rich, Millfield, like any other boarding school in Britain in those days, was not for frivolous students. Life there was conventionally hierarchical and highly authoritarian, with a system of fagging in place where older students could cane the juniors. Luxuries were not proffered. There were no carpets or curtains in the unheated dormitories, and the food was revolting. His classmate, Rupert Christiansen, described Vajiralongkorn during his school days in *The Telegraph* in 2019 as being "tubby and clumsy." This is a part of what Christiansen wrote about Vajiralongkorn:

> He suffered from one of the most violent twitches I have ever seen—one side of his face would seize up once every 30 seconds or so, as if electrocuted. … Nobody really wanted him as their friend, and at every meal he sat himself next to the matron, the gaunt and censorious Miss Wilkins, who clearly found him a bore and stared blankly into the middle distance as he prattled on. Eating was his comfort: he guzzled compulsively, supplementing the ghastly institutional cuisine with Thai specialties and sweetmeats stored in a bottomless trunk kept under his bed. … He wasn't clever, he wasn't in any teams and despite a previous sojourn at a prep school in Seaford, his English remained imperfect and idiosyncratic. But what marked him most was his enthusiasm for the Combined Cadet Force, a Friday afternoon misery that everyone else loathed. Here, he so excelled in the meticulous wearing of kit, the parade-ground drills, the shouting and saluting that he was promoted to some sort of officer status, allowing him to lord it over the rest of us rotten long-haired pacifist slackers. Like others whose sense of superior status is

toxically combined with insecurity and isolation, Mahidol could suddenly drop his pretense of amiable normality and become a vile bully. Indeed, his behavior might now be described as bipolar.[4]

Christiansen's report suggests, on the one hand, a tendency in Vajiralongkorn to behave as a troubled child. It also unveils, on the other hand, his passion and enthusiasm for orders, disciplines, and commands, guiding him into his future career in the air force. After Millfield, Vajiralongkorn moved to Australia, to the King's School in Parramatta. He became the first high-ranking member of the Thai royal family to have further studied in Australia, a relatively low-key country, both in terms of its importance in the Cold War strategy and its political significance for Thailand. In 1970, Australia, while aligning with the Free World in the battle against communism, was not at the epicenter of the conflict. To an extent, Australia provided a security for Vajiralongkorn, and, at the same time, a peaceful environment for him to focus on his studies. Vajiralongkorn proved to be an active student as he joined the King's School First Soccer team in 1971. But his time at the King's School was brief. In 1972, he continued his education at the Royal Military College, Duntroon, in Canberra. His study at Duntroon was divided into two parts, a military training by the Australian Army and a bachelor's degree course at the University of New South Wales.[5] It was also in 1972 when King Bhumibol granted the title of crown prince (*makutrachakumara*) to his son at the age of twenty, through a ceremony at the Ananta Samakhom Throne Hall in Bangkok. Australia officially became an educational ground for the future king of Thailand.

The military training at Duntroon lasted for four years. During this time, Vajiralongkorn enjoyed being an independent man, often seen driving a fast car between Canberra and Sydney and dipping into the socialite scenes the two cities had to offer. Back in Duntroon, Vajiralongkorn was a hardworking student. Although, right at the beginning, according to Paul M. Handley, he could not keep up physically and academically. Vajiralongkorn was never prepared for this course.[6] If Millfield nurtured his love for soldierly exercise, Duntroon further entrenched his enthusiasm in militarism. The Thai-Australian Association, under his patronage, was granted permission by King Bhumibol to publish a hagiography that promoted his activities in Australia. Marshall Johnson, then Australian ambassador to Bangkok, reiterated that his participation in the Australian communities greatly cemented bilateral ties.[7] It is noteworthy that Vajiralongkorn's time at Duntroon coincided with the peak of the Cold War. Thailand was busy defending its borders against raging communism in Indochina. At the same time as King Bhumibol was forging intimate relations with the United States ultimately for the consolidation of the royal institution against internal and external threats, Vajiralongkorn occasionally took breaks from the military training at Duntroon to participate in counter-insurgency campaigns back home. From 1973 to 1976, Vajiralongkorn accompanied his father to visit far-flung provinces of Thailand, areas in which communist troops often encroached, to render support for the vulnerable population as well as security officers. It can be said that Australia, in particular Duntroon, offered useful military training during which time national agendas like protecting national security, national sovereignty, and territorial integrity ranked high in many countries around the world.

Duntroon did not just shape his view regarding the Cold War, however. For the most part, it shaped his personality too. Duntroon has been known to train future leaders of the Australian army, and its training program and fieldwork are rigorous. The dropout rate for students is as high as 40 percent at any time during the four-year course. But the prestige of the college ironically runs parallel with other darker aspects. Established in 1911 in preparation for an anticipated European war, Duntroon sank into scandal as early as 1913 with several allegations of ragging. When Vajiralongkorn was at Duntroon, there emerged cases of bastardization, corruption, rape, and sexual assaults. For example, as reported in Australian media, junior cadets were forced to run naked in Canberra's chilly evenings to Bridges's nearby grave and memorize its inscription, which began "A gallant and erudite solider" (Major-General Sir William Throsby Bridges is the founding commandant of Duntroon).[8] In the chapter by Gregory Raymond in this volume, he said that it was likely that Vajiralongkorn witnessed different kinds of abuse at Duntroon. Although the crown prince might not have partaken in abusive acts, the brutality could have had a lingering effect on him. A crucial question is whether Duntroon could be held responsible for his behavior later in his life.

Looking back at Vajiralongkorn's father, Bhumibol was raised mostly in Lausanne, Switzerland, with his mother-cum-mentor, Sangwan, and his siblings, Galyani and Ananda. Mahidol children received both home schooling and Western education. Sangwan ensured that her children were taught some Siamese royal practices as well as royal *savoire vivre*. By then, her eldest son, Ananda was already king. Hence, it was her responsibility to groom Ananda to become a dutiful monarch.[9] But Vajiralongkorn grew up in a different setting as he spent time mostly on his own overseas. Untamed and unrestrained, Vajiralongkorn's view of royal practices was certainly more relaxed. Being away from home during his formative years further distanced him from the duties and etiquette of the royal family. Handley said succinctly, "None of Bhumibol's children were raised with the discipline of his own childhood. Vajiralongkorn grew up surrounded by fawning palace women, including Sirikit (his mother), who granted his every desire."[10] Vajiralongkorn completed his study at Duntroon in 1975. For the next six months, he was trained at the Special Air Service Regiment in Perth, before returning to Thailand in 1976. Back in Bangkok, he took up his duties as an officer in the Directorate of Intelligence, Royal Thai Army. In December that year, at the age of twenty-four, Vajiralongkorn became engaged to M.L. Soamsawali Kitiyakara, his own cousin. The two were married on 3 January 1977—it was the beginning of family headaches that have colored the life of Vajiralongkorn ever since.

International Recognition

Historically, some monarchies of the world survived tumultuous political crises thanks to the support of foreign powers. During the Bhumibol era, it was evident that the Thai monarchy had grown to become authoritative because of the solid backing of the United States. The context of the Cold War explained the situation in which the survival of Bhumibol depended crucially on the role of the United States in the kingdom and the region. The rise of royal hegemony was possible owing partially to the Cold War ideological conflict. Right at the beginning of the war, Thailand made its position clear—it sought an international alliance, not neutrality. Thailand's ties with the United States blossomed rapidly as the Cold War was advancing. Born in the United States, Bhumibol represented himself as the perfect vehicle with which to augment US relations. Already united negatively against communism, the two nations would enjoy a positive source of unity in "an American king."[11] For the United States, communist threats in Southeast Asia were real and thus had to be eliminated. For the Thai state, the domestic enemies, discursively painted as communists, were a serious challenge to the well-being of the throne. From this perspective, the political interests between the United States and Thailand were forever intertwined. As a frontline state vis-à-vis communists in the region, Thailand implemented a pro-US, anti-communist, pro-monarchy, and pro-military policy, a standpoint that placed Washington at the heart of Thai affairs. The United States had since become a keen supporter of royal politics in Thailand, committing to safeguard the royal institution and, in so doing, finance the Thai army in battling against the communists and crushing any other political opponents. Benjamin Zawacki rightly perceives the United States as a kind of member *ex officio* of network monarchy, a network of royalists consisting of the military, senior bureaucrats, big businesses, and parts of Bangkok's middle class.[12]

King Bhumibol paid two official visits to the United States during his reign, the first time in 1960 at the invitation of President Dwight D. Eisenhower and the second time in 1967 when invited by President Lyndon B. Johnson. During his first trip, Bhumibol and Sirikit turned up at Paramount Pictures studio, on the set of *G.I. Blues* in which a meeting with rock and roll superstar Elvis Presley was arranged. Through hard and soft powers, the United States was able to solidify its relations with Thailand, a strategic ally on mainland Southeast Asia, through a personal connection with the king. For Bhumibol, international recognition, particularly from the world's superpower, was vital, not only as a significant factor reinforcing his throne against communist threats, but also as a part of the king's lifelong project of royal hegemonization. The United States' endorsement of the monarchy gave a legitimacy to such royal hegemonization. But with the Cold War finally over, the United States was no longer alone in dominating world politics. As the face of the communists disappeared, the palace struggled to identify threats to justify royal hegemony, especially in the context of maintaining international alliances. Meanwhile, the United States has shown at times a disinterest in Southeast Asia. Arguably, it has only recently promoted its pro-Asia policy simply because of the rise of China. However, the renewed policy of the United States lacks consistency. The shift of international politics has contributed to bringing about a new reality in which the Thai monarchy has been allowed to behave with fewer obligations.

In the post–Cold War period, there are no "common enemies" that the monarchy could exploit to warrant its international alliance. Communists in the neighborhood have been reassigned as pivotal trading partners.

Defending the monarchy from foreign threats is therefore superfluous. Certainly, countries like the United States and China continue to acknowledge the importance of the monarchy in their respective bilateral relationship. But this importance is no longer strategic. The view of the United States on the Thai monarchy has shifted. Washington's perception of Vajiralongkorn is greatly different from that of Bhumibol. Vajiralongkorn lacks the intellect, charm, curiosity, and diplomatic skill of his father. Bhumibol put them to good use in guaranteeing support from the United States. Without Bhumibol, the change in the United States' strategic calculation vis-à-vis Thailand is inevitable. Vajiralongkorn is not enthusiastic in diplomacy, particularly in playing the role of his country's ambassador of goodwill. The missing personalized connection with the United States, created by Bhumibol, has effectually remolded the Thai-US bilateral relationship to become one that is dully official.

Standing in the backdrop of the changing Thai-US relationship is China. China has risen to challenge the American influence in Thailand. Thailand normalized its diplomatic relations with China in 1975 in the wake of the American departure from the Vietnam War. The regional circumstances forced Thailand to reposition itself in the war against communists. China was reinvented into a new kind of communist—one that was amicable and beneficial. Bilateral relations between Thailand and China have thrived precipitously over the decades. Whether under a democratic or a military regime, Thailand has reached out to China to seek the latter's political and economic support, at least at the governmental level. As the intensifying rivalry between the United States and China has come to define the current international system, Thailand has adopted a policy of balance of power, taking the benefits from the Sino-US competition. From this viewpoint, international recognition of the monarchy may still be desired. But the rivalry between the two powers has offered more room for manoeuvre for Vajiralongkorn. Comparatively, Bhumibol operated in a much-restrained manner merely because of his obligations with the United States. In the multipolar world of today, Vajiralongkorn is afforded more choices, yet ironically these are making him more reactive, and even lacklustre to his surroundings, sometimes at the detriment of his international reputation.

The Tokyo Incident

Vajiralongkorn commenced his career in the army soon after leaving Australia. Bhumibol, while mastering his own diplomatic skills, sought to promote his son, then heir apparent, at the international level. Occasionally, he assigned Vajiralongkorn to represent him at international events. By that time, Bhumibol had already firmly established his authority at home as well as respect and good reputation beyond Thailand's borders. The Thai monarchy stood shoulder to shoulder with other monarchies of the world, from Great Britain in Europe to Japan in Asia. The pinnacle of Bhumibol's international image was manifested in the sixtieth anniversary celebrations of his accession in 2006. Of the 29 reigning monarchs of the world, 25 accepted the government's invitation to join the celebrations in Thailand: 13 sovereigns were themselves in attendance, while 12 sent representatives. Absent were the now-deposed Gyanendra of Nepal, owing to his country's internal political turmoil, and Abdullah of Saudi Arabia, due to ill health.[13] The success reflected long years of tremendous efforts of the Thai palace in lifting the level of prestige and reverence of Bhumibol to international recognition.

Back in 1987, Vajiralongkorn was requested by his father to visit Tokyo to mark the centennial of Thai-Japanese relations. Japan, meanwhile, dispatched Prime Minister Yasuhiro Nakasone to Bangkok to celebrate the occasion there. The two events were simultaneously broadcast live on national television. The Thai and Japanese prime ministers exchanged platitudes on the Bangkok end and Vajiralongkorn and the Japanese crown prince did likewise from Tokyo. Yet, what was supposed to be a festive occasion ended with Vajiralongkorn cutting short his planned eight-day visit by three days, claiming "important duties awaiting him in Bangkok." The Thai Foreign Ministry demanded an official apology from the Japanese government for the allegedly "inappropriate treatment" accorded Vajiralongkorn during his trip. It was reported that his Japanese hosts had managed to infuriate Vajiralongkorn. Among other things, he was angry that a Japanese driver in his motorcade stopped on the side of a highway to urinate. The Japanese government later claimed that that the Japanese chauffeur felt ill and had to be replaced, forcing the motorcade to stop at a motorway tollbooth.[14] It was also reported that Vajiralongkorn was given an inappropriate chair to sit on, forcing him to reach down to the floor to pick up a cord to unveil a memorial.[15] Paul Handley, in his chapter in this volume, informs that in fact Vajiralongkorn was furious because Sujarinee, née Yuvadhida Polpraserth, was not invited to travel with him since she was only an unofficial consort.

A diplomatic storm blew up between Thailand and Japan over what the Thai-language newspapers reported as "slights" to Vajiralongkorn. The furor compelled Prime Minister Nakasone to issue a public statement. "We sincerely offered as much hospitality as possible [to the prince] as an official guest," he said. "However, during his stay in Japan there was some trouble." Nakasone added, "I regret that the trouble made the crown prince uncomfortable." Nakasone was clearly keen to prevent the matter from damaging Thai-Japanese relations. Thailand eventually retracted its demands for an apology after Vajiralongkorn released a letter indicating that he "wished to see the matter dropped so as to preserve good bilateral relations." The Japanese were clearly relieved.[16] Subsequent events, however, suggested that Vajiralongkorn apparently harbored a lingering grudge. He finally took revenge against Japan in 1996. In March of that year, Thailand hosted the leaders of Asian and European nations at a summit meeting. Bhumibol put on a grand reception for the visiting presidents and premiers. But Vajiralongkorn gave Japanese Prime Minister Ryutaro Hashimoto a rather different kind of welcome. Hashimoto's Boeing 747 landed at a Thai airport and began taxiing toward the red carpet laid out for the plane's high-ranking guests. But then the jumbo jet was conspicuously blocked by three F-5 fighter planes led by Vajiralongkorn himself. Photographers at the arrival point were forced to put down their cameras as the prince held the Japanese delegation on the tarmac for 20 minutes before breaking away. "The Prince was apparently avenging his alleged mistreatment on his Japan visit in 1987," Handley noted.[17] Both the Thai and Japanese governments were hugely embarrassed, and the Japanese diplomatically let the incident stand without protest or comment.

Vajiralongkorn's relationship with Japan was never repaired, at least not until 2017 when Emperor Akihito and Empress Michiko visited Thailand to pay their respects to the grand coffin of Bhumibol, who passed away in October 2016.[18] They also held a private discussion with Thailand's new king. The Japanese Imperial Household Agency declared afterward that Vajiralongkorn went out of his way to treat the visiting royals as his honored guests. After the royal audience, Vajiralongkorn was seen bowing deeply toward the emperor and empress as their car pulled away from the entrance of the royal residence. But some observers, citing the briefness of the encounter, concluded that it was not exactly warm.[19]

Undiplomatic and Unapologetic

Vajiralongkorn taking revenge against Japan in 1996 underlined certain problems within the Thai royal establishment. First, it appeared that Vajiralongkorn continued to be so unrestrained by diplomatic regulations that he was willing to offend his Japanese guest at the risk of the two countries' bilateral relationship. It also showed that Bhumibol was unable to control his son, and consequently stirred up a sense of anxiety within the royal court about the future of the throne. Two decades earlier, Bhumibol complained to his friends of his frustration in controlling his son. He understood that Vajiralongkorn was troublesome but was at a loss to understand how his son turned out to be so unmanageable.[20] In 1972 Vajiralongkorn wrote a poem in honor of his father's birthday on 5 December admitting his drawbacks:

ชั่วชีวิต ที่ผ่านมา จนบัดนี้
เข้าใจดี ชายผิดพลาด ดื้อสับสน
เคยสร้างความ ยุ่งยาก ให้กังวล
พ่อสู้ทน ให้อภัย แก้ไขมา

Throughout my life until now,
I understand well I have made mistakes, been stubborn
    and confused.
I have caused headaches and worried you.
But father has been patient and forgiving.[21]

This poem might sound contrite. In reality, Vajiralongkorn's behavior remained out of control. Arguably, the unrivalled achievements of Bhumibol provided a pretext for Vajiralongkorn to behave in such a way, which was often explained away in the shadow of his father's *barami*. This attitude is still prevalent among the royalists who are not necessarily approving of Vajiralongkorn's behavior but continue to lend him support because they love and respect his late father.

Precisely also because of his father's immeasurable *barami*, Vajira-longkorn took it for granted that he would have international recognition since the world had already recognized his father and thereby the Thai monarchy. To Vajiralongkorn's benefit, the idea of international recognition also became less imposing because of the shift of the international system in the post–Cold War era, as alluded to earlier. This explains how his other adventures overseas, before and after the Tokyo incident, remained largely uninhibited. In the early 1980s, Bhumibol arranged more military training for Vajiralongkorn in the United States. He attended special operations school at bases in North Carolina and Georgia. He was very troublesome, often refusing to take orders.[22] By then, Vajiralongkorn was already entangled in marital problems, openly having a mistress, Sujarinee, even when his relationship with the first wife, Soamsawali, had not ended. The two turned up in the United States, causing pain to diplomats on both sides, Thai and American. As one example, Soamsawali crashed her car near Fort Bragg in North Carolina. Even Vajiralongkorn's mother, Queen Sirikit, had to admit to the American media: "My son the crown prince is a little bit of a Don Juan. He is a good student, a good boy, but women find him interesting, and he finds women even more interesting."[23] In 1996, Vajiralongkorn "kidnapped" his own daughter, Sirivannavari Nariratana, formerly known as Busyanambejra Mahidol, during which time he was divorcing Sujarinee. The incident took place in England, giving rise to a complicated litigation between the two parties that immensely exhausted the host country.[24]

In my interview with an American diplomat, who requested to remain anonymous, in Washington, DC, on 23 July 2019, on the US perception of King Vajiralongkorn, I was informed that the United States was ready to strengthen its ties with Thailand—whether these ties would be kept in a Cold War style of alliance or restructured into something new. At the time, the United States had no official position on Vajiralongkorn, according to the diplomat. The main concern of the United States vis-à-vis Vajiralongkorn had been the latter's view regarding China. The diplomat said boldly: "If Vajiralongkorn favors China over us, we will not go the extra mile to support him." The diplomat was convinced that Thailand would continue to prioritize its friendship with the United States over China. "China is not a friend of Thailand, but a big brother," he said. He added, "And members of the Thai royal family are still regular guests to our country. They have paid more visits to the United States than to China."[25] On 7 December 2021, I returned to

Washington, DC, and interviewed two senior officers responsible for the Thai desk at the State Department. Although by then the United States had a new president, Joe Biden, the American position vis-à-vis Vajiralongkorn remained largely the same—that is, the idea that Thailand would maintain its close ties with the United States and that the new monarch would not jeopardize his relationship with Washington.[26] It is evident that the future direction of relationship between Thailand and the United States depends much upon Vajiralongkorn's position in the Sino-US competition. A greater question is whether Vajiralongkorn has any position at all in this tug-of-war game between the two powers.

China, in the meantime, has long forged its ties with the monarchy to influence the kingdom. Although Bhumibol never paid an official visit to China, he openly endorsed his daughter, Princess Maha Sirindhorn, to act as the palace's ambassador in consolidating relations with Beijing. She first visited China in 1981 and met with then paramount leader Deng Xiaoping in Beijing. Across four decades, Sirindhorn has become one of the first elites in Thailand to visit China, and more importantly, she helped alter the Thai perception about the country. She was also among few people in Thailand to have traveled to all of China's provinces.[27] She took up Mandarin lessons. She performed Chinese calligraphy. In 2000, she received China's inaugural Language, Culture, and Friendship Award.[28] In 2019, she was one of six recipients of the Friendship Medal bestowed as China celebrated its seventieth anniversary.[29] Although Vajiralongkorn, as crown prince, had several opportunities to become acquainted with Chinese leaders, he appeared content to let his sister take the lead in cultivating Thai-Sino relations. Vajiralongkorn has over the years met with top leaders of China, although those meetings were mostly not publicized. For example, he held talks with then Vice President Xi Jinping and Prime Minister Wen Jiabao in 2011 in Bangkok. But Vajiralongkorn's interactions with China have remained limited, indicating his lack of initiatives in foreign policy. Since assuming the throne, Vajiralongkorn has continued to work with China on a routine basis. For example, in January 2020, the king sent a telegram of sympathy to President Xi on the epidemic caused by COVID-19.[30] A month later, Vajiralongkorn dispatched medical products and equipment to China as a gesture of goodwill.[31]

Just as Bhumibol invested himself in the United States, Sirindhorn has invested herself in China. Vajiralongkorn has expressed no particular interest in any specific country. Although he has chosen Germany as his long-term residence, there is no such special relationship at the state level. Hence, it is unlikely that Vajiralongkorn would desire to go further in upgrading Thai relations with China. As for China, while treasuring its friendship with the Thai palace, its political alignment with Bangkok is diverse. China has also befriended Thaksin Shinawatra, a former prime minister overthrown in a coup in 2006 allegedly because of his disrespect for the monarchy. Thaksin has visited China several times and even used Hong Kong as a launching pad against his enemies in Bangkok. In another example, Thailand was left out of the Belt and Road Initiative Summit in 2017. Pongphisoot Busbarat argues that there are two possible reasons for that exclusion. The first is the delay in the Sino-Thai high-speed railway project. The project started in 2012, but the political situation in Thailand terminated the deal due to parliamentary disapproval and then the coup in 2014. Despite Beijing's endorsement of the military government in Bangkok, Thailand renegotiated the deal, the process of which dragged on until 2019. (In October 2020, Thai and Chinese officials finally signed an agreement for a US$1.62 billion segment of a high-speed rail line, part of Beijing's Belt and Road cross-border infrastructure initiative.) The second reason may be related to Prime Minister General Prayuth Chan-ocha accepting US President Donald Trump's invitation to visit the White House in 2017. Beijing may want to signal to Bangkok that it will not tolerate being treated as the second choice in Thailand's diplomatic games.[32] These examples reveal that the intimate relations between the palace and the Chinese leadership can never guarantee that the latter will readily respond to the political and economic needs of the Thai state.

A Crop-Top King in the News

Living in England and Australia were for Vajiralongkorn a necessary preparation for his role as the king of Thailand. But it is the love of Germany's Bavaria that ultimately drew Vajiralongkorn back time and again over the years. Today, it serves as his long-term residence. Vajiralongkorn spends more time in Germany than in his kingdom, Thailand. In 2017, Vajiralongkorn ordered the constitution to be amended in sections related to the royal powers. The constitution was earlier endorsed through the national referendum. Yet, nobody dared to criticize his constitutional intervention. He amended the provision in which he no longer needs to appoint a regent to rule in his stead when he resides outside Thailand.[33] In other words, he remains the king of Thailand even when he reigns from Germany, metaphorically via remote control.

There are several theories of why Germany was selected as his main home. Perhaps the primary reason is his need for regular medical check-ups. Also, he has found the region relatively peaceful and far away enough from the hectic atmosphere he normally encounters elsewhere. Withdrawing from maddening crowds provides him privacy. When King Frederick of Prussia yearned for a private residence where he could strip away royal ceremonies and customs, he ordered the construction of a palace called Sans Souci (Without Worries) in Potsdam, near Berlin, in 1745. At Sans Souci, Frederick was living a secret life in an all-male society away from the public eye, like what was seen within the royal court of King Vajiravudh. Sans Souci lent its idea to King Prajadhipok (Rama VII), who built a summer royal residence outside Bangkok in Hua Hin—construction commenced in 1926 and finished in 1933. Prajadhipok called the new palace Klai Kangwon, a Thai translation of Sans Souci. Vajiralongkorn's familiarity with Munich in Bavaria was formed during the years he spent with his former consort, Srirasmi, whom he divorced in late 2014. It is also important to mention that the Crown Property Bureau once had the majority holding in the Kempinski Hotels group, and Vajiralongkorn often stayed at the Kempinski Munich (see the chapter by Michael Ruffles), before he purchased an ultra-luxurious mansion in Lake Starnberg for 12 million Euros. Named Villa Stolberg, it has a living area of 1,400 square meters, houses at least 15 rooms, and serves as his main home in Bavaria. Located about 30 kilometers southwest of Munich, the villa sits adjacent a beautiful lake.[34]

While in search of a tranquil environment in Germany, what Vajiralongkorn ran into was nothing but endless controversies that further tarnished his reputation. In 2011, the German court impounded a Boeing 737 aircraft at Munich Airport that belonged to Vajiralongkorn, as compensation for a long overdue debt of 30 million Euros the Thai government owed a now-defunct German construction company for the Don Muang Tollway. The Thai government subsequently agreed to pay a deposit of 20 million Euros to bail out the aircraft. Meanwhile, Vajiralongkorn took steps to prevent his Mercedes-Benz SLK being confiscated after the aircraft was seized, hiding it in a private parking garage inside the Munich Kempinski, where it was protected by a dozen bodyguards.[35] Like his father did, Vajiralongkorn loves fast cars. German paparazzi often get snapshots of him driving expensive cars in the Bavarian region. For example, he was once spotted in Erding with a white Porsche 911 Turbo that costs almost 200,000 Euros. His extravagant and peculiar lifestyle has become a major attraction for the German media. Vajiralongkorn often makes headlines, even with seemingly insignificant stories. For example, the German press once reported a dispute between Vajiralongkorn and a restaurant owner in Germany. Vajiralongkorn made a reservation at the restaurant, and the owner, eager to please him, closed the entire place for the privacy of the Thai royalty. But Vajiralongkorn turned up very late and did not order a lot of food, thus upsetting the owner who claimed to have lost a substantial profit that evening.[36] In 2017, a thirteen- and a fourteen-year-old German boy shot an air pistol at Vajiralongkorn as he was cycling in the suburb of Munich. The teenagers' mischief almost amounted to a diplomatic incident as Vajiralongkorn complained about the attack via official channels.[37] Vajiralongkorn, in the end, did not take any legal action against the boys.[38]

Recently, sets of photos of him wearing a skimpy, undersized singlet barely covering massive Yakuza-styled tattoo stickers on his back, chest, and arms deeply shocked the Thai public, even among the hardcore royalists. He was seen wearing the bizarre cropped tank top on several occasions, such as at the Munich Airport alongside his girlfriend, who is now Queen Suthida, nicknamed Nui, as well as at various locations with his other wife, Sineenat Wongvajirapakdi, also known as Koi.[39] He has frequently provided much sought-after stories to feed the appetite and curiosity of German tabloid readers. Although Vajiralongkorn is protected by Article 112 of the Thai Criminal Code, better known as lèse-majesté, these photos were shared widely on social media. In the age of social media, the private life Vajiralongkorn really aspires to is nowhere to be found in Bavaria. In Thailand, many Thais lack opportunities to see their king going wild in traditional media, as it is forbidden in Thailand to print news, reports, or photos that potentially damage the reputation of the monarchy. But he is in Germany, and there can be nothing to stop the German media from publishing his eccentric lifestyle fads or from spreading images through social media networks.

At the eve of the outbreak of COVID-19, in April 2020, Vajiralongkorn remained in Europe and continued to make sensational headlines when he

booked the entire Grand Hotel Sonnenbichl with special permission to break
the lockdown in the Alpine resort town of Garmisch-Partenkirchen. But he
was not alone. He isolated from the coronavirus along with a troop of 20
women.[40] The controversy did not stop at the alpine hotel. On 5–6 April
2020, he flew back to Thailand amid the no-fly policy during the pandemic,
prompting the Thai government to close the airport to facilitate his visit. He
was obliged to be in Bangkok to commemorate Chakri Day, the day the
Rattanakosin dynasty was founded. This less-than-a-day event and other
unconventional lifestyle choices of Vajiralongkorn has stirred up a sense of
resentment, particularly among the younger generation. They took to Twitter
to voice their disapproval of the king. For days, the hashtag #มีกษัตริย์ไว้ทำไม
or #WhyDoWeNeedKing remained the top Twitter hashtag in Thailand,
having been retweeted more than one million times.[41] This segment of Thai
youth grew up during a time when the Bhumibol influence started to wane.
Without recollection of the greatness of Bhumibol as propagated by the
palace, they are not handcuffed by the demand for unconditional love for
the monarchy, particularly as Vajiralongkorn has failed to build his own
moral authority to win the hearts and minds of the younger population. The
long-held reverence Thai people had for their monarch is fast eroding.

Vajiralongkorn's activities in Germany eventually sparked a bilateral
issue concerning the possible exercise of power of Vajiralongkorn on German soil. This was caused by his long stay in Germany, during which time
he endorsed many official documents that appeared in the *Royal Gazette*. In
October 2020, the German government released a remarkable warning to
Vajiralongkorn. "If there are things that we consider to be illegal, then that
will have immediate consequences," said Foreign Minister Heiko Maas to
journalists.[42] Needless to say, Germany does not allow foreign governments
or heads of state to conduct their affairs from its soil. The German rebuke
came amid an extraordinary wave of anti-government protest in Thailand.
Also in October, thousands of protesters gathered in front of the German
embassy in Bangkok, where they presented a letter to the German ambassador urging his government to revoke the king's residency status and
declare him persona non grata. The letter was backed up by a public petition
signed by more than 210,000 people.[43]

In my interview with Frithjof Schmidt, a member of the German parliament for the Green Party, he explained that he had asked the government
to make a formal inquiry into the king's status in Germany, specifically,

whether Vajiralongkorn has violated German sovereignty by exercising royal authority during his stay. Schmidt told me that the Foreign Ministry was investigating the case and that the government could move quickly if it determined the king's actions to be inappropriate. Aside from infringing on German sovereignty, such activity also raised the question of whether documents signed in a foreign land were valid under Thai law. Schmidt also said that, regardless of Vajiralongkorn's status, he was forbidden to carry out any political activities in Germany.[44] The role of foreign countries is crucial in shaping the current protests in Thailand. But while Germany was critical of Vajiralongkorn, Australia celebrated its ties with the king at the height of the protests. In March 2021, the Australian government produced a documentary showcasing historical footage of Vajiralongkorn's student time in Australia. It was shown at a special screening at the Australian Embassy in Bangkok and aired on Thai TV over three nights. The event was widely criticized as "untimely" at a point when the monarchy has become the subject of the protests as well as a spike in lèse-majesté cases.[45]

The Kingdom of Fear

If Bhumibol reigned with his moral authority, then what is the tool of Vajiralongkorn in steering his kingdom? Fear. This chapter supports the argument of Claudio Sopranzetti in his discussion of fear as royal governance under Vajiralongkorn. Without his own *barami*, Vajiralongkorn has exercised fear to command those serving him instead of trusting or convincing them to work for him based on love and respect.[46] Vajiralongkorn has used fear to build order, harking back to his old days at Millfield and Duntroon. Obsessions for orders and commands are now visibly noticed in the physical appearance of those working under him—their uniform must be crisp, and hair perfectly cropped. The chief of the army and the police, and even some members of the Thai cabinet, sport the same hairstyle. At a deeper level, Vajiralongkorn reigns as a monarch whose authority is based upon fear, and as one who cares little about people around him. Fear is a tool to threaten his subordinates and drive them to the edge to keep them compliant and docile. He has kept his subordinates in line with unnecessary, yet rigid, rules, from strict physical appearance to a tough fitness regime. Even prior to the death of Bhumibol, Vajiralongkorn relied on fear for his own rearrangement of power. He allowed a faction under his control to purge others perceived to be disloyal to him, as seen in the cases of Suriyan Sucharitpolwong, or Mor Yong, Police Major Prakrom Warunprapha, and Major General Phisitsak Seniwongse na Ayutthaya—all of whom worked for Vajiralongkorn, most visibly in the "Bike for Mom" project. They died while under detention without a clear explanation.[47]

Within Vajiralongkorn's palace, Dhaveevatthana, a prison was built. The Ministry of Justice, during the Yingluck administration, announced on 27 March 2013 that a 60-square-meter plot of land within Dhaveevathana was allocated for the building of what is now called the Bhudha Monthon Temporary Prison. This "temporary" prison has been legalized, potentially allowing the king to detain anyone legally. Adjacent to the prison is a crematorium.[48] Meanwhile, his former consort, Srirasmi, has been put under house arrest in a Rachaburi house, shaved and dressed as a nun. The German tabloid *Bild* published a report of Srirasmi under house arrest at the eve of his coronation in May 2019.[49] Her family members and relatives were imprisoned on dubious charges. Pongpat Chayaphan, a former Royal Thai Police officer who was the head of the country's Central Investigation Bureau, was convicted in 2015 for profiting from a gambling den, violating a forestry-related law, and money laundering. Srirasmi is his niece. Earlier in 2014, Police General Akrawut Limrat, a close aide to Pongpat, was found dead following a mysterious fall from a building.[50] Recently, Vajiralongkorn punished one of his close confidants, Police General Jumpol Manmai, a former deputy national police chief, labeling him as an extremely evil official to justify the humiliation caused to him. Jumpol was arrested and imprisoned. His head was shaved, as were Mor Yong's and Prakrom's, and he was sent to undergo a military training within the Dhaveevatthana Palace. Like Pongpat, he was found guilty of forest encroachment.[51] And also like Mor Yong and Prakrom, he died while under detention, supposedly from a lung infection, in November 2022.[52]

Promotion and demotion have become routine occurrences within the walls of the palace. Speedy promotions in the military and the police were enjoyed by the king's new favorites. Those irritating him were thrown out—but before that, they were humiliated on the pages of the newspapers. Vajiralongkorn purged the entire Vajarodaya clan, one of the most prominent families of palace officials serving under Bhumibol. Distorn Vajarodaya was stripped of his power in the palace, forced to re-enter military training at the age of fifty-three, and is now working as a house servant who serves drinks to guests of the new king.[53] Years before, after divorcing his second wife, he disowned his four sons, Juthavachara, Vacharaesorn, Chakriwat, and Vatcharawee, who now live in exile in the United States with their mother Sujarinee. The last time they met, in haste, was in New York in 2004.[54] They were banned from coming home (Vacharaesorn returned to Thailand in August 2023). These extreme punitive measures reiterated the fact that fear once again functions as a controlling device over his subjects, even those with royal blood. Fear—for one's own freedom, or one's own personal safety—is a key weapon of Vajiralongkorn's in keeping elites around him in line. When he stripped Sineenat of the title of royal consort only a few months after anointing her, the media around the world asked one important question: What has happened to her since her downfall?[55] There was no answer from the Thai palace.

Has fear been extended to prevent the intrusion of international media and foreign critics? In the Bhumibol era, lèse-majesté law was used to curb foreign critics and, although it seemed effective, it also caused great damage to the monarchy. In 2009, the entire board of the Foreign Correspondents' Club of Thailand was accused of lèse-majesté for providing a venue for Jakrapob Penkair, a minister in the Thaksin administration, who gave a talk with a supposedly anti-monarchist content.[56] Paul Handley, the author of *The King Never Smiles*, was banned from Thailand, as was his book.[57] Joe Gordon, a Thai-born American citizen, was jailed for translating a few paragraphs of Handley's book.[58] Oliver Jufer, a fifty-seven-year-old Swiss, was prosecuted in March 2007 and given a 10-year imprisonment for drunkenly spray-painting posters of King Bhumibol in Chiang Mai. After he admitted his guilt, he was set free a month later.[59] In another incident, Australian writer Harry Nicolaides was given a three-year prison sentence for publishing a book that supposedly offended the royal family. He was released after serving six months in jail.[60] Both Jonathan Head from the BBC and Richard Lloyd Perry from the *Times* were once accused of lèse-majesté for writing reports critical of the monarchy.[61] With the pervasive use of the lèse-majesté law, foreign journalists are extremely cautious in writing about the monarchy. This has effectively cultivated a culture of "self-censorship" among foreign journalists based in Thailand.

In an apparent shift of the approach on lèse-majesté, possibly to safeguard the royal image and thus sustain the royal power, Vajiralongkorn ordered the reorientation of the lèse-majesté usage. In a meeting with Vajiralongkorn in 2018, social critic Sulak Sivaraksa told the media that it was the initiative of the new king that no new lèse-majesté cases be filed. "The present king is impatient, he said 'no more,'" Sulak said. Sulak also said, "He has a bad public image, he acknowledges. He is shy but he is knowledge-able. He is very concerned with the survival of the monarchy, and very concerned about whether this country could be really democratic." Sulak opined, "I think the king is wise. He wants the monarchy to be more open and more transparent. He has gained a lot of confidence since he assumed power."[62] Arguably, the shift in the approach in dealing with critics of the monarchy was a result of Vajiralongkorn's own concerns over the survival of the monarchy and his public image. The concerns were finally translated into action but did not last long. Lèse-majesté cases, ceased since 13 October 2017, have made a comeback toward the end of 2020.[63] Unlike other protests in the past, the current demonstration has broken a taboo on the discussion of the monarchy. Even in the presence of the lèse-majesté law, protesters challenged the monarchy by directly criticizing Vajiralongkorn. The state has once again exploited the lèse-majesté law to threaten the protesters, hoping to put an end to the unrest. Almost all the key protest leaders have been charged with lèse-majesté.[64] The inconsistency under the reign of Vajiralongkorn highlights a great discrepancy between the need to protect his image at home and overseas and the growing absolutist nature of the new reign as well as the king's bizarre lifestyles that have found their way to hurt the image he wanted to protect in the first place.

Conclusion

What accompanies the advent of King Vajiralongkorn is not only the possible return of a royal absolutism, but also the decrease in the divinity of the monarchy in a country that has long revered its monarchs. Bhumibol was very successful in fortifying his throne based on broad popular support. Vajiralongkorn, on the contrary, is reigning Thailand with fear. This chapter has investigated Vajiralongkorn's contacts with the outside world, first as a young prince and now as an aged monarch. It examined his childhood past, set in a strict environment of boarding schools, that had effectively influ-enced his personality, as he sought to break free from rigid rituals to become widely unrestrained, thinly veneering a darker side of himself that is intimidating or even violent. His obsession with orders and discipline paved the way for his future path in the army and as a military-like king. As always, the paradox lies deep in the behavior of Vajiralongkorn: his allure for orders and instructions versus his yearning to break free and bouts of hedonism. But it is a familiar pattern that Vajiralongkorn shares with other Thai and world leaders, from Field Marshal Sarit Thanarat to Burma's Ne Win and US President John F. Kennedy, who were famous for their sexual exploits.[65] This paradox is set in stone as the global political landscape has changed in the post–Cold War era. Thailand was once a significant ally of the United States in the war against communism. The needed international alliance in turn was beneficial for the monarchy and the military to uphold their tight grips of power. Hence, the Thai establishment and the United States knitted their ties based on mutual interests. But when the ideological conflict ran its course, international alliance became less demanding. For once, the Thai monarchy enjoyed more freedom, and this possibly allowed Vajiralongkorn to behave without diplomatic obligations.

Vajiralongkorn does not treat the conduct of foreign policy and diplomacy as a part of his role as a monarch. Unlike his father, Vajiralongkorn has never invested in any foreign country upon whom he could rely in crisis. But perhaps, crisis of the monarchy has not yet reached its peak and until then dependency on support from foreign powers is unnecessary. Thais have witnessed him acting undiplomatically and unapologetically toward Japan, the drama of his family break-up in England, and the four disowned sons taking exile in the United States. As Vajiralongkorn moved to Germany, the headaches followed. His activities were sensationalized on the front pages of newspapers not just in Germany but across the globe. In the world of social media, Thais, particularly the younger and more tech-savvy population, witnessing their king going wild overseas, have started to question his divine status, normally a taboo topic encapsulated within the draconian lèse-majesté law. Social media now serves as a platform that hosts anti-monarchist voices rather openly.[66]

The paradox continues alongside the palace's attempt to reconstruct Vajiralongkorn in a positive light. From "Bike for Mom" and then "Bike for Dad," a strategy has been adopted to present an energetic and engaging king. This included the initial downplaying of the use of lèse-majesté law to create a new persona of Vajiralongkorn as civilized and modern. But it is a failed attempt right at the start. The outdated law of lèse-majesté has returned since the end of 2020. Vajiralongkorn has continued to act absurdly abroad, which serves to discredit his own endeavor in image making. In the meantime, international media has found his routine life far from dull. His stories sell. But the incessant media reports on Vajiralongkorn may not in the end alter the situation, as it seems they assist in developing immunity for him in front of the eyes of the world despite intense scrutiny. The world does not need the Thai monarchy to help fix problems it is facing today. The consequence is unfortunately the making of a king who acts with no bounds.

Notes

1 Puangthong, "The Foreign Press' Changing Perceptions of Thailand's Monarchy," 25.

2 Vajiravudh attended school in England from 1893 to 1901, starting at Sandhurst to a period in the Durham Light Infantry and his studies at Oxford University. See Reynolds, "Homosociality in Modern Thai Political Culture," 271. However, there is no evidence that Vajiravudh attended Eton College. Reynolds told the author in 2016 that Vajiravudh's Eton education is one of many historical inaccuracies handed down from generation to generation.

3 Galyani, *Mae Lao Hai Fang*, 179.

4 Christiansen, "What It Was Like to Board at Millfield School with the King of Thailand."

5 According to some accounts, Vajiralongkorn graduated with an arts degree from the University of New South Wales. See Sahni, *King of Thailand and His Connections to Parramatta*. Meanwhile, Paul Handley disputed that Vajiralongkorn may have completed Duntroon but never received a diploma, presumably because he could not truly pass the coursework. See Handley, *The King Never Smiles*, 250.

6 Handley, *The King Never Smiles*.

7 Thai-Australian Association, *H.R.H. The Crown Prince*, 8.

8 Pemberton, "Defense and ADFA Need to Open up on History of Abuse and Accept Royal Commission."

9 Winyu, *Somdej Ya Maefah Luang*, 54.

10 Handley, *The King Never Smiles*, 248.

11 Zawacki, *Thailand: Shifting Ground between the US and Rising China*, 34.

12 Zawacki, *Thailand*, 188.

13 Berger, "Royals Gather for Thai King's Diamond Jubilee Party."

14 See Memorandum for the Director of Foreign Broadcast Information Service.

15 Crossette, "Bangkok Journal."

16 "Nakasone Says Japan Did Best for Thai Prince," *The Straits Times.*

17 Handley, *The King Never Smiles*, 402.

18 Ono and Kotani, "New Thai King Receives Japanese Emperor."

19 Pavin, "Why Thailand's New King has a Troubled History."

20 Handley, *The King Never Smiles*, 250.

21 Chirapha, *Somdej Phra Boroma Orasathiraj Chaofa Maha Vajiralongkorn Sayammakutrachakumara*, 109.

22 Handley, *The King Never Smiles*, 302.

23 Branigin, "Thais Ban Asian Wall Street Journal for Story Critical of Monarch."

24 Online interview with one of the Vivacharawongses, 5 April 2020.

25 Interview with an American diplomat from the US State Department, Washington, DC, 23 July 2019.

26 An interview with two senior officers from the US State Department, Washington, DC, 7 December 2021.

27 Jitsiree, "Thailand's Long-Time Sinophile Princess Sirindhorn to Receive China's Friendship Medal."

28 Zawacki, *Thailand*, 78.

29 For more details on the relationship between the Thai monarchy and ethnic Chinese from a historical perspective, see Wasana, *The Crown and the Capitalists.*

30 "King Maha Vajiralongkorn of Thailand Sent a Telegram of Sympathy to President Xi Jinping of China," Embassy of the People's Republic of China in the Kingdom of Thailand.

31 "Nailuang Phrarachatan Wechaphan Hai Chine Namsongprom Kruangbin Rap 149 Khon thai Krabbaan," *Matichon.*

32 Pongphisoot, "Why Was Thailand's Prime Minister Absent in the Belt and Road Initiative Summit?."

33 "Thai Parliament Approves King's Constitutional Changes Request, Likely Delaying Elections," *Reuters.*

34 Thailand's Crown Property Bureau sold a 60 percent stake in the Kempinski Hotels Group for 1 billion to the Bahraini royal family. Since 2004, Thailand's crown had owned 80 percent of the 122-year-old group, and Bahrain held the other 20 percent. According to the agreement struck in mid-2016, the shareholdings would swap: Bahrain paying out the Thai royal house to take on the larger, 80 percent share of the company. See Sanderson, "Stuck between Two Kings."

35 Pavin, "A Crown Prince and German Affairs."

36 Pavin, "A Crown Prince and German Affairs."

37 Oltermann, "German Teenagers Who Shot Toy Gun at Thai King Spark Diplomatic Incident."

38 "Thailand King Vajiralongkorn Shot at with Air Pistol," *BBC*.

39 Koi eventually fell from grace after being elevated to the position of royal consort a few months earlier. See "Thai King Sacks Six Royal Officials over 'Evil Actions.'"

40 Brown, "King of Thailand 'Isolates' from Coronavirus with 20 Women."

41 Berthelsen, "Thailand's Controversial King Outrages Subjects."

42 Solomon and Bender, "Thailand's King Becomes a Foreign Relations Challenge for Germany."

43 Colitt and Thanthong-Knight, "Germany Warns of 'Consequences' if Thai King Breached Law."

44 Interview via Zoom with Schmidt, 20 October 2020.

45 Ford, "The Australian Government Made a Documentary about Thailand's King."

46 Sopranzetti, "From Love to Fear."

47 "Thai Fortune Teller Held under Royal Defamation Law Found Dead," *The Guardian*.

48 Pavin, "Dhaveevatthana Prison."

49 "Is This Third Ex-wife under House Arrest Here?," *Bild*.

50 Sanitsuda, "Mor Yong's Death Breeds Mistrust."

51 "Ex-Deputy Police Chief among 3 Charged with Encroachment," *The Nation*.

52 "Ex-Deputy National Police Chief Jumpol Dies Age 72," *Bangkok Post*.

53 "Royal Gazette Announces Dismissal of Former Grand Chamberlain Distorn Vajarodaya," *Thai PBS*.

54 Online interview with one of the Vivacharawongses, 5 April 2020.

55 Bernstein, "Thailand's Playboy King Isn't Playing Around."

56 "FCCT Board Members Accused of Lèse-majesté," *International Federation for Human Rights*.

57 Walker, "The King Never Smiles?."

58 "Thai King Pardons US Man Jailed for Royal Insult," *BBC*.

59 MacKinnon, "Swiss Man Jailed for 10 Years for Insulting Thai King."

60 MacKinnon, "Australian Teacher Jailed for Three Years after Insulting Thai King."

61 "Lèse-majesté and Harry Nicolaides," *The Nation's State*. Also see Philp, "Richard Lloyd Parry and Thaksin Shinawatra Accused of Lèse-majesté."

62 Ruffles, "Lèse-majesté Is Dead."

63 Streckfuss, "Lèse-majesté within Thailand's Regime of Intimidation," chap. 10.

64 "Criminal Cases Mount against Thailand's Protest Leaders," *Reuters*.

65 For a related topic on Vajiralongkorn and his women, see Gray, "Magic Families."

66 See the discussion on social media and Thai contemporary politics in Aim, *Opposing Democracy in the Digital Age*.

References

Aim Sinpeng. *Opposing Democracy in the Digital Age: The Yellow Shirts in Thailand*. Ann Arbor: University of Michigan Press, 2021.

Berger, Sebastien. "Royals Gather for Thai King's Diamond Jubilee Party." *The Telegraph*, 13 June 2006. https://www.telegraph.co.uk/news/worldnews/asia/thailand/1521190/Royals-gather-for-Thai-kings-diamond-jubilee-party.html, accessed 3 June 2022.

Bernstein, Richard. "Thailand's Playboy King Isn't Playing Around." *Vox*, 24 January 2020. https://www.vox.com/2020/1/24/21075149/king-thailand-maha-vajiralongkorn-facebook-video-tattoos, accessed 3 June 2022.

Berthelsen, John. "Thailand's Controversial King Outrages Subjects." *Asia Sentinel*, 6 April 2020. https://www.asiasentinel.com/p/thailands-controversial-king-outrages, accessed 3 June 2022.

Branigin, William. "Thais Ban Asian Wall Street Journal for Story Critical of Monarch." *Washington Post*, 23 January 1982. https://www.washingtonpost.com/archive/politics/1982/01/23/thais-ban-asian-wall-street-journal-for-story-critical-of-monarch/ab6cbf0c-3282-46eb-a30f-f488f5c9da21/, accessed 3 June 2022.

Brown, Lee. "King of Thailand 'Isolates' from Coronavirus with 20 Women." *New York Post*, 30 March 2020. https://nypost.com/2020/03/30/king-of-thailand-isolates-from-coronavirus-with-20-women/, accessed 1 June 2022.

Chirapha Oonruang. *Somdej Phra Boroma Orasathiraj Chaofa Maha Vajiralongkorn Sayammakutrachakumara* [The Crown Prince Maha Vajiralongkorn]. Bangkok: Lion Dusit Club, 1972.

Christiansen, Rupert. "What It Was Like to Board at Millfield School with the King of Thailand." *The Telegraph*, 4 May 2019. https://www.telegraph.co.uk/men/thinking-man/like-board-millfield-school-king-thailand/, accessed 1 June 2022.

Colitt, Raymond, and Randy Thanthong-Knight. "Germany Warns of 'Consequences' if Thai King Breached Law." *Bloomberg*, 27 October 2020. https://www.japantimes.co.jp/news/2020/10/27/asia-pacific/germany-thailand-king/, accessed 3 June 2022.

"Criminal Cases Mount against Thailand's Protest Leaders." *Reuters*, 8 March. 2021. https://www.usnews.com/news/world/articles/2021-03-08/factboxcriminal-cases-mount-against-thailands-protest-leaders, accessed 1 June 2022.

Crossette, Barbara. "Bangkok Journal; Once upon a Time a Good King Had 4 Children ...." *New York Times*, 15 December 1987. https://www.nytimes.com/1987/12/15/world/bangkok-journal-once-upon-a-time-a-good-king-had-4-children.html, accessed 3 June 2022.

"Ex-Deputy Police Chief among 3 Charged with Encroachment." *The Nation*, 12 February 2017. https://www.nationthailand.com/news/30306239, accessed 1 June 2022.

"Ex-Deputy National Police Chief Jumpol Dies Age 72." *Bangkok Post*, 2 November 2022. https://www.bangkokpost.com/thailand/general/2427620/ex-deputy-national-police-chief-jumpol-dies-age-72, accessed 5 November 2022.

"FCCT Board Members Accused of Lèse-majesté." *International Federation for Human Rights*, 2 July 2009. https://www.fidh.org/en/region/asia/thailand/FCCT-board-members-accused-of-lese, accessed 3 June 2022.

Ford, Mazoe. "The Australian Government Made a Documentary about Thailand's King. But the Timing Has Raised Some Eyebrows." *ABC News*, 21 February 2021. https://www.abc.net.au/news/2021-02-21/australilan-government-makes-a-documentary-for-thailands-king/13171976, accessed 2 June 2022.

Galyani Vadhana. *Mae Lao Hai Fang* [As mother told me]. Chiang Mai: Surawongse Book Centre, 1980.

Gray, Christine. "Magic Families." *New Mandala*, 23 July 2016. https://www.newmandala.org/magic-families-balcony-stage-vanishing-act/, accessed 3 June 2022.

Handley, Paul M. *The King Never Smiles: A Biography of Thailand's Bhumibol Adulyadej*. New Haven, CT: Yale University Press, 2006.

"Is This Third Ex-Wife under House Arrest Here?" *Bild*, 4 May 2019. https://m.bild.de/bild-plus/news/ausland/news-ausland/thailand-koenig-gekroent-sitzt-hier-seine-dritte-ex-frau-im-hausarrest-61675386,view=conversion-ToLogin,oview=amp.bildMobile.html, accessed 3 June 2022.

Jitsiree Thongnoi. "Thailand's Long-Time Sinophile Princess Sirindhorn to Receive China's Friendship Medal." *South China Morning Post*, 22 September 2019. https://www.scmp.com/week-asia/politics/article/3029681/thailands-long-time-sinophile-princess-sirindhorn-receive-chinas, accessed 3 June 2022.

"King Maha Vajiralongkorn of Thailand Sent a Telegram of Sympathy to President Xi Jinping of China." Embassy of the People's Republic of China in the

Kingdom of Thailand, 1 February 2020. http://www.chinaembassy.or.th/eng/ztbd/Coronavirus/t1738731.htm, accessed 3 June 2022.

"Lèse-majesté and Harry Nicolaides." *The Nation's State*, 7 October 2008. http://nationsstate.blogspot.com/2008/10/lse-majest-and-harry-nicolaides.html?m=0, accessed 3 June 2022.

MacKinnon, Ian. "Australian Teacher Jailed for Three Years after Insulting Thai King." *The Guardian*, 19 January 2009. https://www.theguardian.com/world/2009/jan/19/thailand-nicolaides-court-monarchy, accessed 3 June 2022.

———. "Swiss Man Jailed for 10 Years for Insulting Thai King." *The Guardian*, 29 March 2007. https://www.theguardian.com/world/2007/mar/29/ianmackinnon, accessed 3 June 2022.

Memorandum for the Director of Foreign Broadcast Information Service. 5 October 1987.

"Nailuang Phrarachatan Wechaphan Hai Chine Namsongprom Kruangbin Rap 149 Khon Thai Krabbaan" [The king offered medical equipment to China, together with sending a plane to bring home 134 Thais]. *Matichon*, 3 February 2020. https://www.matichon.co.th/foreign/news_1942386, accessed 3 June 2022.

"Nakasone Says Japan Did Best for Thai Prince." *The Straits Times*, 14 October 1987. https://eresources.nlb.gov.sg/newspapers/Digitised/Article/straitstimes19871014-1.2.22.7, accessed 3 June 2022.

Oltermann, Philip. "German Teenagers Who Shot Toy Gun at Thai King Spark Diplomatic Incident." *The Guardian*, 21 June 2017. https://www.theguardian.com/world/2017/jun/21/munich-teenagers-fire-on-thai-king-with-airsoft-gun, accessed 3 June 2022.

Ono, Yukako, and Hiroshi Kotani. "New Thai King Receives Japanese Emperor." *Nikkei Asian Review*, 6 March 2017. https://asia.nikkei.com/Politics/New-Thai-king-receives-Japanese-emperor2, accessed 3 June 2022.

Pavin Chachavalpongpun. "A Crown Prince and German Affairs." *New Mandala*, 14 July 2016. https://nypost.com/2020/03/30/king-of-thailand-isolates-from-coronavirus-with-20-women/, accessed 3 June 2022.

———. "Dhaveevatthana Prison: Hell on Earth in Thailand." *Japan Times*, 2 June 2017. https://www.japantimes.co.jp/opinion/2017/06/02/commentary/world-commentary/dhaveevatthana-prison-hell-earth-thailand/, accessed 3 June 2022.

———. "Why Thailand's New King Has a Troubled History with One of His Country's Most Important Allies." *Washington Post*, 20 November 2017. https://www.washingtonpost.com/news/democracy-post/wp/2017/11/29/why-thailands-new-king-has-a-troubled-history-with-one-of-his-countrys-most-important-allies/, accessed 3 June 2022.

Pemberton, George. "Defense and ADFA Need to Open up on History of Abuse and Accept Royal Commission." *The Sydney Morning Herald*, 27 November 2014. https://www.smh.com.au/opinion/defence-and-adfa-need-to-open-up-on-history-of-abuse-and-accept-royal-commission-20141127-11v2go.html, accessed 3 June 2022.

Philp, Catherine. "Richard Lloyd Parry and Thaksin Shinawatra Accused of Lèse-majesté." *The Times*, 11 November 2009. http://vleeptronz.blogspot.com/2009/11/more-lese-majeste-bullshit-in-thailand.html, accessed 3 June 2022.

Pongphisoot Busbarat. "Why Was Thailand's Prime Minister Absent in the Belt and Road Initiative Summit?" *ISEAS Commentaries* 37, 9 June 2017. https://www.iseas.edu.sg/media/commentaries/why-was-thailands-prime-minister-absent-in-the-belt-and-road-initiative-summit-by-pongphisoot-busbarat/, accessed 7 June 2022.

Puangthong R. Pawakapan. "The Foreign Press' Changing Perceptions of Thailand's Monarchy." *Trends in Southeast Asia* 18 (2015):1–38.

Reynolds, Craig J. "Homosociality in Modern Thai Political Culture." *Journal of Southeast Asian Studies* 45.2 (June 2014):258–77.

"Royal Gazette Announces Dismissal of Former Grand Chamberlain Distorn Vajarodaya." *Thai PBS*, 11 November 2017. https://forum.thaivisa.com/topic/1010899-royal-gazette-announces-dismissal-of-former-grand-chamberlain-%E2%80%9Cdistorn-vajarodaya%E2%80%9D/, accessed 3 June 2022.

Ruffles, Michael. "Lèse-majesté Is Dead. Long Live Lèse-majesté." *The Sydney Morning Herald*, 22 November 2018. https://www.smh.com.au/world/asia/lese-majeste-is-dead-long-live-lese-majeste-20181121-p50hbz.html, accessed 3 June 2022.

Sahni, Neera. *King of Thailand and His Connections to Parramatta.* Research Service, City of Parramatta Council, 23 October 2017. https://historyandheritage.cityofparramatta.nsw.gov.au/blog/2017/10/23/king-of-thailand-and-his-connections-to-parramatta, accessed 3 June 2022.

Sanderson, Paul. "Stuck between Two Kings: A Possible Explanation for Hakeem al-Araibi's Detention." *The Sydney Morning Herald*, 4 May 2019. https://www.smh.com.au/world/asia/two-kings-a-billion-euros-and-an-australian-trapped-in-thailand-20190314-p5146l.html, accessed 3 June 2022.

Sanitsuda Ekachai. "Mor Yong's Death Breeds Mistrust." *Bangkok Post*, 11 November 2015. https://www.bangkokpost.com/opinion/opinion/761020/mor-yong-death-breeds-mistrust, accessed 3 June 2022.

Solomon, Feliz, and Ruth Bender. "Thailand's King Becomes a Foreign Relations Challenge for Germany." *Wall Street Journal*, 26 October 2020. https://www.

wsj.com/articles/thailands-king-becomes-a-foreign-relations-challenge-for-germany-11603733852, accessed 3 June 2022.

Sopranzetti, Claudio. "From Love to Fear: The Rise of King Vajiralongkorn." *Al Jazeera*, 11 April 2017. https://www.aljazeera.com/indepth/opinion/2017/04/thailand-junta-king-vajiralongkorn-170411102300288.html, accessed 3 June 2022.

Streckfuss, David. "Lèse-majesté within Thailand's Regime of Intimidation." In *Routledge Handbook of Contemporary Thailand*, ed. Pavin Chachavalpongpun, 134–44. London: Routledge, 2019.

Thai-Australian Association. *H.R.H. The Crown Prince: His Years in Australia*. Bangkok: Chuanphim Printing, 1977.

"Thai Fortune Teller Held under Royal Defamation Law Found Dead." *The Guardian*, 9 November 2015. https://www.theguardian.com/world/2015/nov/09/thai-fortune-teller-mor-yong-held-under-royal-defamation-law-found-dead, accessed 3 June 2022.

"Thai King Pardons US Man Jailed for Royal Insult." *BBC*, 11 July 2012. https://www.bbc.com/news/world-asia-18792430, accessed 3 June 2022.

"Thai King Sacks Six Royal Officials over 'Evil Actions,' Days after Removing Consort." *The Guardian*, 24 October 2019. https://www.theguardian.com/world/2019/oct/24/thai-king-sacks-six-royal-officials-over-evil-actions-days-after-removing-consort, accessed 1 June 2022.

"Thai Parliament Approves King's Constitutional Changes Request, Likely Delaying Elections." *Reuters*, 13 January 2017. https://www.reuters.com/article/us-thailand-king-constitution/thai-parliament-approves-kings-constitutional-changes-request-likely-delaying-elections-idUSKBN14X0IF, accessed 3 June 2022.

"Thailand King Vajiralongkorn Shot at with Air Pistol." *BBC*, 21 June 2017. https://www.bbc.com/news/world-asia-40355652, accessed 3 June 2022.

Walker, Andrew. "The King Never Smiles?." *New Mandala*, 28 July 2006. https://www.newmandala.org/the-king-never-smiles/, accessed 3 June 2022.

Wasana Wongsurawat. *The Crown and the Capitalists: The Ethnic Chinese and the Founding of the Thai Nation*. Seattle: University of Washington Press. 2019.

Winyu Boonyong. *Somdej Ya Maefah Luang* [The queen mother]. Bangkok: Changthong Publishing, 1996.

Zawacki, Benjamin. *Thailand: Shifting Ground between the US and Rising China*. London: Zed Books, 2017.

Contributors

CHATRI PRAKITNONTHAKAN is a professor of architecture at the Faculty of Architecture, Silpakorn University, and a columnist for *Matichon Weekly*. He received his PhD in history from Chiang Mai University in 2019. Chatri has studied Thai architectural history with a particular emphasis on politics in architecture, historiography of Thai art, and politics in conservation of the historic urban landscape of old Bangkok. His current research focuses on the Art Deco movement in Southeast Asia.

CLAUDIO SOPRANZETTI is an associate professor in the Sociology and Anthropology Department at the Central European University and a Quondam Fellow at All Souls College, Oxford University. He is the author of *Red Journeys* (University of Washington Press, 2012), *Owners of the Map* (University of California Press, 2018), and the award-winning graphic novel *The King of Bangkok* (University of Toronto Press, 2021).

DAVID STRECKFUSS serves as a "foreign expert" at the Faculty of Sociology and Anthropology at Thammasat University and is an honorary fellow of the University of Wisconsin-Madison. He is also an adviser to the online publication *The Isaan Record*. He has lived in Thailand for more than thirty years and is interested in legal history, nationalism, ethnic identities, and social justice. He is the author of *Truth on Trial in Thailand: Defamation, Treason, and Lèse-Majesté* (Routledge, 2011) and a contributor to the biography *King Bhumibol: A Life's Work* (Editions Didier Millet, 2012). He also has had pieces published in the *Bangkok Post*, *New York Times*, *Asian Wall Street Journal*, *Al Jazeera*, and *New Mandala*.

FEDERICO FERRARA is an associate professor at the City University of Hong Kong, in the Department of Public and International Affairs. A graduate of Harvard University, where he was awarded a PhD in political science in 2008, Federico has written on Thai politics and comparative political institutions in a variety of books and academic journals. Most prominently, he is the author of *The Political Development of Modern Thailand* (Cambridge

University Press, 2015) and *The Development of Political Institutions: Power, Legitimacy, Democracy* (University of Michigan Press, 2022).

GREGORY V. RAYMOND is a senior lecturer at the Australian National University researching Southeast Asian politics and foreign relations, with a focus on Thailand and the Mekong states. He is the author of *Thai Military Power: A Culture of Strategic Accommodation* (NIAS Press, 2018) and the lead author of *The United States-Thai Alliance: History, Memory and Current Developments* (Routledge, 2021).

MICHAEL RUFFLES is a journalist and subeditor at *The Sydney Morning Herald*. Along with investigations editor Michael Evans, he wrote an award-winning series of articles exposing a former Thai cabinet minister's drug charges and jail time. He was chief subeditor of the *Bangkok Post Sunday* and its acclaimed Spectrum section from 2013 to the end of 2016.

PAUL M. HANDLEY worked as a journalist in Thailand from 1987 to 2001, for the *Far Eastern Economic Review, Newsweek, Institutional Investor,* and other publications. In 2006 he published *The King Never Smiles: A Biography of King Bhumibol Adulyadej.* He currently works in Washington, DC, as a national security correspondent for Agence France-Presse.

PAVIN CHACHAVALPONGPUN is an associate professor at the Center for Southeast Asian Studies, Kyoto University. He is also the editor of the online journal *Kyoto Review of Southeast Asia* in which all articles are translated from English into Japanese, Thai, Bahasa Indonesia, Filipino, Vietnamese, and Burmese. He is the author and editor of several books, including the most recent *Coup, King, Crisis: A Critical Interregnum in Thailand*, published by Yale Southeast Asia Studies in late 2020.

INDEX

print edition: design, layout, and typography
epub/kindle editions: design and coding
all editions: cover and illustrations
by **H.G. Salome**

Vermont, USA
www.metaglyfix.com

Made in the USA
Monee, IL
03 April 2024

56241323R00174